REPRODUCTIVE ISSUES IN AMERICA

A Reference Handbook

Other Titles in ABC-CLIO's
**CONTEMPORARY
WORLD ISSUES**
Series

Books in the Contemporary World Issues series address vital issues in today's society such as genetic engineering, pollution, and biodiversity. Written by professional writers, scholars, and nonacademic experts, these books are authoritative, clearly written, up-to-date, and objective. They provide a good starting point for research by high school and college students, scholars, and general readers as well as by legislators, businesspeople, activists, and others.

Each book, carefully organized and easy to use, contains an overview of the subject, a detailed chronology, biographical sketches, facts and data and/or documents and other primary-source material, a directory of organizations and agencies, annotated lists of print and nonprint resources, and an index.

Readers of books in the Contemporary World Issues series will find the information they need in order to have a better under-standing of the social, political, environmental, and economic issues facing the world today.

REPRODUCTIVE ISSUES IN AMERICA

A Reference Handbook

Janna C. Merrick
Robert H. Blank

CONTEMPORARY WORLD ISSUES

A B C ☰ C L I O

Santa Barbara, California
Denver, Colorado
Oxford, England

Library of Congress Cataloging-in-Publication Data
Merrick, Janna C.
   Reproductive issues in America : a reference handbook / Janna C.
Merrick, Robert H. Blank.
       p. ; cm. — (Contemporary world issues)
   Includes bibliographical references and index.
   ISBN 1-57607-816-7 (alk. paper); ISBN 1-57607-817-5 (eBook)
   1. Human reproductive technology—United States—Handbooks,
manuals, etc.
   [DNLM: 1. Reproductive Techniques—United States—Handbooks.
2.Reproductive Techniques—United States—Resource Guides.
3. Abortion, Legal—United States—Handbooks.   4. Abortion, Legal—
United States—Resource Guides.   5. Family Planning—United
States—Handbooks.   6. Family Planning—United States—Resource
Guides.   7. Family Planning Policy—United States—Handbooks.   8.
Family Planning Policy—United States—Resource Guides.   9. Genetic
Counseling—United States—Handbooks.   10. Genetic Counseling—
United States—Resource Guides. WQ 39 M568r 2003]   I. Blank,
Robert H.   II. Title.   III. Series.

RG133.5.M47 2003
616.6'9206—dc21

                                                            200300795

08 07 06 05 04 03   10 9 8 7 6 5 4 3 2 1

This book is also available on the World Wide Web as an eBook.
Visit abc-clio.com for details.

ABC-CLIO, Inc.
130 Cremona Drive, P.O. Box 1911
Santa Barbara, California 93116-1911

This book is printed on acid-free paper ∞.
Manufactured in the United States of America

For Candy and Jean

Contents

Preface

As this book goes to press, newspapers are brimming with provocative accounts of dramatic changes in human reproduction. In January 2003, Clonaid, Inc., a company some describe as a cult, announced it had successfully cloned two healthy infants and it would release DNA tests to prove the babies were, indeed, clones. The scientific community dismissed it as a hoax when the promised tests failed to materialize. Shortly thereafter, Dolly the sheep, known as the world's first cloned mammal, was euthanized at age six because of premature lung disease and arthritis. Most of her contemporaries will live twice as long and be healthier along the way. Seemingly, each new day brings a new discovery in the exploration and development of human reproductive technology.

Reproductive Issues in America: A Reference Handbook provides a compass for this journey that explores the most fundamental issue in human life: how we reproduce ourselves. Chapter 1 sets the conceptual framework by analyzing the "rights" that various actors claim along this journey. Some, for example those seeking assisted reproduction, may make a claim that they have a right to have children, and government should assist them in doing so. Others, such as the woman seeking an abortion, may desire to make reproductive choices in private and may claim that government has no right to interfere with those choices.

This book addresses many complex and controversial issues in human reproduction. In addition to establishing the conceptual framework, Chapter 1 considers individuals' choices not to become pregnant through various forms of contraception. It moves on to a discussion of sterilization, both voluntary and involuntary, and concludes with an analysis of abortion methods and policy, including selective abortion in multiple-fetus pregnancies. Chapter 2 focuses on various forms of assisted reproduction, including therapeutic assistance such as in vitro fertilization and social assistance such as surrogate motherhood. It examines the controversial issues of prenatal diagnosis, sex preselection, fetal surgery, genetic screening, coerced obstetrical interventions, prenatal substance abuse, and fetal and embryo research. Chapter 3 is a comprehensive chronology of the major events in human reproductive science and policy from 1873 to 2003, and Chapter 4 provides biographies of the major contributors to these events and of the current scholars who write about these events. Chapter 5 gives readers facts and data about reproductive issues, including texts of specific government acts, and Chapters 6 and 7 provide useful resources about organizations, books, journals, websites, and videos for readers as they map their own analytical journeys.

We are indebted to many people. Research assistants Kathaleen Rust and Jean Celestin read drafts and tracked down research. Delores Bryant and Doris Kearney at the University of South Florida provided excellent secretarial services and Alicia Merritt and Carla Roberts at ABC-CLIO efficiently shepherded the book through production. We would also like to thank our families and friends who were supportive of our work and patient with our long hours at the computer.

Janna C. Merrick
University of South Florida, U.S.A.
Robert H. Blank
Brunel University, London

1

Reproductive Rights

On May 4, 2001, the newspaper headlines proclaimed that the first genetically modified babies had been born. The stories announced that up to thirty babies had been born using a technique in which they received genes from two mothers and one father. Elsewhere are reports of new techniques that allow men with *dead* sperm to father children, women in their sixties to give birth, and couples to preselect the sex of their children. Mothers are carrying the fetuses of their daughters, twins are born six years apart, and there is talk of human cloning and even male procreation.

Barely a day passes without news reports focusing on complex events in human reproduction. These reports demonstrate the rapid advances in human reproductive technologies and often are met with awe. However, such events also give rise to important ethical and public policy dilemmas and raise serious challenges to conventional notions of reproductive rights. They also introduce many third parties to the procreative process and promise to alter the way we perceive children and parents.

The Framework of Reproductive Rights

There are three critical problems inherent to a rights approach, each of which raises questions as to its ultimate value in resolving conflicts: What constitutes a right? Who has rights? How do we resolve conflicts among rights or rights holders? In addition to these generic problems with rights, application of a rights framework to human reproduction raises unique problems. Each of these problems is discussed in relation to reproduction before turning attention to the U.S. context of reproductive rights.

Rights will always be controversial because they impose claims upon others. Many of the most explosive political issues turn on differing interpretations of rights and on the relative weights accorded them. Furthermore, shifts constantly occur that broaden or narrow the scope of rights. Although some theorists attempt to enumerate immutable sets of rights and some contemporary observers advocate absolute sets of human rights, rights represent legal constructs that exist within a particular constitutional or legal framework. The language and rhetoric of rights, therefore, must be interpreted within a complex set of values and structures in a specific time and place.

One basic distinction of rights is that between negative and positive rights. Negative rights are those that impose obligations on others or keep others from interfering with the rights of the bearer. Each person under such conditions has a sphere of autonomy that others cannot violate, but no one is obliged to take positive action to further the exercise of those rights. In contrast, positive rights impose obligations on others or society to provide those goods and services necessary for each individual to carry out his or her rights. For every positive right one has, someone else has a duty to do something. Although the appropriate level of positive rights is not clearly defined, this additional dimension requires the presence of institutions that guarantee a certain level of material well-being through the redistribution of goods and services, if needed.

In addition to the distinction between negative and positive rights, Figure 1.1 demonstrates that reproductive rights potentially have several dimensions, and this complexity can cause disagreement as to what, if any, lines should be drawn. In general, reproductive rights include a right not to have children, a right to have children, and a right to have children of a particular quality and quantity. In turn, each of these major categories has many variations, which require clarification and the setting of boundaries. Much of the disagreement over women's rights centers on the distinctions between the right not to reproduce and the right to reproduce.

Central to reproductive rights is the question of personhood. At what stage does the developing human organism become a person for purposes of rights: at conception, viability, birth, or some point after birth? Furthermore, are there certain character-

Figure 1.1 Defining Reproductive Rights

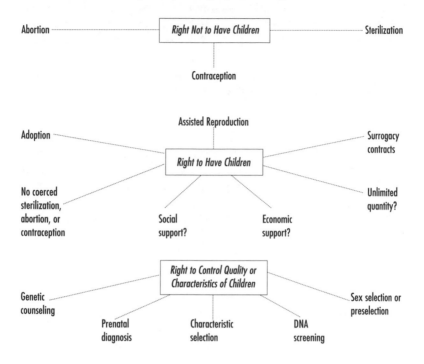

istics that represent minimal requirements for personhood, such as a "near normal" genetic profile, a minimal intelligence quotient (IQ), or other criteria? The decisions made on these questions go far to explain how people approach a broad range of reproductive issues from abortion to fetal research. For instance, the person who believes that the eight-cell human embryo has rights has little to share with the person who believes that personhood and thus rights come only with the live birth of the infant.

The language of rights is often presented as straightforward. Unfortunately, because of the first two problems of defining rights and persons who hold rights, the rights discourse always produces conflict, which takes two basic forms. First, the lack of clear hierarchies or priorities of rights results in conflict among rights themselves. A second and often overlapping conflict occurs when the rights of two individuals clash. For instance, who has the right to raise the child, the genetic father or the surrogate mother? This dilemma is complicated in many reproductive issues by the lack of consensus as to what the right to reproduction entails and whether a fetus has rights that might contradict the right to privacy of a pregnant woman. Figure 1.2 illustrates some of the dimensions of conflict inherent in reproductive rights.

Reproductive Rights in the United States

Few areas of human intervention engender as much intense debate as those relating to human reproduction, which is unsurprising because a primary enterprise of living is reproduction. It satisfies the individual's natural drive for sex and provides continuity with past and future generations. Moreover, because of differing roles between males and females in the reproductive process, reproduction raises fundamental political questions regarding equality, and historically has been a critical factor in discrimination against women based on "biological destiny." Oppressive reproductive policies also create the potential for racial, religious, and ethnic origin discrimination.

Although some limits are placed on reproductive rights in all societies, in most western countries, procreation is viewed as a fundamental right inherent in the very survival of the individual. The U.N.'s Universal Declaration of Human Rights (1948) empha-

Figure 1.2 Potential Parties in Reproductive Arena

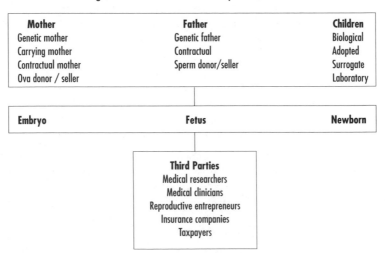

Mother	Father	Children
Genetic mother	Genetic father	Biological
Carrying mother	Contractual	Adopted
Contractual mother	Sperm donor/seller	Surrogate
Ova donor / seller		Laboratory

Embryo	Fetus	Newborn

Third Parties
Medical researchers
Medical clinicians
Reproductive entrepreneurs
Insurance companies
Taxpayers

sizes the right to marry and found a family free from constraint, and it affords special care and assistance to motherhood. According to Article 16, the family is the natural and fundamental unit of society and is entitled to protection by the state. Similarly, in the United States, reproductive rights are viewed as fundamental human rights. Justice William O. Douglas (*Skinner v. Oklahoma* 1942) applied the concept of "fundamental interests" to procreation when he placed compulsory sterilization within the confines of the equal protection clause of the Fourteenth Amendment: "We are here dealing with legislation which involves one of the basic civil rights of man. Marriage and procreation are fundamental to the very existence and survival of the race." Since *Skinner,* the constitutional status of reproductive choice has been expanded. In a concurring opinion in *Griswold v. Connecticut* (1965), Justice Arthur Goldberg viewed the marital relationship as a fundamental area of privacy protected by the Ninth Amendment. The state can interfere with marriage and procreation only upon proof of a "compelling state interest." This point was reiterated in *Roe v. Wade* (1973), in which the U.S. Supreme Court ruled that the right of privacy protects a woman's decision to terminate a pregnancy, and in *Eisenstadt v. Baird* (1972), in which it recognized "the right of the individual, married or single, to be free of unwarranted government intrusion into matters so fundamentally affecting a person as the decision whether to bear or beget a child."

In discussing reproductive rights, there is a danger of vastly oversimplifying what procreation itself entails and a tendency to focus on particular aspects of it at the exclusion of others. Contemporary debate, for instance, has focused on the right of a woman to control her body and terminate an unwanted pregnancy through abortion or, conversely, on the protection of individuals from being sterilized against their will. Procreation, however, is a complex process that develops over time and involves a series of disparate though interrelated decisions. Claims of reproductive freedom logically extend to four components of reproduction: conception, gestation, birth, and child rearing. Only recently has attention focused on the biological experience of bearing children and giving birth as aspects of procreative freedom. Child rearing can be a fulfilling experience deserving respect, whether or not the person who raises the child also provides the child's genes or bears the child. Moreover, there is a tendency to deal almost exclusively with the reproductive choices regarding *who* may conceive, bear, and rear a child, as opposed to those choices involving the conduct that occurs in the process of conceiving, bearing, and rearing.

Considerable effort is needed to clarify the notion of reproductive rights, especially in light of recent advances in genetics and medicine. No longer is the genetic linkage unambiguous. Virtually any kind of combination of germinal material is now possible. Artificial insemination, in vitro fertilization, and various embryo transfer techniques displace the premise that a woman who conceives a child also bears it and raises it. In other words, the process of procreation itself is undergoing continuous change. It is dangerous, therefore, to focus too closely on one dimension of procreative rights at the exclusion of others.

Constraints on State Intervention in Defining Responsible Parenthood

Reproductive freedom is highly valued in the United States, but it is not absolute. The state does have an interest at times in intervening and limiting these freedoms. Most often, it occurs when the parents inadequately care for their children. Under what circumstances is the state justified in intervening directly in the reproductive process through the imposition of restrictions or requirements on parents or potential parents? There are three constitutional rights that limit the power of the state to intervene in the reproductive decisions of a pregnant woman: the right to bodily integrity, the right to make intimate family decisions, and the right of parents to make decisions about how to raise their child. As usual, these legal rights are subject to varying interpretations over time and across jurisdictions.

The Right to Bodily Integrity

The origins of the right to bodily integrity lie in the Fourth Amendment's "right of the people to be secure in their persons, houses, papers, and effects against unreasonable searches and seizures" and in the due process clause of the Fourteenth Amendment. This right to self-determination and bodily integrity has long been applied to decisions involving medical treatment; a doctor who does not obtain consent before treating the patient can be charged with battery (*Schloendorff v. Society of*

N.Y. Hospital 1914). Since that time, consent has come to be interpreted as informed, thus allowing the individual to weigh the risks and benefits of a proposed treatment. Implicit in the concept of informed consent is the right to refuse treatment, even if it might lead to the patient's death (*Bouvia v. Superior Court* 1986).

Although the right to bodily integrity is a basic right, it is a qualified one. The courts have not prohibited all state action that interferes with this right but have applied a balancing test that weighs the invasion of bodily integrity against the legitimate state interest in taking that action. When state action invades an individual's bodily autonomy, however, the courts have required procedural safeguards. The Constitution, then, allows states to intrude into an individual's bodily integrity only if the intrusion is essential to achieve a legitimate state goal that is judged more important than the individual's bodily privacy. For instance, the courts have held that the state's compelling interest in protecting the life or health of a child outweighs a mother's right to bodily integrity (e.g., see *In re President and Directors of Georgetown College* 1964, where the court ordered a blood transfusion for a woman against her will when it found that her death would jeopardize the welfare of her minor children). The state's interest in taking the intrusive action, however, must outweigh the individual's privacy interest. Furthermore, the state must not be able to achieve its goal through any less intrusive means. Additionally, the state must grant the individual adequate procedural rights if her or his rights are adjudicated.

The Right to Make Intimate Family Decisions

In *Griswold v. Connecticut* (1965), the Supreme Court enunciated a right to marital privacy that protects couples from governmental efforts to prevent their use of contraceptives. The Court held that the Bill of Rights implicitly protects a "zone of privacy." Although there is no explicit reference to the term "privacy" by the framers, the Court forged this right from the penumbras emanating from the First Amendment right of association, the Third Amendment prohibition against quartering soldiers in peacetime, the Fourth Amendment prohibition against unreasonable searches and seizures, the Fifth Amendment protection against self-incrimination, and the Ninth Amendment, which vests in the people those rights not enumerated in the Constitution.

In *Eisenstadt v. Baird* (1972), the Court extended the right to use contraceptives to unmarried couples by applying the equal protection clause of the Fourteenth Amendment. The right to autonomy in intimate decision making rests on two principles: a person should be free from governmental intrusion into his or her home or family, and a person has a right to autonomy in making certain personal decisions. The second principle led to the *Roe v. Wade* (1973) decision invalidating the Texas statute prohibiting abortion. The Court elaborated on the principle of autonomy, holding that it prevents a state from interfering in fundamental intimate decisions in the absence of a compelling state interest. The right to terminate pregnancy involves rights "implicit in the concept of ordered liberty" and falls within the zone of privacy protected by the Constitution. To deny a woman the right to make this decision would cause distress and the risk of harm inherent in imposing an unwanted child on the woman. The *Roe* decision concluded that only after the fetus became viable could the state demonstrate a compelling interest to intervene.

In *Harris v. McRae* (1980), however, the Court held that the denial of Medicaid funding, even for medically indicated abortions, does not unduly interfere with the freedom of choice protected in *Roe,* although it makes "childbirth a more attractive alternative, thereby influencing the woman's decision." Freedom of choice does not impose an obligation on the state to subsidize all alternatives equally. Although the Court is adamant in prohibiting any absolute denial of the constitutional right to make autonomous procreative decisions, for lesser intrusions, it is willing to apply a balancing analysis that varies in intensity according to the means employed and the extent of intrusion on privacy rights. It requires considerable care on the part of the state in framing any regulations that affect childbearing decisions, but upon proof of a compelling state interest, the Court is willing to permit lesser forms of interference with procreative rights (*Webster v. Reproductive Health Services* 1989).

The Right to Parental Autonomy in Childbearing

There is a traditional preference in U.S. society for minimal state intervention in childbearing decisions. It is based on the assumption that parents are able to and will pursue the course of action that is in their child's best interest. According to the Supreme Court:

> The law's concept of the family rests on a presumption that parents possess what a child lacks in maturity, experience, and capacity for judgment required for making life's difficult decisions. More importantly, historically it has recognized that natural bonds of affection lead parents to act in the best interests of their children. (*Parham v. J. R.* 1979, 602)

The parent-child relationship, then, is special and comprises deep psychological and social bonding as well as physical and material dependence. When in doubt, the courts have chosen to err on the side of nonintervention to preserve the stability of the parent-child relationship: "[T]he state should usually defer to the wishes of the parents; it has a serious burden of justification before abridging parental authority by 'substituting its judgment' for that of the parents" (*In re Phillip B.* 1979, 51). In a challenge to the law that mandated aggressive treatment of ill newborns over the refusal of parents (*Bowen v. American Hospital Association* 1986), the Supreme Court held that the state should intervene only in "exceptional" cases.

Despite violations in practice, the prevailing value orientation in the United States continues to give preeminence to the right to reproduce with few restrictions as an interest so fundamental that society should not interfere without a compelling reason. There has been some erosion of the assumption that the parents will make good faith efforts to act in the best interests of their children, and increased emphasis, both in case law and literature, on a parental duty to provide a healthy environment so that all children have a minimal chance to succeed. The view that a child has a right to a sound body and mind is growing more prevalent. Although reproductive rights are still highly valued, new pressures for setting limits when their exercise conflicts with the health and life of children, including the unborn, are evident.

Within the context of emerging technologies for procreative control, there is support for the view that society has not only the authority but also the duty to intervene in reproductive decision making. Whether out of concern for affected children, future generations, the health of the gene pool, or some other societal good, there appears to be a growing perception that some constraints ought to be placed on parents when they abuse those rights. Advocates of this approach contend that even if procreation is an inalienable right, it can be regulated by a society that is concerned with the existence of each child and with its own survival as a society. Reproduction in these terms is a right shared with society as a whole and is but part of a larger complex of rights, responsibilities, and obligations. State intervention might be justified under certain circumstances, although each case must be addressed with caution.

The Changing Relationship between Parents and Children

As the number of children preferred by many parents has declined, the expectations for each new birth seem to rise accordingly. Parents who have only one or two children want those children to be as "perfect" as possible, within the meaning of their own value system. The state, too, has a profound interest in the aggregate quality of progeny. One clear predisposition in western society is a fear of those persons who are different—the mentally disabled and, to a lesser extent, the physically disabled. The availability of technologies to treat or reduce the possibility of having a child with such "defects," along with the trend toward fewer children per family, will accentuate the emphasis on the "quality" of progeny.

All reproductive technologies share the ethically acute characteristic of introducing third parties into what has usually been a private matter between the parents. The more complex the intervention, the more mediators become necessary. Embryologists, geneticists, and an array of other medical specialists and lawyers are central to these applications. Although these specialists' desire to help their clients may be genuine, their very presence takes control of procreation away from the parents.

More disquieting is the fact that many of these third parties represent commercial interests. For instance, the shift of fertility research and services from the public sector to the private, profit-making sector heightens concern over the rights of women to privacy in conception. The introduction of economic relationships into human reproduction transforms men and women into consumers of reproductive services and products and, more importantly, commodifies the role of women in producing children for the reproductive marketplace. Commercialization of procreation presents a clear danger of commodifying both women and children through the specialization of reproduction into discrete parts, each controlled by a different agent. Under these conditions, children become consumer goods that can be made to order and purchased on the open market, thus encouraging "an emphasis on acquiring one's own children as property" (Overall 1987, 200).

One critical issue, then, is what role the government should have in the reproductive process. Although the courts by default are active players, elected officials have by and large done everything to avoid the new generation of reproductive issues. This choice is understandable, given that abortion continues to be a political land mine. The fragmented federal system also works against a national policy in contentious areas such as reproduction. The unfortunate result is inconsistent and often conflicting policies, as individual state legislatures and courts shape their responses to new technologies and accompanying novel issues surrounding reproduction.

Fertility Control

The development of oral contraceptives (OCs) and intrauterine devices (IUDs) in the 1960s gave couples increased reproductive control. By the 1990s, there were more than forty different brands on the market in the United States (Knight et al. 2001, 29). Initially, both the pill and the IUD were hailed as offering safe and effective means of fertility control. By 1968, however, the public was being warned that the pill was not as safe as previously suggested and that some users were at risk for a variety of diseases, including breast cancer. Although oral contraceptives still enjoy the highest percentages of favorable opinion among women, concern over health risks is decreasing support. A 1995 Gallup Poll, for instance, found that 75 percent of women surveyed believed the pill caused "serious health care problems." One-third believed it caused cancer, and nearly as many felt it caused heart attacks and stroke.

The IUD suffered a similar fate, in that initial enthusiasm was soon dampened by claims of serious and, in some cases, fatal pelvic inflammatory disease in IUD users. Lawsuits directed primarily at the Dalkon Shield IUD resulted in the near cessation of production of IUDs by U.S. companies that did not want to incur the legal costs of aggressive lawsuits against their products, even though IUDs were found to be of minimal risk to most women. An extensive study concluded that even the indictment of the Dalkon Shield's producers was a mistake and that it, too, is a safe method of fertility control (Mumford and Kessel 1992).

Despite the approval of the injectable hormonal contraceptive Depo-Provera by the U.S. Food and Drug Administration (FDA) in October 1992 and the development of many new OCs, the search for long-term fertility control continues. It is estimated that contraceptive failure leads to 1.5 to 2.0 million accidental pregnancies in the United States each year. Because most couples elect to have small families, they are faced with more than twenty years of fertility control after completion of their family. Rather than using a form of contraception that is at best inconvenient and not fully effective and at worst a significant hazard to the woman's health, more couples have opted for long-term fertility control. Demographic trends indicate that demand for long-term methods of fertility control is likely to intensify over the next several decades as the population ages.

Subdermal Hormonal Implants

One option is the use of subdermal hormonal implants (SHIs), which are rods or capsules that contain a contraceptive steroid. In 1990 Norplant became the first form of SHI approved for marketing in the United States. Developed by the Population Council, it consists of six rods made of Silastic, a type of silicone rubber. Each rod contains 34 milligrams of levonorgestrel, a synthetic progestogen, which permeates the walls of the rods and enters the body over a five-year period. The rods are implanted under the skin inside the upper arm or forearm in a fifteen-minute surgical procedure using local anesthetic. Norplant was 99 percent effective in preventing conception and works by inhibiting ovulation and by thickening the cervical mucus, making it less penetrable by sperm. Since the rods were not biodegradable, they must be physically removed. Although Norplant has been removed from the market, at least two other SHIs (Capronor, a biodegradable rod that is expected to work for eighteen months, and Norplant-2, two rods that last for three years) are under development.

In the United States, some women faced a financial barrier to their voluntary use of the implant. With the average cost of Norplant insertion between $500 and $600 and the cost of removal at approximately $150, the total average cost was about $700. The implant was still less expensive than oral contraceptives, which cost about $1,500 for a five-year period. In the short run, however, Norplant's high initial cost made it difficult to acquire without private insurance or Medicaid coverage, though some family planning clinics provided it on a sliding scale fee basis.

Norplant became especially controversial because some viewed it as a means to address a myriad of social ills. As an instrument of social policy, Norplant was touted as a cure for teenage pregnancy, welfare dependency, and drug-addicted mothers. These efforts at social engineering generated a debate over the power of government to regulate fertility and coerce reproductive choices of teenagers and poor and minority women. Norplant use to control teenage pregnancy raised the issue of whether the implant was a license for promiscuity and whether schools should encourage its use by providing contraceptive counseling and distributing the implant to their students. In addition, these school programs acquired racial overtones when Norplant was provided to inner-city minority teenagers. Its advocates replied that the implant permitted girls to avoid teenage motherhood and complete high school and even college without becoming pregnant.

Norplant's use by women on Medicaid, some 50 percent of all users, raised the question of its use to control the cost of public assistance. Advocates argued that because state governments must support the children of the poor, the implant was one way to reduce welfare costs. To that end, state legislators introduced bills to encourage or require the use of the implant by women on welfare and to address the growing social problems of drug abuse and child neglect and abuse. Some of these bills provided financial incentives to encourage low-income women and substance abusers to use the implant. Others mandated its use as a condition of receiving public assistance and as a condition of probation for women capable of becoming pregnant who had been convicted of felony drug offences or who had had babies born with fetal alcohol syndrome. None of these bills, however, became law.

Whatever the social risks, family planning clinics welcomed Norplant because of the problems they encounter in gaining compliance from women who use contraceptive techniques that require daily self-administration or partner cooperation. Norplant is reliable and effortless to use and provides a reversible method of birth control with no known permanent adverse effect on fertility. Although there was never any clear evidence that women using Norplant suffered long-term health risks of breast or other cancers, there were documented side effects, including menstrual bleeding, intermenstrual spotting, and prolonged episodes of bleeding of more than ten days per cycle. Some women also reported pain at the implant site and other adverse reactions common to hormonal contraceptives, including headache, nervousness, nausea, dizziness, depression, appetite changes, dermatitis, acne, weight gain, fatigue, and weakness. These side effects led 15–19 percent of women to have the implant removed. A series of class action suits by over 50,000 women caused a precipitous decline in Norplant sales after 2000, and in August 2002, despite an FDA advisory in July that said that health concerns were unfounded, Norplant was permanently withdrawn from the market thus leaving a void to be filled by future innovations and a return to more traditional forms of sterilization (Roan 2002).

Sterilization

Data demonstrate that sterilization has become a widely accepted method of fertility control because of its very low failure rates (tubal ligation and vasectomy have failure rates of 0.4 percent and 0.15 percent, respectively), compared with the IUD (6.0 percent), the pill (2.6 percent), and especially condoms (14.2 percent) and diaphragms (15.6 percent). Reinforcing this demand by couples for a fail-safe, permanent method of contraception, many organizations have expended considerable effort to make sterilization services available to individuals who desire them. The Association for Voluntary Surgical Contraception (AVSC) and the Planned Parenthood Federation of America both lobbied for the elimination of statutory constraints on voluntary applications and the provision of such services as part of an overall population-planning program. AVSC emphasizes an individual's right to know about and choose sterilization, and Planned Parenthood presents sterilization as one aspect of an overall family planning program.

The increase in demand for long-term fertility control can also be traced to the refinement of sterilization techniques, especially for females. What once required inpatient surgery under general anesthesia and lengthy recovery periods is now available on an outpatient basis. This medical advance has not only increased the acceptability of sterilization but also decreased its relative cost vis-à-vis the long-term costs of alternative contraceptive methods. An administrative advantage of sterilization for family planning clinics is that it necessitates reaching a client only once rather than on a continuing basis. This one-time-only factor and safety have made sterilization the most frequent means of fertility control in the world.

Involuntary Sterilization

There are two distinct meanings of the term "involuntary" here. The first refers to sterilizations that are involuntary because the subject is legally incompetent to exercise informed consent. For instance, parents who petition the state for permission to have their mentally retarded daughter sterilized are attempting to substitute their consent for hers. Such involuntary applications are always problematic because it is impossible to determine what the subject would choose if she or he were capable of granting informed consent.

The second form of involuntary sterilization might best be defined as compulsory. In this situation, a person legally capable of informed consent is coerced into being sterilized. Sterilization for reasons of eugenics, to punish a criminal, and to keep women on welfare from having more children are examples of this more insidious form of the practice. Legislation in the early twentieth century was motivated primarily by medical theories that postulated that mental illness and other social ills could be alleviated only if "undesirables" were sterilized. Although such eugenic theories fell into disrepute, as of 1991, twenty-one states had statutes providing for involuntary sterilization of some type. Four allow compulsory sterilization of institutionalized persons only, whereas seventeen permit it on persons in the community as well as those in institutions.

Persons addressed by such statutes usually include the mentally retarded or mentally ill and, in a few states, epileptics. The Delaware statute authorizes sterilization of habitual criminals. In fourteen states, parents or legal guardians can initiate steriliza-

tion proceedings, and in Virginia, a spouse or "next friend" also
has that authority. Although all but seven states require a hearing
prior to sterilization, actual procedures vary considerably from
state to state. Four states require only an administrative hearing,
which is usually conducted by the director of the state department with jurisdiction over public institutions, whereas nine
states require a full judicial hearing. They provide for a formal
hearing, the right to counsel, the right to be present and cross-
examine witnesses, and the right to a full record of all testimony,
both written and oral. Eight states permit substituted consent by
a parent or guardian, and several states permit such consent by a
spouse of the person to be sterilized. These more recent sterilization laws clearly demonstrate the move away from eugenic ratio-
nales and toward other justifications. Only four states refer to
eugenic or hereditary grounds for sterilization, and three of them
include other grounds as well. Increasingly, the states refer to
"the inability to care for and support children," the "best interests of the person," or the "welfare of society" as statutory standards for sterilization.

Despite the renewed interest of some state legislatures in
adopting sterilization statutes, the most conspicuous activity to
date is concentrated in the courts. Court activity regarding involuntary sterilization centers on two issues: Are the specific statutory schemes constitutional? In the absence of express statutory
authorization, do the courts have jurisdiction to approve sterilization petitions for persons who are incompetent? The court
response to the first question is a qualified "yes." Although there
is no uniform response from the courts on the second question,
the trend is toward allowing such orders within strict parameters.

The courts tend to agree that involuntary sterilization
statutes are constitutional after the precedent set in *Buck v. Bell*
(1927), in which the Supreme Court upheld eugenic sterilization
under Oliver Wendell Holmes's dictum that "three generations of
imbeciles are enough." They have been active over the years,
however, in narrowing that precedent through rulings that specific statutes lack necessary due process elements such as the right
to counsel, a hearing, or appeal. In these cases, the courts usually
leave it up to the legislature to rewrite laws to ensure both procedural and substantive protections to the targets of sterilization.

In *North Carolina Association for Retarded Children v. State of
North Carolina* (1976), for example, a U.S. district court left stand-
ing the right of state legislatures to enact sterilization laws, but

only within narrow circumstances. The court explicitly dismissed eugenic bases for mandating sterilization but noted that there was considerable medical evidence that sterilization is desirable in extreme cases as a last resort. For instance, it might be warranted in cases of clearly identifiable genetic defects with "significant probability" that offspring will inherit that defect. Also, if a mentally retarded person was incapable of discharging the responsibility of parenthood because of an inability to create a nondetrimental environment for his or her progeny, cause for sterilization might be established. Other justifications for sterilization noted are the inability of a person to understand that the consequence of sexual activity is a child; the inability to use other forms of birth control; and in rare and unusual cases, the medical determination that it would be in the best interests of the mentally retarded person, the state, or both.

Using a different rationale to uphold a state sterilization law, the Oregon Court of Appeals (*Cook v. State of Oregon* 1972) approved the sterilization of a seventeen-year-old girl on grounds it would be a burden to the state if she were to have children. Because of her incapacity to care for any children, they would most likely be neglected and become wards of the state. The court ruled that since she could never be an adequate parent, it was proper to sterilize her. In *Motes v. Hall City Department of Family and Children Services* (1983), however, a Georgia court declared that the state statute providing for involuntary sterilization of mentally incompetent persons was unconstitutional because it denied those persons the right to procreate.

Until 1980, with very few exceptions, courts ruled that they had no authorization to order permanent sterilization of incompetent persons without an express legislative grant of such power. Although the signals coming from the courts are equivocal, there is an evolving pattern in which courts recognize jurisdiction in ordering sterilization of persons incapable of consent. In 1985, the Supreme Court of California (*Conservatorship of Valerie N.*) invoked the jurisprudence of fundamental rights to invalidate a California statute that prohibited the sterilization of mentally retarded persons. In a long opinion with heated dissent by Chief Justice Rose Bird, the court argued that the statute "impermissibly deprives" developmentally disabled persons of privacy and liberty interests protected by federal and state constitutions. By withholding sterilization from an incompetent woman, the statute deprived her of her only realistic opportunity for contraception and, consequently, restricted her chances for self-fulfillment. "Since the right to elect sterilization as a method of contraception is generally available to adult women, restriction on that right must be justified by a compelling state interest" (at 761). This growing court acceptance of jurisdiction over involuntary sterilization is accompanied, however, with a hesitation to order permanent sterilization procedures except in the most extreme cases.

Voluntary Sterilization

The vast majority of sterilizations performed in the United States are voluntary fertility control procedures based on individual choice. The development of less intrusive, safe, and effective sterilization procedures, combined with attitudinal changes in the medical profession and the general public, led to substantial efforts during the 1960s and 1970s to facilitate access to sterilization by those who wanted to terminate their fertility. After a long process of court challenges that gradually eliminated a variety of restrictions, voluntary sterilization is legal in all fifty states. In response to these many legal uncertainties, a number of states enacted voluntary sterilization statutes. Although variation in states' efforts to regulate voluntary sterilization continues to be confusing, most of the specific requirements fall into one of four categories: age requirements, a waiting period (usually thirty days) between time of consent and the procedure, consent of spouse, and second-opinion consultation.

In addition to these legislative actions, a series of court challenges have successfully struck down the most constraining legal restrictions. In *Hathaway v. Worcester City Hospital* (1973), a U.S. court of appeals held that the refusal of a city hospital to permit its facilities to be used for sterilization violated the constitutional rights of a woman who wanted a tubal ligation for contraceptive purposes. Similarly, in *Avila v. New York City Health and Hospital Corporation* (1987), a Bronx County court ruled that an institution receiving federal funds and performing sterilization may not arbitrarily prevent a mentally competent and freely consenting individual from having the operation. In a related case (*Carey v. Population Services International* 1977), the Supreme Court implied that personal autonomy over contraception protected the right to sterilization as well. By invalidating New Jersey's statutory limitation on a minor's access to contraceptives, the court extended this right to all forms of birth control, presumably including sterilization.

Although these statutes and court decisions have clarified the legal right to be sterilized for fertility control, some impediments to the widespread availability of voluntary sterilization remain. Although publicly supported hospitals cannot refuse to perform sterilization, in most states they still can establish their own policies regarding waiting periods, consultation, and spousal consent. Physicians and clinics can also impose their own restrictions as to whom they consider eligible, thus making voluntary sterilization difficult to obtain in some locales. Some physicians, especially those in states that have not addressed the question of minors, require that the patient be over twenty-one, married, and have spousal or parental consent. Others impose waiting periods ranging from seventy-two hours to thirty days (the same as the waiting period for all federally funded sterilizations) to minimize the possibility that a person might change his or her mind after the procedure is completed.

A further complicating factor is confusion in insurance coverage. Although many policies treat contraceptive sterilization as a medical procedure despite its motivation, others discriminate between medically indicated and elective sterilization and reimburse only the former. Other policies specifically exclude coverage of nontherapeutic sterilization. This consideration might discourage or even preclude voluntary sterilization for those individuals with limited monetary resources. Although Medicaid provides recourse in some states for those who qualify, about one-quarter of the states do not include coverage for elective sterilization. We now turn our attention to abortion, an issue that has caused enormous controversy in the U.S. political system.

Abortion: Colliding Rights and Complex Responsibilities

In 1969, Norma McCorvey was an unemployed, twenty-one-year-old high school dropout. She was also pregnant. She sought an abortion and was advised that it was illegal in Texas where she was living; she considered an illegal abortion but decided against it. She gave up her newborn baby for adoption, but before doing so, this poorly educated, poverty-stricken young woman agreed to become the complainant in what would become one of the greatest policy-changing cases in the history of

U.S. jurisprudence. In order to protect her privacy, McCorvey took the pseudonym Jane Roe, and together with young attorneys Sarah Weddington and Lynda Coffee, filed suit to overturn the Texas law prohibiting abortion.

Roe v. Wade (1973) hit the U.S. legal system at a time of great social unrest and change, when Americans were evaluating the role that government played and should play in their personal lives. The women's movement—buttressed by the introduction of low-cost oral contraceptives—was beginning to slowly change how society viewed women and how women viewed themselves. The time was ripe to evaluate whether abortion should be legalized nationally and, if legalized, under what circumstances. Most women of childbearing age today cannot remember a time when abortion was illegal in the United States. Although faced with moral dilemmas about whether to terminate an unwanted pregnancy, unlike women of their mothers' generation, they are not faced with the desperation of searching for illegal abortionists or traveling to foreign countries (Bonavoglia 1991).

Abortion reaches to the core of how individuals define personhood and how they view their rights and responsibilities as women and men and as mothers and fathers. It is more ethically complex than contraception because it involves the fetus, which some view as a human life. At first glance, abortion seems to be about a woman's right to choose and a fetus's right to be born. But there are other people who may not have legal rights in this debate but surely face moral dilemmas. Fathers, grandparents, health care providers, and even taxpayers have interests when an abortion is performed; all have views—some deeply held—about whether abortion is moral or immoral. The 1992 U.S. Supreme Court decision in *Planned Parenthood v. Casey* illustrates this potential conflict of interests:

> Abortion is a unique act. It is an act fraught with consequences for others: for the woman who must live with the implications of her decision; for the persons who perform and assist in the procedure; for the spouse, family, and society, which must confront the knowledge that these procedures exist, procedures some deem nothing short of an act of violence against innocent human life; and, depending on one's beliefs, for the life or potential life that is aborted. (*Planned Parenthood v. Casey* 1992, 2807)

The nation is divided on this issue, and for more than three decades its citizens have taken sides in the great moral debate about what constitutes a human being and when, if ever, it is appropriate to terminate a pregnancy. The battle lines were drawn primarily by the loosely defined prochoice and prolife movements. The prochoice movement organized in the 1960s as part of a larger movement to increase women's rights, and thus it is woman-based and centers on a woman's right to control her body, a negative right preventing others from restricting her choices. The prolife movement organized in response to *Roe* and is fetus-based, holding that life begins at conception and abortion constitutes the murder of a helpless unborn child.

The Incidence of Abortion in the United States

In the United States, it is estimated that 43 percent of women will have at least one abortion in their lifetimes (AGI 2002). In 2000, one-quarter of pregnancies ended in abortion, which amounted to 1.31 million abortions (Finer and Henshaw 2003). The numbers seem high, but the incidence of abortion is on the decline. Longitudinal data provided by the Alan Guttmacher Institute (AGI) show that although the percentage of pregnancies ending in abortion rose steadily from 19.3 percent in 1973 to 30.4 percent in 1983, that number is declining (Henshaw 1998, 1–6. See also Finer and Henshaw 2003).

The incidence of abortion among teenagers aged fifteen to nineteen is also on the decline, as is the rate of pregnancy. Although many groups and political leaders advocate adolescent abstinence, 80 percent of U.S. females have had sexual intercourse before the age of twenty (Singh et al. 2000, 21–28, Table 2). Among girls aged fifteen to nineteen, the incidence of pregnancy declined by 9 percent between 1990 and 1996, and the percentage of pregnancies ending in abortion declined from 46 percent in 1990 to 35 percent in 1996 (Henshaw and Feivelson 2000, 272–280).

Although abortion is legal in the United States until the point of fetal viability outside the womb, access to abortion services is not universal. Most abortions are performed in clinics rather than hospitals, but many communities have no abortion services whatsoever. In 1996, 86 percent of counties had no known provider, and 32 percent of women of reproductive age lived in these counties. More than half of metropolitan counties and one-third of U.S. cities also had no providers (Henshaw 1998, 263–270).

The type of procedure used to terminate a pregnancy depends largely upon the length of the pregnancy. Several surgical procedures are used, although each is minimally invasive. The Centers for Disease Control report that about 90 percent of abortions in the United States take place in the first trimester (twelve weeks) of pregnancy (*Stenberg v. Carhart* 2000), with the most common method being dilation of the cervix and suctioning of the fetus. About 10 percent of abortions are performed during the second trimester (twelve to twenty-four weeks), and the most common procedure is dilation of the cervix and evacuation of the fetus (D&E) with surgical instruments. If the head presents first, the doctor will collapse the skull and remove the fetus. If the feet present first, the doctor pulls the fetus through the cervix and then collapses the skull. The latter is referred to as dilation and extraction (D&X) and is sometimes characterized by laypeople and the news media as partial-birth abortion. Although there is debate in the medical community about which procedure is safest, the American College of Obstetricians and Gynecologists argues that D&X abortion "presents a variety of safety advantages over other abortion methods" (*Stenberg v. Carhart* 2000).

After many years of debate and legal wrangling, the FDA approved the French abortion drug mifepristone, also known by its trade name RU-486, in September 2000 for use during the first seven weeks of pregnancy. Used in Europe since the late 1980s, it is administered orally in the physician's office or clinic in conjunction with a second drug (misoprostol). Another oral medication, methotrexate, has been FDA-approved for treatment of cancer for many years and causes abortion if administered in combination with misoprostol during the first seven weeks of pregnancy (Center for Reproduction, Law, and Policy 2001). Therefore, nonsurgical "medical" abortions have been available for a number of years, despite the FDA's long-term ban on RU-486.

Although medical abortions currently represent a small percentage of total abortions, the AGI predicts a rapid increase in the future. It estimates that 4,200 medical abortions were performed in 1996 but that 4,300 were performed in the *first half* of 1997 (Henshaw 1998, 263–270). Data from the U.S. clinical trials for approval of mifepristone compared the views of women having mifepristone abortions with those having surgical abortions at the same gestational point (fifty-one to fifty-two days). Ninety-one percent of women using mifepristone said they would choose it again, compared to only 58 percent of women using surgical abortion (AGI 2000). Use of mifepristone in Europe has shown that it is safe and effective. A British clinical study reported 96 percent of women using mifepristone had complete abortions and did not require any surgical intervention ("In Clinical Use" 2001).

The Politics of Abortion

Some readers may be surprised to learn that throughout much of U.S. history, abortion was both legal and a socially accepted business practice. By 1900, however, virtually all states had outlawed it, primarily because of reforms in the medical profession (Mohr 1978). Elective abortion was illegal in all fifty states in 1962, when Sherri Finkbine, a young, pregnant Arizona mother, took the tranquilizer Thalidomide. The drug was banned in the United States, but Finkbine's husband obtained it in Europe, and when news reports there indicated it caused major fetal deformities, she sought an abortion. Her obstetrician agreed and reserved the operating room.

As an effort to warn others about the dangers of Thalidomide, Finkbine agreed to an anonymous newspaper interview, but her identity quickly became known, the hospital denied the abortion, and she was fired from her job as the host of a children's television program. Under intense media coverage, she fled to Sweden for the abortion. It was later reported that the fetus was severely deformed and most likely would have died had it been carried to full term (Craig and O'Brien 1993, 41; Tribe 1990, 37). The Finkbine case was followed by a three-year epidemic (1962–1965) of rubella, during which time 15,000 children were born with birth defects (Tribe 1990, 37).

These two events helped those who supported a woman's right to terminate her pregnancy, and the prochoice movement was born. It is important to understand what the prochoice movement is and is not. The prochoice movement does not advocate abortion. Rather it seeks to ensure a legal climate in which a woman has the right to choose whether to terminate a pregnancy and not face criminal or civil penalties for doing so. Beginning in the 1960s, support for the right to choose came from various established institutions, including the United Church of Christ, United Methodist Church, United Presbyterian Church, and the Episcopal Church (Tribe 1990, 37–49). New groups organized and mobilized, including the National Association for the Repeal of Abortion Laws (founded in 1969).

Change came slowly at first. By the early 1970s, five states (Alaska, Hawaii, New York, Colorado, and Washington) and the District of Columbia had legalized elective abortion. Thirteen states provided for abortion when the woman's physical or mental health was endangered, and Mississippi allowed abortion when the woman had been raped. Twenty-nine states allowed abortion only in cases in which the mother's life was endangered, and Louisiana, New Hampshire, and Pennsylvania prohibited all abortions (Craig and O'Brien 1993, 75).

But change came quickly in the aftermath of the dramatic decision in *Roe v. Wade* (1973). The Supreme Court ruled that states could not prohibit a woman from having an abortion during the first two trimesters of pregnancy. As discussed earlier in this chapter, it found that abortion falls within the zone of a woman's right to privacy and that

> this right of privacy . . . is broad enough to encompass a woman's decision whether or not to terminate her pregnancy. The detriment that the State would impose upon the pregnant woman by denying this choice altogether is apparent. Specific and direct harm medically diagnosable even in early pregnancy may be involved. Maternity, or additional offspring, may force upon the woman a distressful life and future. Psychological harm may be imminent. Mental and physical health may be taxed by child care. There is also the distress, for all concerned, associated with the unwanted child, and there is the problem of bringing a child into a family already unable, psychologically and otherwise, to care for it. In other cases, as in this one, the additional difficulties and continuing stigma of unwed motherhood may be involved. All these are factors the woman and her responsible physician necessarily will consider in consultation. (*Roe v. Wade* 1973, 153)

The Court placed some restrictions on the right to secure an abortion. It ruled that in the first trimester, the decision was left to the pregnant woman and her attending physician, and during the second trimester, the states could regulate abortion in ways that were reasonably related to maternal health. During the third trimester, the states could regulate and in fact proscribe abortion, except in cases in which pregnancy threatened the mother's life (*Roe v. Wade* 1973, 114). Thus the Court decision provides a negative right, in which the government cannot prevent the abortion during the first two trimesters.

A companion case, *Doe v. Bolton* (1973), challenged a Georgia statute based on the American Law Institute's Model Penal Code. The code, adopted by about one-quarter of the states, allowed for abortion in cases in which the pregnancy endangered the woman's life or health, the fetus was seriously deformed, or the pregnancy was the result of rape. Two physicians in addition to the woman's personal physician had to confirm that these conditions had been met, a hospital committee had to approve the abortion, and the abortion had to be performed in a hospital accredited by the Joint Commission on Accreditation of Hospitals (JCAH). The Supreme Court overturned the Georgia statute by holding that not all abortions should be required to be carried out in JCAH-accredited hospitals and neither hospital committees nor additional physicians need approve the abortion.

The prolife movement was quick to organize in the aftermath of *Roe* and *Doe*. The Catholic Church took the lead in mobilizing prolife activities through its parishes (Petchesky 1990, 252) and was joined in the late 1970s by the New Right, a broadly based movement dominated by fundamentalist religious groups and other conservative organizations. The New Right's members had diverse backgrounds and sometimes incompatible views and goals. Moreover, the conservative New Right was at odds with the more liberal Catholic Church on many issues (Petchesky 1990, 254–260; Tribe 1990, 159–160). Nevertheless, they reached common ground on their opposition to the legalization of abortion and forged a loose alliance.

The prolife movement pursued three strategies to overturn *Roe* and *Doe*. It attempted to amend the Constitution, brought new cases to the courts, and sought to make it uncomfortable for pregnant women and others to enter abortion clinics (Craig and O'Brien 1993, 43). The Catholic Church took the lead in seeking a constitutional amendment. The first actual vote on the Human Life Amendment occurred in the Senate in 1976, and when that vote failed (Bopp 1984, vii), it quickly became apparent that there was insufficient congressional support to gain the two-thirds vote

needed to send the amendment out for state ratification. The prolife strategy then shifted to electing more antiabortion candidates
to the House and Senate. These efforts paid off in 1978 and 1980,
but the electoral gains did not immediately translate into policy
changes, and the Human Life Amendment was never passed by
both houses of Congress (see Hershey and West 1983, 54).

With the elections of anti-*Roe* Presidents Ronald Reagan
(1980 and 1984) and George H. W. Bush (1988), the prolife movement had an opportunity to influence the selection of federal
judges. Together, Reagan and Bush appointed at least 60 percent
of federal judgeships, and the *New York Times* reported that Reagan appointees supported abortion restrictions in approximately
77 percent of the cases before them (Lewis 1992). Although prolife supporters were dismayed at the 1981 appointment of Sandra
Day O'Connor to the Supreme Court because of her track record
on abortion as an Arizona legislator, they rejoiced in the 1986 ele-
vation of conservative William Rehnquist from associate justice
to chief justice and in the appointments of conservatives Antonin
Scalia in 1986 and Clarence Thomas in 1991.

The prolife movement was making headway. Although it
had not overturned *Roe* and *Doe*, its allies in Congress, the state
legislatures, the Reagan and Bush administrations, and the
nation's courts would erect major roadblocks to obtaining abortions, and those roadblocks would be especially high for poor
women. Until 1976, approximately 300,000 legal abortions, about
33 percent of all legal abortions, were funded annually by Medicaid (Tribe 1990, 151). However, in 1976 Congress began prohibiting the use of federal Medicaid funds for abortion, except in
extremely limited circumstances. These limitations, usually
referred to as the Hyde Amendments, were upheld by the
Supreme Court in *Harris v. McRae* (1980).

There were other efforts as well. Congress barred the use of
federal funds for a number of programs in which abortion was a
method of family planning; prohibited judges or public officials
from ordering recipients of federal funds to perform abortions if
doing so was against the recipients' beliefs; barred lawyers in
federally funded legal-aid programs from providing assistance in
procuring "nontherapeutic" abortions; barred recipients of federal funds from discriminating against job applicants because of
their reluctance to counsel, assist, or participate in performing
abortions; prohibited funding for organizations involved in providing abortions but allowed religious organizations to receive

funds to promote "self-discipline" (i.e., abstinence) as a form of birth control; and provided that employers would not have to pay health insurance benefits for abortion except to save the life of the mother (Craig and O'Brien 1993, 112–113). The Reagan administration issued administrative regulations in 1988 that disallowed funding for organizations providing abortion counseling (Craig and O'Brien 1993, 188). The so-called gag rule was upheld in *Rust v. Sullivan* (1991) but was lifted by President Bill Clinton, via executive order, shortly after his inauguration in 1993 and then reinstated in 2001 by his successor, President George W. Bush.

State legislatures and sometimes city councils also sought to restrict access to abortion in the post-*Roe* period through a variety of provisions, including parental notification or consent, spousal notification, and waiting periods. Also included were requirements that abortions be performed in hospitals rather than clinics (thereby substantially increasing the costs), along with denial of public funds. The Supreme Court upheld some restrictions while overturning others. (For more extensive discussions of abortion litigation, see Craig and O'Brien 1993. For a discussion of the impact of waiting periods on the timing of abortion, see Joyce and Kaestner 2000.)

The record of the Supreme Court has been complex and sometimes contradictory. The Court overturned a Missouri law requiring that abortions after the twelfth week be performed in licensed hospitals (*Planned Parenthood of Kansas City v. Ashcroft* 1983) and overturned a city ordinance that disallowed abortions in all but licensed hospitals (*City of Akron v. Akron Center for Reproductive Health* 1983). It upheld parental notification statutes and consent statutes if they contained judicial bypass provisions (*Bellotti v. Baird* 1976, *H. L. v. Matheson* 1981, *Planned Parenthood of Kansas City v. Ashcroft* 1983, *Hodgson v. Minnesota* 1990, *Ohio v. Akron Center for Reproductive Health* 1990, and *Planned Parenthood v. Casey* 1992), but spousal notification was found to be unconstitutional (*Planned Parenthood v. Danforth* 1976; *Planned Parenthood v. Casey* 1992). Requirements that abortion patients receive extensive *informed consent* information regarding fetal development, alternatives to abortion, availability of child support, and so forth were overturned in *City of Akron v. Akron Center for Reproductive Health* (1983) and *Thornburgh v. American College of Obstetricians and Gynecologists* (1986) but upheld in *Planned Parenthood v. Casey* (1992).

In addition to notification/consent provisions and informed consent information, some states required waiting periods, thus typically necessitating at least two visits to the abortion clinic. Waiting periods were overturned in *City of Akron v. Akron Center for Reproductive Health* (1983) but upheld in *Planned Parenthood v. Danforth* (1976) and *Planned Parenthood v. Casey* (1992). States and cities also restricted public funding for abortions by limiting the circumstances under which Medicaid would pay for abortions (upheld in *Maher v. Roe* 1977 and *Beal v. Doe* 1977), denying poor women access to nontherapeutic abortions in public hospitals (upheld in *Poelker v. Doe* 1977), and prohibiting use of public facilities for abortions not necessary to save the mother's life.

In *Webster v. Reproductive Health Services* (1989), the Court ruled that states could require physicians to conduct viability tests to ensure that abortions were not performed on fetuses that would be viable outside the womb. Justice Blackmun, the author of *Roe*, filed a strongly worded dissent writing that *Webster* was an invitation to further restrict abortion rights. The signs were evident, he wrote, and a chill wind was blowing. That chill wind blew even colder in 1992, when a sharply divided Supreme Court reconsidered the basic legal principles of *Roe*. In *Planned Parenthood v. Casey* (1992), it abandoned the trimester approach, ruling that a woman had the right to an abortion prior to fetal viability, but the right was not without limitations, including provisions for informed consent, a twenty-four-hour waiting period, parental notification, and record keeping.

> Regulations, which do no more than create a structural mechanism by which the State, or the parent or guardian or a minor, may express profound respect for the life of the unborn are permitted, if they are not a substantial obstacle to the woman's exercise of the right to choose. . . . Unless it has that effect on her right of choice a state measure designed to persuade her to choose childbirth over abortion will be upheld if reasonably related to that goal. Regulations designed to foster the health of a woman seeking an abortion are valid if they do not constitute an undue burden. (*Planned Parenthood v. Casey* 1992, 2821).

In addition to supporting policymakers who opposed abortion, the prolife movement mounted a highly visible direct action campaign to deter women from obtaining abortions and deter employees from working in abortion clinics. Demonstrators picketed abortion clinics, harassed individuals who attempted to enter those clinics, and vandalized property. Direct action turned violent with the 1993 murder of Dr. David Gunn in Pensacola, Florida, and the 1998 murder of Dr. Barnett Slepian in Amherst, New York. A 1994 survey reported violence—including blockades, invasions, bomb threats, bombing, arson threats, arson, chemical attacks, death threats, or stalking—at 52 percent of abortion clinics nationwide (Feminist Majority Foundation 2000). The National Organization for Women (NOW), Planned Parenthood, and abortion clinics and organizations sought to use an 1871 civil rights law, often referred to as the Ku Klux Klan Act, against prolife protestors whose organized activities included blocking access to abortion clinics. Their efforts, however, were rebuffed by a divided Supreme Court in *Bray v. Alexandria Women's Health Clinic, et al.* in 1993.

NOW filed a second suit claiming that a coalition of antiabortion groups was conspiring to use "force, violence or fear to induce clinic employees . . . to give up their jobs" and that such extortion constituted racketeering in violation of the Racketeer Influenced and Corrupt Organizations (RICO) chapter of the Organized Crime Control Act of 1970. The U.S. District Court dismissed the action on the grounds that the prolife groups were political opponents, not commercial opponents, and the Court of Appeals affirmed. The Supreme Court, however, disagreed, unanimously finding that the racketeering statute could be used as the legal basis for suing organizations within the prolife movement (*NOW v. Scheidler* 1994). The case was remanded to District Court, where a jury found for the plaintiffs and ordered the defendants—including the Pro-Life Action League and Operation Rescue—to pay monetary damages to several women's health organizations. The Court of Appeals affirmed; however, the U.S. Supreme Court reversed the decisions of the district and appeals courts, finding that the defendants had not committed extortion because they had not obtained property from the plaintiffs (*Scheidler v. NOW* 2003).

Another next major test for the Court involved a Nebraska statute intended to criminalize partial-birth abortions and mandating punishment of up to twenty years in prison for the person performing the abortion. As noted above, the term "partial-birth abortion" has no clinical definition but is generally used to describe D&X abortions and sometimes D&E abortions, the most common method used during the second trimester. In a 5 to 4 decision, the Supreme Court struck down the Nebraska statute, finding that it would outlaw both D&X and D&E abortions and therefore impose an undue burden on the woman by forcing her to choose riskier methods. It would also create a climate in which "all those who perform abortion procedures using (the D&E) method must fear prosecution, conviction, and imprisonment" (*Stenberg v. Carhart* 2000).

Abortion and Multiple-Fetus Pregnancies

The battle over abortion took a new twist in the 1990s because of the increased number of multiple-fetus pregnancies resulting from improvements in and greater use of assisted reproductive technologies, the details of which are discussed in Chapter 2. Between 1989 and 1998, the number of twin births rose by 23 percent, and the number of triplet and quadruplet births grew nearly threefold (Congressional Information Service 2001).

Many issues come into play when prospective parents are faced with a multiple pregnancy, particularly when there are three or more fetuses. Although singletons and twins have similar patterns of morbidity and mortality, the risks increase dramatically when three or more fetuses are involved. Despite the extensive news coverage in 1997 showing a positive outcome for the McCaughey septuplets conceived after use of fertility drugs, many serious problems may arise during multiple-fetus pregnancies and births, including premature delivery, respiratory distress, vision problems, developmental delays, risk of a hemorrhage, and delivery by cesarean section. The Multiple Births Foundation in Great Britain reports that triplets are six times more likely than singletons to be stillborn, twelve times more likely to die during the first year of life, and forty-seven times more likely to have cerebral palsy (Multiple Births Foundation 1993). Risk to the mother's health also increases with higher order pregnancies.

The financial costs of multiple-fetus births can be extraordinary. The media reported the costs for the McCaughey septuplets to be in excess of $1 million (Schlotzhauer 1999), and research in the *New England Journal of Medicine* found that the per-baby hospital costs of a triplet birth were nearly four times the costs of a singleton birth (Callahan et al. 1994). The costs of raising multiples are much higher than for a singleton, particularly if there are birth defects, and the time and energy demands of caring for multiples may be excessive and strain the stability of a family unit. These concerns have led many couples to selectively abort some fetuses with the intent of carrying others to delivery. Both the terminology and techniques differ from traditional abortion. Embryo reduction—also referred to as multifetal pregnancy reduction—is generally accomplished during the first trimester by the injection of potassium chloride into the fetal heart. The dead fetus remains in the womb and is delivered with the live fetus(es).

The ethical issues involved in embryo reduction differ somewhat from those in traditional abortion. The latter usually involves an unplanned and unwanted pregnancy. Most often in embryo reduction, however, the prospective parents have gone to great lengths to achieve the pregnancy through assisted reproduction, and if they are well informed about the potential for multiple fetuses, understand prior to conception that one or more of the fetuses may be aborted. They enter the world of assisted reproduction with a plan to abort. A second ethical issue involves the purpose of the reduction. Pregnancies involving more than three fetuses are extremely risky. Thus reducing to the more manageable situation of two or three fetuses is more or less a "lifeboat" approach to saving the pregnancy (Rorty and Pinkerton 1996). Recent advances in reproductive technology called "blastocyst transfer" have allowed successful pregnancies with only two embryos implanted, and thus in the future, fewer in vitro procedures may result in triplets, quadruplets, or sextuplets. Blastocyst transfer, however, would have no impact on the incidence of multiple-fetus pregnancies caused by fertility drugs. Regardless of whether assisted reproduction has been used, how do we deal with prospective parents who want to reduce the pregnancy to a singleton, when diagnostically twins or triplets could result in a positive pregnancy outcome? Or what if they want a fetus of one gender or one with certain characteristics?

A third ethical issue involves the role of the clinician and her or his obligation to fully inform the patient of the likelihood of multiple fetuses and then respect the patient's decision about the number of embryos to be implanted. An interesting case arose in

Great Britain, when Patricia Thompson requested the implantation of two embryos, but doctors implanted three, and she
became pregnant with triplets. She and her husband eventually
decided to carry the triplet pregnancy forward, despite the risks
to her health and to the pregnancy itself. Subsequently, however,
she successfully sued the fertility center.

The debate over abortion—whether termination of a pregnancy or *part* of the pregnancy—will remain with us for many
years to come. The overwhelming majority of Americans support
legalized abortion under certain circumstances (Gallup Organization 2002), but it is unclear whether abortion will remain legal
in the future. President George W. Bush, elected in 2000, is a vocal
opponent and may have the opportunity to reverse *Roe* through
appointments to the Supreme Court. The current right to abortion is a negative one; it is a right in which the government may
not prevent a woman from securing an abortion, so long as the
fetus is not viable outside her body. The state is not required to
assist her and in fact may raise barriers making it difficult for her
to exercise this right. Prochoice and prolife activists are firm in
their beliefs and their commitments, and the battle over whose
rights to guarantee rages on.

The area of human reproduction is fraught with conflicting
interests and conflicting rights. We view this conflict as a paradigm of positive and negative rights, in which positive rights
impose obligations on others to assist in guaranteeing rights and
negative rights offer protection against interference from others
in the exercise of rights. The foregoing discussion of fertility control relies on the enforcement of negative rights that prohibits
others from interfering with a woman's right to contraception
and abortion. What follows in Chapter 2 is a discussion of the
right to have children, focusing on the question of what obligations others may incur to assist the infertile couple in the creation
of a family.

References

AGI (Alan Guttmacher Institute). 2000. "Most Abortion Patients View
Their Experience Favorably, but Medical Abortion Gets a Higher Rating
Than Surgical." *Family Planning Perspectives* 32 (5): 2000. http://
www.agi-usa.org/pubs/journals/3226400.html. Accessed July 24, 2001.

———. 2002. "Induced Abortion." http://www.agi-usa.org/pubs/fb_
induced_abortion.html. Accessed September 29, 2002.

Avila v. New York City Health and Hospitals Corporation, 518 N.Y.S.2d 574, 136 Misc. 2d 76 (Sup. Ct. Bronx City, 1987).

Beal v. Doe, 432 U.S. 438 (1977).

Bellotti v. Baird, 428 U.S. 132 (1976).

Bonavoglia, Angela. 1991. *Choices We Made*. New York: Random House.

Bopp, James, ed. 1984. *Restoring the Right to Life: The Human Life Amendment*. Provo, UT: Brigham Young University Press.

Bouvia v. Superior Court of Los Angeles County, 179 Cal. App. 3d 1127 (1986).

Bowen v. American Hospital Association, 106 S. Ct. 2101 (1986).

Bray v. Alexandria Women's Health Clinic, et al. 113 S. Ct. 753 (1993).

Buck v. Bell, 274 U.S. 200 (1927).

Callahan, Tamara L., Janet E. Hall, Susan L. Ettner, Cindy L. Christiansen, Michael F. Greene, and William F. Crowley. 1994. "The Economic Impact of Multiple-Gestation Pregnancies and the Contribution of Assisted-Reproduction Techniques to Their Incidence." *New England Journal of Medicine* 331 (4): 244–249.

Carey v. Population Services International, 431 U.S. 678 (1977).

Center for Reproduction, Law, and Policy. 2001. "The Facts: Medical Abortion: An Alternative for Women." http://www.crlp.org/pub_fac_medabor.html. Accessed July 23, 2001.

City of Akron v. Akron Center for Reproductive Health, 426 U.S. 416 (1983).

Congressional Information Service. 2001. "Numbers of Twin, Triplet, Quadruplet, and Quintuplet, and Other Higher Order Multiple Births: United States, 1989–98." http://www.lexis-nexis.com/universe.

Conservatorship of Valerie N., 219 Cal. Rptr. 387, 707 P.2d 760 (Cal.1985).

Cook v. State of Oregon, 495 P.2d 768, 9 OR. App. 224 (1972).

Craig, Barbara Hinkson, and David M. O'Brien. 1993. *Abortion and American Politics*. Chatham, NJ: Chatham House.

Doe v. Bolton, 410 U.S. 179 (1973).

Eisenstadt v. Baird, 405 U.S. 438 (1972).

Feminist Majority Foundation. 2000. www.feminist.org/news/pressstory.asp?id=4523. Press release dated January 18. Accessed July 25, 2001.

Finer, Lawrence B., and Stanley K. Henshaw. 2003. "Abortion Incidence and Services in the United States in 2000." *Perspectives on Sexual and Reproductive Health* 35 (1): 6–15.

Forrest, Jacqueline Darroch, and Susheela Singh. 1990. "Public-Sector

Savings Resulting from Expenditures for Contraceptive Services." *Family Planning Perspectives* 22 (1): 6–15.

Gallup Organization. 2002. Poll conducted May 6. Published online by Nexis-Lexis, Roper Center at the University of Connecticut Public Opinion Online.

Griswold v. Connecticut, 381 U.S. 479 (1965).

Harris v. McRae, 448 U.S. 297 (1980).

Hathaway v. Worcester City Hospital, 475 F.2d 701 (1st Cir. 1973).

Henshaw, Stanley K. 1998. "Abortion Incidence and Services in the United States, 1995–1996." *Family Planning Perspectives* 30 (6): 263–270, 287.

Henshaw, Stanley K., and Dina J. Feivelson. 2000. "Teenage Abortion and Pregnancy Statistics by State, 1996." *Family Planning Perspectives* 32 (6): 1–6, 272–280.

Hershey, Marjorie Randon, and Darrell M. West. 1983. "Single-Issue Politics: Prolife Groups and the 1980 Senate Campaign." In *Interest Group Politics,* Allan J. Cigler and Burdett A. Loomis, eds. Washington, DC: Congressional Quarterly Press.

Hodgson v. Minnesota, 497 U.S. 417 (1990).

"In Clinical Use, Low-Dose Medical Abortion Method Proves Highly Successful." 2001. *Family Planning Perspective* 33(3). http://www.agi-usa.org. Accessed July 24, 2001.

In re Phillip B., 156 Cal. Rptr. 48 (1979).

In re President and Board of Directors of Georgetown College, Inc., 331 F.2d 1000 (D.C. Cir.), cert. denied 377 U.S. 978 (1964).

Joyce, Ted, and Robert Kaestner. 2000. "The Impact of Mississippi's Mandatory Delay Law on the Timing of Abortion." *Family Planning Perspectives* 32 (1): 4–13.

Knight, Kevin, Eileen Reyes, Joel Wallace, Chiun-Fang Chiou, Sally Wade, and Jeff Borenstein. 2001. "Cost-Effectiveness Analysis of Long-Term Contraceptives for Women." Cedars-Sinai Health System, Los Angeles, CA.

Lewis, Neil A. 1992. "Selection of Conservative Judges Ensures a President's Legacy." *New York Times,* July 1, p. A13.

Maher v. Roe, 432 U.S. 464 (1977).

Mohr, James C. 1978. *Abortion in America: The Origins and Evolution of National Policy, 1890–1900.* New York: Oxford University Press.

Motes v. Hall City Department of Family and Children Services, 251 a. 373, 306 S.E.2d 260 (1983).

Multiple Births Foundation. 1993. "Multiple Pregnancy and Multiple Birth." http://www.multiplebirths.org.uk. Accessed September 2, 2001.

Mumford, Stephen D., and Elton Kessel. 1992. "Was the Dalkon Shield a Safe and Effective Intrauterine Device?" *Fertility and Sterility* 57 (6): 1151–1176.

North Carolina Association for Retarded Children v. North Carolina, 420 F. Supp. 451 (M.D. N.C. 1976).

NOW v. Scheidler, 510 U.S. 249 (1994).

Ohio v. Akron Center for Reproductive Health, 497 U.S. 502 (1990).

Overall, Christine. 1987. *Ethics and Human Reproduction: A Feminist Analysis.* Boston: Unwin Hyman.

Parham v. J. R., 442 U.S. 584 (1979).

Petchesky, Rosalind P. 1990. *Abortion and Woman's Choice: The State, Sexuality, and Reproductive Freedom.* Boston: Northeastern University Press.

Planned Parenthood Association of Kansas City v. Ashcroft, 462 U.S. 476 (1983).

Planned Parenthood of Central Missouri v. Danforth, 428 U.S. 552 (1976).

Planned Parenthood of Southeastern Pennsylvania v. Casey, 112 S. Ct. 1791 (1992).

Poelker v. Doe, 432 U.S. 519 (1977).

Roan, Shari. 2002. "Concerns Are Unfounded, but Norplant Being Taken Off Market." *Knight Ridder Tribune*, August 26.

Roe v. Wade, 410 U.S. 113 (1973).

Rorty, Mary V., and JoAnn V. Pinkerton. 1996. "Elective Fetal Reduction: The Ultimate Elective Surgery." *Journal of Contemporary Health Law and Policy* 13(53).

Rust v. Sullivan, 111 S. Ct. 1759 (1991).

Scheidler v. N.O.W., 123 S. Ct. 1057 (2003).

Schloendorff v. Society of New York Hospital, 105. N.E. 92 (1914).

Schlotzhauer, Anna. 1999. "The Ethics of Selective Termination Cases." *Journal of Legal Medicine* 20(40). http://www.lexisnexis.com. Accessed September 24, 2001.

Singh, Sushella, Deirdre Wulf, Renee Samara, and Yvette P. Cuca. 2000. "Gender Differences in the Timing of First Intercourse." *International Family Planning Perspectives* 26 (1): 21–28, 43.

Skinner v. Oklahoma, 316 U.S. 535 (1942).

Stenberg. v. Carhart, 530 U.S. 914 (2000).

Thornburgh v. American College of Obstetricians and Gynecologists, 476 U.S. 747 (1986).

Tribe, Laurence H. 1990. *Abortion: The Clash of Absolutes*. New York: W. W. Norton.

Webster v. Reproductive Health Services, 109 S. Ct. 3040 (1989).

2

Issues in Conception and Pregnancy

In this chapter, we shift attention from the right not to have children to less clearly established rights to have children and to maximize the "quality" of our children—to design them by choosing their sex and other characteristics. We summarize issues in assisted reproduction, fetal surgery, and genetic intervention, concerns surrounding the behavior of the pregnant woman, and the role of the government in ensuring healthy children. Finally, we briefly examine advances and issues in fetal and embryo research as they relate to rights of the various parties.

Although the application of these procedures varies both in terms of technical capabilities and the motivation behind their use in specific cases, they generate similar issues concerning the role of third parties in the reproductive process, the commodification of children and women, and the commercialization of procreation. Furthermore, because they introduce many third parties, they complicate the rights of the participants and raise new areas of potential conflict. They also create conflict over access to these expensive interventions and bring into focus the positive rights dimension of reproduction and the role of government and society in providing the means necessary to exercise the right to reproduce.

Assisted Reproductive Technologies

Infertility is a growing problem for many men and women in the United States: in 1998, an estimated one in six couples was infertile. The causes of infertility are complex and not fully understood, but they include environmental, heritable, pathological, and sociobehavioral factors. Contemporary social patterns, including deferring childbearing until well into one's thirties or forties, and increased sexual contact of young women with a variety of partners, are linked with increased infertility in women. The epidemic proportions of herpes simplex II and chlamydia among young women accentuates this problem. Although drug therapy and microsurgical intervention may be effective in treating some forms of infertility, increasingly couples are turning to an expanding selection of assisted reproductive technologies.

Artificial Insemination

The oldest and most widely used form of assisted reproductive technologies is artificial insemination (AI). Although AI is a relatively simple procedure, its success depends on a number of technical factors such as quality of the semen specimen and the timing of the insemination. An 80 percent success rate within several months of the start of the treatment is usual in AI. There are two basic types of AI, depending on whether the sperm used is the husband's (artificial insemination by husband, or AIH) or a donor's (donor insemination, or DI). Although procedurally it is irrelevant whether the semen is the husband's or a donor's, the ethical, psychological, and social problems surrounding DI are more complicated. DI brings into the reproductive process third parties and others and introduces the concept of collaborative conception.

Although the first child conceived via DI was born more than a century ago, use of DI expanded near the end of the twentieth century because of the introduction of cryopreservation techniques to freeze and preserve indefinitely a semen sample by immersion in liquid nitrogen. Cryopreservation led to the establishment of commercial sperm banks, which advertise their "products" to the public. At least seventy banks across the United States give men the opportunity to store semen prior to a vasectomy or to chemotherapy or radiation therapy as a form of "fertility insurance." Some, such as the Repository for Germinal Choice, which inseminates women of "high intelligence" with sperm from "superior men," represent eugenics programs.

In Vitro Fertilization

In vitro fertilization (IVF) is the procedure by which eggs are removed from a woman's ovaries and fertilized outside her body. The resulting embryos are kept in a culture medium for approximately two days until they reach the four- to eight-cell stage, at which point they are transferred via catheter into the uterus of the woman. When successful, the embryos will implant within six to nine days, resulting in a pregnancy. Usually, the retrieval of the mature eggs via laparoscopic surgery is preceded by ovulation induction, in which the woman takes a combination of hormones that stimulate her ovaries to "superovulate" and produce an abnormal number of eggs to be fertilized, thus increasing the chances of conception. This procedure is indicated when the oviducts are blocked, preventing eggs from passing through the fallopian tubes to be fertilized.

One variation of IVF is gamete intrafallopian transfer (GIFT), in which sperm and eggs are transferred separately to the fallopian tubes. Because fertilization takes placed in the fallopian tubes instead of a petri dish, GIFT is more acceptable than IVF to members of some religions. A second variation is zygote intrafallopian transfer (ZIFT), in which the embryo is placed in the fallopian tube about eighteen hours after fertilization. All these techniques can use donor ova and sperm where appropriate and increasingly make use of frozen embryos.

The movement of conception from the secrecy of the womb to a dish under the microscope in the laboratory also enables a wide range of pre-embryo research possibilities, as well as genetic screening, selection, and modification of embryos as these techniques develop. One technique termed "twinning" physically splits the embryo to create identical twins, thus permitting screening or other manipulation of one of the embryos prior to transfer to the womb. Cryopreservation of eggs and embryos, in addition to sperm, permits combination of germinal materials from persons across generations.

IVF illustrates the speed at which these technologies become diffused. In 1978, the first baby conceived via IVF, Louise Brown, was born in England. In January 1980, after considerable political debate, Norfolk General Hospital in Virginia obtained governmental approval to make the technique available. On December 28, 1981, Elizabeth Carr became the first baby conceived with the help of IVF in the United States. By 1990, the number of clinics offering IVF had expanded to over 300. Moreover, most clinics continue to have waiting lists of women who are willing to pay thousands of dollars for a chance of becoming pregnant. Often the total expenses may be more than $50,000, after a series of attempts at pregnancy, travel, lodging, and loss of employment for the duration of the treatment. Despite this investment, up to 80 percent of the women who undergo IVF will not have a child.

Because the IVF process is designed to override natural reproductive mechanisms, questions have been raised about its safety. To date, however, it appears that the overall rate of congenital abnormalities for IVF babies is not higher than for those conceived naturally, although there are risks associated with a heightened proportion of multiple births and low birth weight deliveries. Other potential sources of damage, however, could be tied to development of the ovum (especially if superovulation is employed), the selection of sperm (the female reproductive tract selects against some types of abnormal sperm), fertilization itself, and the use of freezing techniques to preserve gametes or embryos.

In addition to these currently used techniques, new applications appear frequently. One technique is micromanipulation of sperm into an egg, which allows for the insertion of one selected sperm into the egg's outer membrane. Intracytoplasmic sperm injection (ICSI) uses this approach when the man has few or severely impaired sperm. Reproduction assistance technologies also overlap with screening and selection technologies. Sperm separation techniques used in conjunction with DI and IVF now provide the means to maximize the conception of a child of the desired sex.

It is estimated that there is a potential clientele of more than 100,000 women who, for a variety of medical reasons, could benefit from ovum donation (Braverman 1993, 1216). Since its inception in 1983, the use of donor oocytes (female eggs before maturation) has increased dramatically, with more than 100 programs now in operation. Unlike sperm donors who receive smaller fees, women who donate eggs must endure uncomfortable procedures and can earn approximately $3,000 per donation, though some programs and couples are willing to pay substantially more, reportedly as high as $50,000 to $100,000 (Gurmankin 2001). The growing use of ovum donation raises issues surrounding the impact on the offspring and the families created through ovum donation, as well as questions of consent and parentage. Andrea Gurmankin (2001) also found that many oocyte donation centers minimized or misrepresented the risks when they recruited donors.

The already substantial demand for IVF services is certain to intensify as IVF pregnancy success rates increase and its availability to the population expands. As is illustrated by the passage of state laws mandating insurance coverage for IVF and other fertility services, pressures are mounting for insurance companies to cover all or part of the costs of the procedure (Ingram 1993). Although these statutes exempt payment by Medicaid for individuals without insurance, claims for such coverage are inevitable. Moreover, if the costs become reimbursable in whole or in part by third-party payers, the demand for such services will intensify.

The transformation of procreation from an intimate matter between two persons to yet another market enterprise raises serious conceptual concerns. When the most private of human endeavors becomes a matter of entrepreneurship, it is imperative that we carefully analyze how this revolution in thinking, as well as technique, affects human relationships. How will this trend alter our views of parental responsibility, children, and women? How far can we proceed in this direction without entering a "brave new world" of procreation as a manufacturing process?

Surrogate Contracts and the Creation of New Families

One aspect of this brave new world is the creation of families through surrogacy agreements. The traditional concept of surrogacy most often involves an infertile couple contracting with a surrogate who agrees to be artificially inseminated with the sperm of the husband and to surrender the child upon delivery to the intended couple. It is a misnomer to characterize the pregnant woman as a surrogate because she is providing half the genetic material. In reality, she is the biological mother, but to avoid confusion, we will refer to her as the biological surrogate.

With advances in assisted reproductive technology, a number of newer variations are available. If the intended father and mother are fertile, but the wife cannot carry the pregnancy, they may opt for gestational surrogacy, in which their sperm and egg are combined through in vitro fertilization and implanted in a gestational surrogate. In this case, the intended parents are simultaneously the biological parents, and the surrogate has no maternal biological relationship to the fetus. In donor gestational surrogacy, the egg and/or sperm are donated and combined through in vitro fertilization. If both the egg and the sperm are donated, the resulting child will not be the biological child of either the surrogate or the intended parents. In this case, it is possible for the child to have three mothers (the egg donor, the surrogate, and the intended mother) and three fathers (the sperm donor, the surrogate's husband, and the intended father).

The modern commercial surrogacy industry began in California in the 1970s and has now grown into a lucrative business with about sixty centers nationwide. (See Kerian 1997 for a detailed history.) The center typically advertises for surrogates and serves as a broker between them and intended parents. Optimally, the center will screen all potential participants, provide the contract, and assist with counseling prior to any agreement being reached so that all participants give informed consent before signing the contract and initiating the pregnancy. The Center for Surrogate Parenting (CSP) in Beverly Hills is one of the oldest surrogacy centers in the United States. Between 1980 and 2000, CSP facilitated 747 surrogacy births. In 2001, CSP charged nearly $62,000 for artificial insemination and more than $75,000 for in vitro fertilization with egg donation. The surrogate was paid $18,000 regardless of which procedure was used; CSP received $18,000; and the remaining costs were attributed to legal fees, insurance, medical care, and counseling (CSP, 2001). Historically, surrogates relied on their own health insurance to cover medical costs, but recently, health insurance providers, including Kaiser Permanente, Health Net, Foundation Health, and Blue Cross of California have excluded surrogacy expenses from their policies (Kelliher 1999).

Several studies were conducted in the 1980s regarding the profiles of surrogates and intended parents. Philip Parker's study reported that 40 percent of surrogates were unemployed or receiving financial aid, 25 percent had had an abortion, 9 percent had previously relinquished a child for adoption, and 89 percent would not have served as surrogates without a substantial fee (Parker 1983, 118). The U.S. Office of Technology Assessment (OTA) found that most intended parents were in their thirties or early forties and were middle class in both lifestyle and income. Surrogates, however, were in their mid-twenties, only 60 percent were married, and their reported incomes were substantially below those of the intended parents (OTA 1988, 274). Hilary Hanafin, a psychologist at CSP, found that 72 percent of surrogates enjoyed being pregnant, 68 percent wanted to help a childless couple, and 54 percent were motivated by the fee they would receive. Thirty-seven percent had previously had abortions (Hanafin 1987).

Lori Andrews's research, based on anecdotal interviews rather than surveys, paints a picture of mutual cooperation and respect between surrogates and intended parents. She characterizes surrogates as referring to the fetus as the intended parents' "baby" and loving it in much the same way they love a niece or nephew but not as they love their own children. Her research points to the psychological benefits these surrogates receive because of the feeling that they are helping someone else meet a joyous life goal; many viewed themselves as feminists because they had exercised their reproductive choices and demonstrated an ethic of care (Andrews 1995, 2352–2354).

In Chapter 1, we analyzed the rights that various people have or may have in terms of their reproductive freedom. In surrogacy, the stage is potentially set for an intense conflict of rights, both positive and negative. The children in these arrangements are the most vulnerable, and their rights clearly need protection. The child born of the surrogacy agreement, like children born in more traditional ways, needs care, love, nurturing, and security. Intended parents clearly want children and have generally made substantial financial commitments to obtain them through surrogacy agreements. But what happens when something unintended confronts the intended parents? In some cases, intended parents have refused to accept children because they wanted a single child and the pregnancy resulted in twins, or they were disappointed with the sex of the child. Rejection has also resulted when infants had birth defects or serious illnesses, or when the intended parents divorced prior to delivery.

Another issue is whether the fees paid to a surrogate constitute baby selling, a practice illegal in all fifty states to protect children from being bought and sold like commodities. The issue of potential baby selling is most problematic in cases of biological surrogacy, in which the surrogate provides half the genetic material and is in fact the biological mother. It is less problematic in gestational surrogacy, in which the intended mother is also the biological mother, and in donor gestational surrogacy, in which the donor is typically far removed from the birth. Although the issue is controversial and open to dispute, we would argue that so long as the surrogate is paid the same fee for her services regardless of whether there is a live birth or a stillbirth, such payment does not constitute baby selling. Moreover, fees to cover expenses are often paid to mothers who surrender their children through traditional adoption proceedings. The overriding concern should be for the best interests of the child, not whether a fee is paid. Andrews agrees, arguing that "there is no evidence that the couple who pays $10,000 to a surrogate is any more likely to treat the child as a commodity than the couple who pays $10,000 for a biological mother's expenses during an adoption, or the couple who pays much more than $10,000 to an in vitro fertilization doctor" (Andrews 1995, 2361).

Concern should also be expressed for the "other" children in the surrogacy arrangement, the existing children of the surrogate. Although current data are not available nationwide, it is clear that many surrogates—probably most surrogates—have children prior to entering surrogacy arrangements. CSP, for example, considers only surrogate applicants who already have children. We wonder what young children think as they watched their mother grow large with a baby that will never be part of their family and also wonder how they will explain the situation to their playmates. Will their sense of security be weakened when the baby is given away to another family, and will they be fearful that they might also be given away?

The welfare of the adults in the surrogacy arrangement is less problematic. Each enters the agreement with the understanding, although not necessarily a guarantee, that the surrogate and her husband will relinquish any claims they might have regarding parental status and turn the child over to the intended parents. Some would argue that surrogacy exploits the surrogate, and clearly there have been such cases. It would seem that the potential for exploitation might be substantially reduced if surrogacy brokers follow guidelines regulating who can serve as a surrogate. Women who are exceedingly vulnerable because of poverty, illiteracy, low levels of education, mental instability, and so forth ought not to be surrogates. Neither should women who have not had a child, because they are unaware of the demands of pregnancy and delivery and the attachment they may develop to a child.

Another potential area of conflict involves contractual restrictions placed on the surrogate's lifestyle and also the potential demand for abortion or selective abortion in cases of a multiple-fetus pregnancy. All parties have moral obligations to protect the fetus to the best of their abilities, but should they also have legal obligations? Surrogates should be honest about their lifestyles prior to entering surrogacy agreements, and once pregnant, should follow guidelines involving tobacco, alcohol, drugs, and so forth. Legally enforcing these clauses, however, is problematic, particularly since smoking and alcohol are most detrimental to the fetus during the early months of pregnancy, so even if the surrogacy center or the intended parents resorted to the courts for enforcement, time would not be on their side. Moreover, it is questionable whether the courts would enforce these restrictions. An even more problematic issue is whether the clauses providing for abortion on demand by the intended parents are enforceable under *Roe v. Wade* (1973).

Surrogacy and the Law

In response to well-publicized lawsuits throughout the nation as well as a model uniform statute recommended in 1988 by the National Conference of Commissioners of Uniform State Laws, many states considered legislation to either disallow or accommodate surrogacy arrangements, although not all states enacted legislation. The result is a patchwork of conflicting and inconsistent statutes and state supreme court decisions. As of December 2000, about half the states had established policies either through statutes or case law. Six states void agreements, eight states ban compensation, and two have judicially refused to recognize the agreements (UPA 2000; see also OPTS 2001). In 2000, the National Conference of Commissioners of Uniform State Laws recommended to state legislatures a revised model statute (a copy of which is reproduced in Chapter 5) supporting commercial surrogacy.

Although the percentage of surrogacy agreements tested in the courts is quite low compared to the total number of children born through these agreements, those that have reached the courts have addressed important issues. Three cases have been decided by state courts; none has been heard by the U.S. Supreme Court. In 1986, the Kentucky Supreme Court found that commercial surrogacy did not violate its baby-selling laws if agreements were made prior to conception and the mother was allowed to change her mind before relinquishing her parental rights (*Surrogate Parenting v. Commonwealth ex. rel. Armstrong*). The Kentucky legislature subsequently banned surrogacy agreements.

The most famous case to date is that of *Baby M,* decided by the New Jersey Supreme Court in 1988. William Stern, a biochemist with a Ph.D., and his wife, a pediatrician, contracted with Mary Beth Whitehead, the homemaker wife of a sanitation worker, to bear a child using Stern's sperm and Whitehead's egg. At birth, the Sterns named the infant Melissa, Whitehead named her Sara, and a legal war began. A few days after the birth, Whitehead appeared at the Sterns' home and asked to take the baby for a week, but then fled to Florida, where she and the baby were located by police officials. The Sterns filed for custody, which the trial court awarded along with a termination of Whitehead's parental rights (*In Re Baby M* 1987).

On appeal, the New Jersey Supreme Court ruled unanimously that the contract between Whitehead and the Sterns was unenforceable because it violated New Jersey laws prohibiting baby selling, monetary inducement for adoption, and prebirth adoption agreements.

> Mr. Stern knew he was paying for the adoption of the child; Mrs. Whitehead knew she was accepting money so that a child might be adopted; the Infertility Center knew that it was being paid for assisting in the adoption of a child. . . . (*In the Matter of Baby M* 1988, 1241)
>
> [It is] the sale of a child, or, at the very least, the sale of a mother's right to her child, the only mitigating factor being that one of the purchasers is the father. Almost every evil that prompted the prohibition on the payment of money in connection with adoptions exists here. (1248)

The court ruled that it was in the best interest of Baby M to live with the Sterns; Whitehead was found to be the legal mother and was granted visitation.

Although issues in *Baby M* focused on traditional surrogacy, those in *Anna J* focused on gestational surrogacy. Mark and Crispina Calvert, he Caucasian and she of Filipino descent, contracted with Anna Johnson, an African American single mother, because Crispina had undergone a partial hysterectomy. Mark's sperm and Crispina's eggs were fertilized in vitro, three zygotes were implanted in Johnson, and on September 9, 1990, a healthy baby boy was born. The Calverts named him Michael Ryan, Johnson named him Matthew, and once again, a legal war began.

The trial court upheld the enforceability of the contract, granted legal parenthood to the Calverts, and denied Johnson's claims to parenthood. The California Court of Appeals affirmed, and Johnson appealed to the California Supreme Court, which ruled that both women presented acceptable proof of maternity because Calvert provided the genetic material and Johnson provided gestation, labor, and delivery. The court then turned to the contract to determine intent, finding that it clearly indicated that all parties intended for Crispina to serve as the child's mother. Although statutory law

> recognizes both genetic consanguinity and giving birth as means of establishing a mother and child relationship, when the two means do not coincide in one woman, she who intended to procreate the child—that is, she who intended to bring about the birth of a child that she intended to raise as her own—is the natural mother under California law. (*Johnson v. Calvert* 1993, 782)

The court also found that statutory prohibitions on payment for consent to adoption were not violated because gestational surrogacy differs in crucial respects from adoption and the surrogacy payments were not intended as payments in exchange for surrendering parental rights but as compensation for Johnson's services in gestating the fetus and undergoing labor. Johnson's arguments regarding involuntary servitude were dismissed, as were arguments regarding the exploitation of women and the commodification of children. Crispina Calvert was declared to be the legal mother, and Johnson's claims to motherhood were dismissed (Blank and Merrick 1995).

In addition to those cases decided by state supreme courts is a complex case of donor gestational surrogacy decided by the California Court of Appeals. John and Luanne Buzzanca sought to have a child through surrogacy. After efforts with five different surrogates failed, daughter Jaycee Buzzanca was conceived from an embryo created in vitro from a donated egg and donated sperm implanted in gestational surrogate Pamela Snell (Capron 1998, 22). Jaycee was not biologically related to either intended parent or to the surrogate. Several weeks before Jaycee's birth, John Buzzanca filed for divorce and claimed not to be the legal father to avoid child support obligations, arguing that surrogate Pamela Snell and her husband were the legal parents. Luanne Buzzanca took physical custody of Jaycee shortly after her birth and sought custody and child support from John.

In a decision that many viewed as extraordinary, the trial court found that Jaycee had no legal parents. Neither the sperm donor nor the egg donor was identified in the court proceedings, and the Snells stipulated that they were not the parents. The trial court found that Luanne was not the legal mother because she had neither contributed the egg nor given birth. John was not the legal father because his sperm was not used, and therefore he had no biological relationship with the child. In effect, the trial court found that Jaycee Buzzanca was an orphan of technology and surrogacy.

In a sharply worded decision, the California Court of Appeals reversed the trial court by analogizing the donation of an embryo to donation of sperm:

> Just as a husband is deemed to be the lawful father of a child unrelated to him when his wife gives birth after artificial insemination, so should a husband and wife be deemed the lawful parents of a child after a surrogate bears a biologically unrelated child on their behalf. In each instance, a child is procreated because a medical procedure was initiated and consented to by intended parents. (*In re Marriage of Buzzanca* 1998)

The Court of Appeals found that Luanne Buzzanca was the legal mother and John Buzzanca the legal father; it reversed the trial court's judgment that John Buzzanca was not obligated for child support.

There is considerable debate in the academic literature regarding whether such disputes should fall within family law or contract law. Richard Epstein makes a forceful argument for the latter. Even though he focuses primarily on traditional surrogacy, in which the surrogate provides half the genetic material, he argues that people know their own interests and contracts are mechanisms for achieving mutual gain and should be enforced, including clauses for abortion on demand from the intended parents.

> It is the father who has, under contract, the long-term obligations for the child, and it cannot be regarded as unjust or unwise that his decision should determine whether the abortion should take place for precisely

those reasons that are so important to ordinary married couples. Indeed it would be quite extraordinary if any contract would allow the separation between risk and reward that is created by allowing the surrogate to carry the baby to term when the obligations of care devolve thereafter on the father. . . . Allowing the surrogate to carry the child to term against the wishes of its father is inconsistent with the basic contractual design. (Epstein 1995, 2336)

He supports paid surrogacy, arguing that money

only converts the transaction from a voluntary donation of parental rights to a sale of parental rights. It does not make the transaction corrupt; it does not carry with it the conclusive mark of fraud, concealment, or misrepresentation, which cannot be inferred from the payment of money in this context any more than it can in any other. The most that can be said is that the money may create some kind of conflict of interest between parent and child, so that the sale will be made to a higher bidder when the child is better off in the care of a lower bidder. (Epstein 1995, 2333)

It is the latter issue—the welfare of the child—that troubles us about Epstein's argument, and because of this concern, we argue that contested surrogacy arrangements should be decided by family law principles. The state's paramount interest in surrogacy arrangements should be the welfare of the child rather than the enforcement of the contract. It is the same interest that the state upholds in adoption, custody, and child abuse cases, and children born of surrogacy arrangements should be treated likewise.

Regulating Reproductive Technologies

The proliferation of reproduction assistance services, the trend toward commercialization of these services, and the potential conflicts among the many parties to these new reproduction methods raise concerns over regulation. In general, the issues surrounding these innovations have been handled by case law only when legal conflicts, primarily over custody, have arisen. Although Congress has held many hearings on reproductive assistance technologies, they have not led to a national policy. Despite the appearance of this issue on the national agenda in the late 1980s, regulation of infertility services has largely rested in the states through their authority to protect health and their power to regulate familial relations, medical practice (including licensing health personnel and facilities), and contracts. As a result, regulation of assisted reproductive services and surrogacy is inconsistent and at times contradictory from one state to the next. As methods have evolved from DI, which has been practiced for a century, to more recent and provocative innovations such as IVF and GIFT, statutory regulation has become scarcer.

In many ways, public policymakers have turned to professional organizations to develop and apply guidelines for assisted reproductive services. The two most active organizations on promulgating relevant standards of practice are the American Fertility Society (AFS) and the American Association of Tissue Banks (AATB). Since 1986, AFS has prepared sets of ethical guidelines governing these technologies, issued position papers on insurance coverage of infertility services, and published revised procedures for conducting DI, IVF, GIFT, and other relevant services (AFS 1988a, 1988b). Most recently, it has published guidelines for therapeutic donor insemination (AFS 1993b), for oocyte donation (AFS 1993a), and for minimal genetic screening for gamete donors (AFS 1993c).

Although the standards promulgated by professional organizations are valuable and provide some control over the use of these technologies, the problem with guidelines, as opposed to regulations, is that there is no legal authority behind the guidelines to ensure compliance. Instead of the force of law, association guidelines rely on accreditation privileges and ethical sanctions. There is little to stop the establishment of unsanctioned cryobanks, fertility clinics, or DI/IVF/GIFT services. One strategy for the states is to restrict practice of these services to those facilities that comply with AFS, American College of Obstetricians and Gynecologists (ACOG), or AATB guidelines. Another strategy would be to use these guidelines as a framework for shaping public policy.

Assisted Reproduction and Reproductive Rights

Assisted reproduction shifts emphasis from the right not to have children to the question of whether there is a complementary right to have children and, if so, what limits might be imposed as to the number or "quality" of those progeny. For instance, is there a duty of persons who carry genetic disease to refrain from having children from their own germinal material and to use collaborative conception technologies such as DI or embryo transfer? If there is a right to have children, to what extent does it include a claim for access to reproduction assistance technologies? These technologies have the potential to expand the right to have children significantly, but only if those persons who need them have access to them.

Reproductive technologies raise the logical extension of reproductive autonomy as a positive right—a claim upon society to guarantee, through whatever means possible, the capacity to reproduce. If the right to procreation is interpreted as a positive one, then an infertile couple could argue a constitutional claim for access to these technologies. Under such circumstances, individuals who are unable to afford those treatments necessary to achieve reproductive capacity could expect society to guarantee access. A woman with blocked fallopian tubes would have a claim to corrective surgery or IVF. An infertile man would be ensured access to DI or corrective surgery, where possible.

Once procreative rights are stated as positive, however, drawing reasonable boundaries becomes difficult. Does a woman who is unable to carry a fetus to term because of the absence of a uterus or a high-risk condition have a legitimate claim for a surrogate mother? Wherever the lines are drawn, some individuals are likely to have limited opportunity to have children. Shifts toward a positive rights perspective accentuate the already growing demand for these technologies, encourage entrepreneurs to provide a broad variety of these reproductive services, and, importantly, put increasing pressures on the government to fund these services.

Technologically assisted reproduction then has widespread implications for the exercise and scope of reproductive rights. Although these technologies give hope to many infertile persons and provide the means to exert more control over the characteristics of their progeny, they also raise potential conflicts among the rights of the many parties involved in the process. Also, depending on the specific application, these technologies can either extend or constrain the reproductive rights of the users. Each practice has a variety of possible clinical, social, and eugenic applications that depend upon the primary motivation behind its use.

Court cases have involved the legal rights of "orphaned" embryos, the rights of a couple to custody of "their" embryos held by a fertility clinic, the rights of a widow to be inseminated with the frozen semen of her deceased husband, and the rights of death row prisoners to have children via artificial insemination so as to pass on their genes. These and other emerging cases represent but the first wave of a proliferation of challenging and unfamiliar legal dilemmas.

The delineation of legal parentage and parental rights, therefore, is becoming increasingly difficult, and even though most participants do not end up in court, when they do, novel legal dilemmas arise. In addition to the conflicts over rights arising from particular applications of assisted reproduction, cumulatively these new capabilities raise more general concerns for the rights of certain categories of people. Attention now is turned to an analysis of the impact of reproductive technologies on children and women and to the corollary issue of access.

The Children of Technologically Assisted Reproduction

Conspicuously absent from much of the debate over reproductive technologies is concern over the impact of these innovations on children, both as products of specific applications and as concepts. In dealing with any assisted reproductive application, a child is the person most affected by the decision to utilize the technique, but the child is not a party to the decision. Of course, a case can be made that the child would favor the decision of the parent(s) to use the technology because otherwise he or she would never have existed, but the development of more powerful genetic interventions may weaken this argument. The desired outcome of assisted reproduction is the deliberate creation of a child, often with specific genetic characteristics. Although some applications of assisted reproduction reinforce the genetic link by enabling infertile persons to have "a child of their own," other practices such as DI, egg donation, and embryo transfer challenge the notion that genetic parenthood guarantees familial relationship. The increased use of these practices raises the question of whether children have a right to know the identity of their genetic parents. Recently, there have been reports in the media of children of DI now searching for their genetic fathers, the semen donors who were guaranteed anonymity. As stated by one donor opposed to these searches, "I did not do it to get fifty cards on Father's Day; I did it for the money."

Another issue regarding the fate of children related to assisted reproduction revolves around the social value we place on the child. Until recently, parents had children for a variety of personal reasons, but in the absence of the procreative technologies available today, by and large they took responsibility for the children they bore. When fate dealt them a child with imperfections, they accepted it and coped as well as they could. Today, within the context of the expanding selection of intervention possibilities, many persons are no longer satisfied with a child viewed as less than the best. Even the average does not seem good enough for many parents.

This emphasis on technological "perfection" raises questions concerning the purpose of children in this generation. It is not surprising that terms such as "quality control" over the reproductive process and children as "products" of particular techniques are commonplace. This possible commodification of children, then, must be contrasted with the reproductive rights of the potential parents who will use these techniques.

Rights and Access to Assisted Reproduction

The diffusion of assisted reproduction services has raised critical questions of access, especially in the market-oriented U.S. health care system. These issues of access turn on the prevailing conceptions of reproductive rights. If there is a positive right to have children, to what extent is a woman or a couple entitled to the aid of the medical community or the government in providing the resources necessary to carry out that right? The high costs of many of these techniques, especially IVF, have created economic barriers, which means that at least initially, only those persons with adequate personal resources are able to undergo treatment. With the proliferation of clinics offering these services, however, has come the heightened concern over access and the presence, in effect, of an economic screening mechanism to determine which infertile couples will have the opportunity to have children.

Although there currently are no comprehensive data on the proportion of assisted reproduction costs paid out of pocket as compared to that reimbursed by private insurers, an increasing number of carriers provide routine coverage for IVF and other reproduction assistance treatment if it is medically indicated. For instance, employees with Blue Cross/Blue Shield coverage in Delaware have an option to purchase IVF coverage (no minimum waiting period, $25,000 lifetime maximum). Many group insurance plans, however, do not cover IVF, usually on grounds that it is experimental. This inconsistency in coverage of IVF from one plan to the next has led to efforts by groups such as RESOLVE (affiliated with the National Infertility Association) to lobby for state legislation that mandates third-party coverage.

To date the courts have given mixed signals regarding insurance coverage. In *Witcraft v. Sundstrand Health and Disability Group Benefit Plan* (1988), for instance, the Iowa Supreme Court held that the dysfunction of the insured's reproductive organs was an illness. Since the plan covered "expenses relating to" illness, the court held the claim for IVF expenses valid. In *Kinzie v. Physician's Liability Insurance Company* (1987), however, an Oklahoma appellate court denied recovery on grounds that IVF was elective and was not required to cure or preserve the insured's health. Moreover, the court did not deem it medically necessary to a woman's health to give birth to a child (Ingram 1993, 104).

At least ten states have adopted legislation mandating that insurance carriers operating in their states either provide coverage for IVF and related infertility services (Arkansas, Hawaii, Illinois, Maryland, Massachusetts, New Jersey, Rhode Island) or offer such a package (California, Connecticut, Texas). Massachusetts, for example, enacted legislation (Act H. 3721, 1987) that required all insurance plans covering pregnancy-related benefits to include medically indicated expenses of diagnosis and treatment of infertility to the same extent that benefits are provided for other pregnancy-related procedures. Under the regulations promulgated by this act, insurers must provide benefits for all nonexperimental infertility procedures (211 C.M.R. 37.01 to 37.11). They include AI, IVF, and other procedures characterized as nonexperimental by the AFS or other infertility experts recognized by the state commissioner of insurance, but surrogacy, reversal of voluntary sterilization, and procurement of donor eggs and sperm are specifically excluded from coverage. The insurers may establish reasonable eligibility requirements, which are to be made available to the insured.

Although expansion of insurance coverage for fertility treatment will expand accessibility, there is little evidence that Medicaid recipients or the millions of women without health insurance will have access to IVF, even though on average poor women have a higher prevalence of infertility than middle-class women. Whatever happens with private insurance, there has been little activity by the states or by Congress to fund assisted reproduction, and it is unlikely to happen in times of continued budget scarcity. For those women who are unable to obtain assisted reproduction for lack of economic resources, reproduction as a positive right remains unfulfilled.

Even the negative right to have children, however, is problematic for some women, who are denied access to assisted reproduction services because they are not married, especially if they are lesbian. Although these women might have the financial means, they are effectively barred from using services that are open only to married couples or heterosexual couples in "long-term stable relationships." Some observers argue that this practice is a violation of these women's fundamental rights to procreate and bear a child under the Fourteenth Amendment, but as stated earlier, the right to have children has not been firmly established and remains controversial even among feminists. As a result, it is doubtful that the courts will actively intervene to guarantee access to commercial fertility services.

These exclusionary practices based on marital status or sexual orientation have forced some women into third-party arrangements with known or anonymous donors. Unfortunately, women denied professional services with their accompanying anonymity and screening capabilities are more at risk for legal and possibly health problems. For instance, in one case the court upheld a semen donor's request for visitation rights with a child born to a lesbian mother (*Jhordan C. v. Mary K.* 1986). The court stated that the woman could have avoided this situation if a physician had obtained the semen as provided by statute, but it did not query whether as a lesbian she would have had access to such professional services.

Reproductive technologies promise to revolutionize the family structure even more if the demands of some transsexual groups are ultimately met. These persons are genetic males who have undergone hormonal and surgical treatment to become females. Increasingly, some of these individuals are demanding more government funding of research into male procreation and rapid development of applications so that they can experience "womanhood to its fullest." As noted earlier, male procreation is likely to be possible in the near future. If transsexual women have access, it seems unlikely that other men who desire to experience "motherhood" can be denied it.

Ultimately, the resolution of these issues regarding access to assisted reproduction technologies depends on how broadly we define the right to have children, if, indeed, we agree there is such a right. Because of the need for access to professional services and, in some cases such as IVF, teams of medical specialists, procreation is no longer a private matter, nor it is inexpensive. This situation raises serious questions concerning the allocation of medical resources. What priority should these costly treatments have, compared to preventive measures and research to discover the underlying causes of infertility? Although society has put a high priority on reproductive rights, debate continues over the exercise of this right when it requires significant public resources.

Prenatal Diagnosis

Prenatal diagnosis has become an important component of clinical prenatal care and is now a medical standard for women with "high-risk" pregnancies. To reduce the incidence of birth defects, many prenatal diagnostic technologies are currently used in the United States. One technique for detection of genetic disorders is amniocentesis, which is usually administered between sixteen and eighteen weeks after the beginning of the last menstrual period. The procedure involves inserting a long thin needle attached to a syringe through the lower wall of the woman's abdomen and withdrawing approximately 20 cubic centimeters (cc) of the amniotic fluid that surrounds the fetus and contains some live body cells shed by the fetus. These cells are placed in a laboratory medium and cultured for approximately three weeks. Karyotyping of the chromosomes is then conducted to identify any abnormalities in the chromosomal complement as well as the sex of the fetus. If needed, specific biochemical assays can be conducted to identify up to 120 separate metabolic disorders and neural-tube defects. More than 90 percent of women undergoing amniocentesis are informed that the fetus is normal. In the event a fetus is diagnosed as having a severe chromosomal or metabolic disorder, the mother may opt for a therapeutic abortion. At present, nearly all amniocenteses are done on pregnant women who are over thirty-five years of age because of the strong association between increased maternal age and heightened chromosomal abnormalities (see Table 2.1).

In another technique, chorionic villus sampling (CVS), a biopsy is taken from the placenta, which has deoxyribonucleic acid (DNA) identical to that of the fetus. Transabdominal CVS extracts a small amount of placental tissue through a needle that is inserted into the pregnant woman's abdomen. The advantage of CVS over amniocentesis is that CVS can be conducted as early as the ninth week of pregnancy, thus providing the pregnant woman with information at a time when a much safer abortion is possible than the midterm abortions associated with amniocentesis.

A widely used technology that has become indispensable in prenatal diagnosis is ultrasound, or sonography. This procedure directs high-frequency sound waves into the abdomen of the pregnant woman to gain an echo-visual image of the fetus, uterus, placenta, and other inner structures. It is noninvasive and painless for the woman. Extensive studies have found no harmful long- or short-term hazards to the fetus from ultrasound, although its routine use should be weighed against the possibility of false positive or negative diagnoses and the considerable monetary investment involved in screening large numbers of low-risk pregnancies. In addition to its use in conjunction with amniocentesis to determine fetal position and age, ultrasound can be used to observe fetal development and movement and detect spina bifida, some musculoskeletal malformations, and major organ disorders.

Table 2.1 Relation between Maternal Age and Estimated Rate of
Chromosomal Abnormalities

Age	Risk of Down's Syndrome	Risk of Chromosomal Abnormality
20	1/1,667	1/526
25	1/1,250	1/476
30	1/952	1/385
35	1/385	1/202
37	1/227	1/129
40	1/106	1/65
45	1/30	1/20
49	1/11	1/7

Source: D'Alton and DeCherney 1993, 115.

Potentially, a wide variety of hereditary disorders, including hemophilia and possibly Duchenne muscular dystrophy, might be identifiable through fetoscopy, an application of fiber optics technology that allows direct viewing of the fetus in the womb. The fetoscope is inserted through an incision in the woman's abdomen, usually under the direction of ultrasound, and is maneuvered around in the uterus to examine the fetus section by section.

Fetoscopy can also be used to sample fetal blood from a vessel on the surface of the placenta and has direct therapeutic use in the intrauterine transfusion of fetuses. It also offers considerable potential for introducing medicines, cell transplants, or genetic materials into fetal tissue to treat genetic diseases. Despite substantial progress in fetoscopy, it is still considered applied research because of the hazards it poses for the fetus, including escalated rates of premature birth and miscarriages.

Yet another prenatal diagnostic technique is maternal serum alpha-fetoprotein (AFP) testing, which is used to detect neural tube defects and Down's syndrome. The level of AFP is determined either from amniotic fluid or maternal serum, which is usually collected between the twelfth and twentieth weeks of pregnancy. Although the Food and Drug Administration approved the sale of diagnostic kits, controversy arose concerning the high rate of false positives and the possibility that women might be encouraged to abort fetuses solely on the basis of this preliminary screening device.

The cutting edge of diagnostic techniques is pre-implantation embryo testing on a cell removed from a four- to eight-celled embryo produced by IVF before it is transferred to the uterus. Although it may be possible in the near future to diagnose some inherited diseases in human embryos by noninvasive methods, pre-implantation diagnosis currently entails the biopsy of one or more cells from each embryo. If the biopsied cell is free from the disorder, the embryo is transferred to the women. However, if the cell has the flawed gene, the embryo is either destroyed or frozen for later study.

Although pre-implantation screening offers distinct advantages over conventional techniques to couples at risk for genetic disease, two sets of ethical objections are raised. The first focuses on embryo status and the manipulations required, and the second turns on its eugenic implications and its potential for positive engineering of offspring traits. Despite these concerns, the potential benefits have helped fuel significant government support for the Human Genome Initiative discussed later.

Sex Preselection

Interest in sex selection is not new. Infanticide has long been practiced in many cultures to choose gender. As couples have fewer children, there is evidence that they are willing to use technologies that offer control over the characteristics of their progeny. Although preference for a particular sex is less clear in the United States than it is in many other cultures, the availability of sex preselection techniques, combined with the trend toward one- and two-child families, may produce a broader demand as easy and effective techniques become available.

Current approaches that offer the best chance of success are based on the fact that each sperm cell carries either an X chromosome or a Y chromosome and that the sex of the progeny is determined by which type of sperm fertilizes the egg. The goal of sex preselection is to control this process. To aid in reaching this objective, some recently discovered characteristics of these two types of sperm are invaluable. First, in any male ejaculation, there are more Y-bearing sperm than X-bearing sperm. In addition to being more numerous, Y-bearing sperm are smaller, less dense, and faster moving than their X-bearing counterparts. Conversely, the Y-bearing sperm die sooner and are more readily slowed down by normal acidic secretions of the vagina. However, once past the vagina, they are less inhibited than the X-bearing sperm by the alkaline environment of the uterus.

Within the context of this new knowledge about the sperm, most sex preselection research is aimed at developing accurate and reliable sperm separation techniques. Once the desired sperm concentrations are isolated, they are inseminated into the recipient woman's uterus using artificial insemination techniques. At least seventy clinics in the United States use variations of the sperm separation procedure to select sex-specific sperm. Although the scope of sex preselection in the United States is unclear and no simple, reliable, and usable method enjoys wide acceptance by the research community, demand for services is accelerating as fragmented reports of success are covered by the mass media. Unlike IVF and other techniques, the potential market for a reliable and less intrusive method is not limited to a small proportion of the public. It also seems to be an area in which latent desires of many persons to control the gender of their offspring could be exploited by an industry that markets sex selection products and services.

Policy Issues in Prenatal Diagnosis

Since the early 1980s, there has been a continual expansion of the prenatal diagnostic techniques available to women to identify fetal anomalies. Amniocentesis, CVS, and ultrasound have become standard clinical procedures, in some cases before their safety and efficacy have been fully evaluated. Although these technologies might enhance a woman's reproductive freedom by providing information that helps her decide how to manage the pregnancy, as with all reproductive technologies, anything that can be done voluntarily can also be coerced.

Moreover, coercion can take many forms, from subtle "pressures" to conform to standard medical practice and the technological imperative to legally defined duties. Barbara Rothman (1986, 114) notes that the new images of the fetus resulting from prenatal technologies are making us aware of the "unborn" as people, "but they do so at the cost of making transparent the mother." Furthermore, a "diagnostic technology that pronounces judgments halfway through the pregnancy makes extraordinary demands on women to separate themselves from the fetus within" (Rothman 1986, 114). Even in the absence of legal coercion, then, the culturally imposed sanctions favoring medicalized pregnancies appear strong.

One dilemma surrounding current use of these techniques is that although they give us the ability to reduce the incidence of genetic disease, they do so primarily by eliminating the affected fetus through selective abortion, not by treating the disease. Future developments in gene therapy might shift emphasis toward treatment, but prenatal diagnosis will continue to expand maternal choice only to the extent it allows the pregnant woman to terminate the pregnancy of an affected fetus. Thus, it will continue to be a policy issue congruent with abortion.

The dilemma becomes more immediate, however, if therapy is available in conjunction with the diagnosis. Robertson (1983, 448) points out that "the issue in such a case would be whether the mother's failure to seek a test was negligent in light of the risks that the test posed to her and the fetus and the probability that the test would uncover a correctable defect." Technically, prenatal diagnosis could be directly mandated by state statute, with criminal sanctions for women who fail to comply with the law.

Fetal Surgery

Until the early 1980s, the only options offered by the prenatal diagnosis of a fetal disorder were to carry the affected fetus to term or abort it. Now, however, there are three basic approaches to treating the endangered fetus. The first entails administering medication or other substances indirectly to the fetus through the mother's bloodstream. Second, timely delivery can be induced so that the infant's problem can be treated immediately in a neonatal unit. The third approach is surgery on the fetus in the womb. Fetal surgery has been made possible by new developments in ultrasound and fetoscopy and also by sophisticated surgical instrumentation designed specifically for these intricate procedures on fetuses.

The first reported fetal surgery was performed in 1981 on a thirty-one-week-old fetus twin suffering from a severe urinary tract obstruction. In a similar case, surgeons treated a urinary tract obstruction in a twenty-two-week-old fetus by draining an accumulation of fluid from a large cyst that threatened the life of the fetus. Also under ultrasound, doctors at several locales have implanted miniature shunting devices in the brains of fetuses diagnosed as having hydrocephalus, a dangerous buildup of fluid in the brain. Other applications of fetal surgical methods have drained collapsed lungs and removed excess fluid from the chest and abdomen of a fetus. Fetal surgery is practical because it takes place in a surgical field (the amniotic fluid) that is sterile and because fetal wounds heal without the scarring, inflammation, fibrosis, or contraction that affect adult wound healing (Pergament 1993, 141).

The most dramatic type of fetal surgery was conducted on a twenty-four-week-old fetus to repair a diaphragmatic hernia (Harrison et al. 1990). After surgically opening the abdomen of the mother, the left side of the fetus was brought outside the uterus. After a fifty-four-minute surgery, the uterus was closed in three layers with fibrin glue applied between them and the amniotic fluid was replenished. At thirty-two weeks gestation, seven weeks after surgery, a healthy baby boy was delivered via cesarean section.

Notwithstanding these successes, all fetal surgeries remain high-risk procedures limited to fetuses in danger of dying before or soon after birth without the surgery. Also, for many disorders it is improbable that effective treatment will be developed in the foreseeable future. The threat of precipitating preterm delivery or abortion remains a severe constraint on all but the most routine fetal interventions. Risk also confronts the mother in any fetal surgery. Another dilemma of fetal surgery is that in "saving" a fetus that otherwise would die, a seriously disabled newborn may survive (Pergament 1993, 144).

One of the most difficult legal issues to be faced in the near future will be how to balance the rights of the mother and the medical needs of the fetus when they are contradictory. The basic issue here is whether the fetus is a patient separate from its mother in cases in which the fetus can be treated either medically or surgically. Prior to recent developments in fetal surgery, the fetus was considered a medical patient, and certain problems were treated with medicines administered to the mother or directly into the amniotic fluid. Although these procedures required the cooperation of the pregnant woman, they were not as physically intrusive or potentially risky as surgery. The difficulty with fetal surgery is that any treatment of the fetus can be accomplished only by invading the physical integrity and privacy of the woman. She must consent to surgery, not only on her unborn child, but also on herself. However, pressures on the pregnant woman to use available fetal therapies will likely increase as the techniques are transformed from experimental status to routine therapeutic procedures. For instance, even though Sherman Elias and George Annas view forcible medical treatment as "brutish and horrible," they concede:

> When fetal surgery becomes accepted medical practice, and/if the procedure can be done with minimal invasiveness and risk to the mother and significant benefit to the fetus, there is an argument to be made that the woman should not be permitted to reject it. Such rejection of therapy could be considered "fetal abuse" and, at a late stage in pregnancy, "child abuse," and an appropriate court order sought to force treatment. (1983, 811)

One problem with this argument is the danger in our medicalized society that new technologies might be offered to or even forced upon pregnant women without adequate proof of benefit. Our dependence on technological solutions, reinforced by a medical community trained in the technological imperative, often gives us a false degree of security as to what medicine can accomplish. Many therapies come into widespread use without adequate assessment as to their risks and benefits. Increasingly, as demand for medical solutions escalates, the line between experimentation and therapy becomes a tenuous one. Arguments that a pregnant woman has a legal duty to use "established" medical procedures, therefore, must be approached critically.

The rapidly developing advances in a variety of treatments, including fetal surgery, accentuate a subtle but real shift toward the recognition of an independent self of the fetus. Technologies that help visualize the growing organism as human; amniocentesis, which labels that entity as a "boy" or a "girl"; and prospects of a wide variety of direct surgical interventions certainly provide the developing fetus with recognition as an individual of some importance. Although it does not seem feasible to speak of the fetus as a fully autonomous person, it takes on broader human characteristics that lead to a redefinition of parental responsibility to the "unborn patient." One of the most difficult legal issues to be faced in the near future will be how to balance the rights of the mother and the medical needs of the fetus. Although in most cases the interests of the mother and the fetus are likely to be congruent, in some cases their interests will be in conflict.

Genetic Screening and Diagnosis

In the early 1970s, genetic screening was elevated to the national policy agenda after some states instituted mandatory sickle cell screening programs targeted at black populations. These screening programs led to considerable stigmatization and discrimination against individuals who were identified as having the sickle cell trait. In response, Congress passed the National Sickle Cell Anemia Control Act in 1972, under which states received federal funding only if their screening program was voluntary.

Until recently, diagnosis of genetic disorders focused on screening for carrier status for a handful of single-gene recessive diseases, most prominently sickle cell anemia and Tay-Sachs disease. Once identified, individuals with the trait could be educated as to the risk of having an affected child or offered prenatal diagnosis, if available for that particular disease. Although innovations over the last two decades in carrier screening and prenatal diagnosis have been impressive, the recent development of a broad array of new molecular techniques promises dramatic new possibilities for human genetic intervention.

One particularly sensitive area of research is directed toward discovering which genes are associated with intelligence. Work on the "fragile-X" chromosome, which is associated with mental retardation, is the first wave of this investigation. The discovery of genetic markers for some forms of Alzheimer's disease suggests hypotheses for genetic linkages to a range of neurological disorders. Eventually, genetic tests may allow scientists to identify not only the course of genetic abnormalities but also traits that put certain individuals at higher risk for susceptibility to a host of environmental factors.

We are currently in a transition period regarding genetic tests. Although advances in human molecular genetics have made it possible to identify individuals at risk for an array of conditions, the development of a battery of molecular probes is still in infancy. The commercial development and marketing of accurate and inexpensive tests, however, is imminent. Such genetic tests are likely to become as routine as contemporary health screening indicators. For example, companies might include such tests as part of their health promotion or preventive medicine programs. Then persons identified through those programs as having a genetic proclivity toward hypertension or malignant melanomas could be put into early diagnosis programs. Importantly, however, the same tests might be used as the basis to fire that person to reduce health care expenditures for the company.

Although human gene therapy is still in its infancy, the growth of such research has been "phenomenal" (Healy 1993). Gene transfer techniques will correct genetic defects, not by environmental manipulations, but instead by acting directly on the DNA in the affected person's cells. The research emphasis today is on somatic cell therapy, in which genes are inserted into particular body cells other than the germinal cells (the sperm, the egg, and those cells that give rise to them). Because somatic cell gene therapy does not affect the germ line, the genes conveyed through the procedure will not appear in the recipient's children. A considerably more controversial type of gene therapy is the intervention in germ-line cells, which contribute to the genetic heritage of offspring.

This move from diagnostic to therapeutic ends of genetic intervention calls into question the role the government ought to play in encouraging or discouraging its research and application. It also extends the ethical questions concerning parental responsibilities to one's children, societal perceptions of children, the distribution of social benefits, and the definition of what it means to be a human being. Furthermore, the availability of technologies for prenatal diagnosis, screening, and selection may heighten discrimination against children born with congenital or genetic disorders. In this atmosphere, such individuals might be perceived increasingly as unfortunate persons who would not have been born if only someone had gotten to them in time. Parents might feel tremendous guilt or resent the child, especially if social pressures and stigma are directed against them. The right to be born healthy is misleading if it means that only healthy persons have a right to be born. The choice of those affected is not between a healthy and unhealthy existence but rather between an unhealthy existence and none at all.

The technologies of prenatal intervention and human genetics raise critical policy dilemmas that increasingly require public attention. On the one hand, these innovations promise to alleviate the individual and social costs of genetic disease and give us more control over the destiny of future generations. On the other hand, widespread use of these technologies expands considerably the ability to label and categorize individuals according to precise genetic factors. The newfound capacity to predetermine the sex of progeny, to select the frozen embryo that best meets one's expectations, and through DNA tests to identify and possibly modify "undesirable" characteristics have the potential to dehumanize us, despite giving the appearance of expanding individual choice.

Obstetrical Procedures and the Courts

Throughout this chapter, we have discussed the dramatic improvements in prenatal technologies. Ultrasound and microscopic cameras have allowed us visual entry into the womb. Seeing the developing fetus within its mother's body has led many to view it as a patient separate from the pregnant woman. This is a difficult and complex proposition because one can only treat the fetus by invading the body of the woman. The law is clear that the health care provider cannot treat the woman without her informed consent; to do so constitutes battery by the provider against the woman. A competent adult can refuse treatment even if it results in her death; the fetus, however, cannot give either informed consent or informed refusal, and herein lies the potential for an enormous ethical dilemma. What standards should be applied and what procedures followed when a woman refuses to consent to treatment that physicians feel is in the best interest of the fetus and possibly in the best interest of the woman as well?

In this debate, one question is key: does a fetus have rights? The U.S. Supreme Court in *Roe v. Wade* (1973) ruled that the state has a legitimate interest in potential life after the point of fetal viability, and in *Webster v. Reproductive Health Services* (1989, 3057), the Court upheld mandated viability tests, finding that they "permissively further the state's interest in protecting potential human life." A number of lower courts have also ruled on the fetal rights issue, usually in the context of the fetus becoming the born child. In 1980, a Michigan court of appeals ruled that a born child could be compensated for injuries received in utero because of the mother's use of tetracycline during pregnancy (*Grodin v. Grodin*), and an Illinois appellate court upheld the right of a child to be compensated for automobile injuries received in utero (*Stallman v. Youngquist* 1984). The strongest legal statement on the rights of the fetus, as discussed below, came from the South Carolina Supreme Court, which ruled in 1997 that the viable fetus is a "child" for purposes of the state's child abuse and endangerment statute (*Whitner v. State*). Although the precedent is not completely clear, the general pattern outside South Carolina is that the fetus does not have rights; it is the born child who has rights and may have a cause of action for injuries suffered while in the womb.

Most women will go to enormous lengths to ensure the development of a healthy baby, but there are occasions when a woman refuses to have surgery or objects to a procedure because of religious or cultural values or a disagreement regarding the diagnosis or treatment plan or because she feels the procedure will endanger her life or the well-being of the fetus. She may also be poor and uninsured and therefore unable to pay for expensive procedures. Should she accept a blood transfusion, even though she is a devout follower of a religious denomination that believes transfusion is a sin? Although committing this sin might be minimally invasive physically, it might be highly invasive emotionally.

And what of the more invasive procedures such as in utero surgery or delivery by cesarean section? The latter deserves special attention because of the high rates of cesarean deliveries in the United States. A cesarean section is major surgery entailing a painful recovery for the new mother, and it has significantly higher risks of both maternal and newborn mortality compared to vaginal delivery, although the risks are still low. Some of the common conditions for which cesarean deliveries are recommended include placenta previa (the placenta blocks the birth canal), fetal sepsis (infection), fetal distress, or fetal breech position. If the diagnosis of one or more of these conditions is correct and the cesarean section is not performed, the fetus or newborn may be seriously compromised or die, and the mother may die as well. Thus the stakes are very, very high. If a woman refuses to submit to a cesarean delivery, she is entering the arena of complex ethical debate and possibly complex legal debate. The physician or hospital may seek a court order to compel her to comply. There are a significant number of cases on record in which hospitals have sought court orders, the diagnoses proved incorrect, and healthy children were born through vaginal delivery.

Perhaps the most dramatic and devastating case to date is that of Angela Carder, who had fought cancer since age thirteen, undergoing numerous treatments, including a leg amputation. Her cancer was in remission when she married and became pregnant. In June 1987, during her twenty-sixth week, she was admitted to George Washington University Hospital (GWUH), where doctors found a large tumor and advised her that she was near death. Her long-time oncologist recommended experimental chemotherapy or radiation in an effort to extend her life for two weeks to improve the chances of survival for both mother and infant. However, staff at GWUH determined that the fetus should be extracted through cesarean section, and shortly thereafter, a trial court convened at the hospital to determine whether the surgery could take place without Carder's consent. At the time of the hearing, Carder was heavily sedated and did not testify. Carder's oncologist was not consulted or even informed of the hearing and later indicated that he would have opposed the surgery, had he known about it. It is reported that the medical staff of the unit opposed the surgery, as did Carder's mother, who testified against it. Nevertheless, an order authorizing the cesarean delivery was issued (Spruce 1998).

By the time the hearing had concluded, Carder was alert and lucid. When informed of the order, she clearly stated twice that she did not want the surgery performed (Spruce 1998). The hearing reconvened, the judge reaffirmed his order, and a hastily assembled panel of appellate judges confirmed it. Baby Lindsey Carder died three hours after her delivery, and mother Angela Carder died two days later, never having given consent.

Despite the fact that the baby and mother had died, the District of Columbia Court of Appeals in 1990 reversed the trial court's order to perform the surgery and also made a strong statement on behalf of all patients, particularly pregnant patients, to make decisions for their own medical care. Regarding cesarean deliveries, it found that "in virtually all cases the question of what is to be done is to be decided by the patient—the pregnant woman—on behalf of herself and the fetus" (*In re: A. C., Appellant* 1990, 1110). The notion of maternal obligation to "rescue" the fetus was clearly ruled out: "[The] courts do not compel one person to permit a significant intrusion upon his or her bodily integrity for the benefit of another person's health. . . . Surely . . . a fetus cannot have rights in this respect superior to those of a person who has already been born" (1990, 1123).

Although the jurisdiction of the appellate court in the Angela Carder case applies only to the District of Columbia, some thought that it would have national impact because of the widespread reporting of the case in the news media and the extensive analysis of it in law journals. Unfortunately, other cases would follow, and the issue of court-ordered obstetrical intervention would not be resolved on a nationwide basis. When one looks at such cases, several problematic patterns are discernible. A 1986 survey of obstetricians showed a greater likelihood that orders for procedures such as cesarean sections, hospital detentions, and intrauterine transfusions would be sought for minority women than for white women. Of twenty-one cases reported, 81 percent involved black, Asian, or Hispanic women, and 24 percent involved women who did not speak English as their primary language (Kolder, Gallagher, and Parsons 1987, 1193).

A second pattern is that physicians and courts have rushed to judgment. The data from Kolder, Gallagher, and Partsons report that in 70 percent of the cases studied, hospital administrators and lawyers were aware of the situation for a day or less before the order was pursued. In 88 percent, court orders were obtained in less than six hours, and in 19 percent, the orders were issued in less than one hour. The speed at which these orders are sought is complicated by the fact that sometimes diagnoses are inaccurate. In six of the sixteen cases in which orders were sought for a cesarean delivery, the diagnosis of harm to the fetus proved inaccurate (Kolder, Gallagher, and Parsons 1987).

Most people agree that parents-to-be should, to the best of their abilities, protect the fetus that is to become the born child. In light of the absence of a national policy, what should the various people do when disagreements arise? The issue of court-ordered obstetrical intervention is frequently characterized as a conflict between the pregnant woman and the fetus. This description is inaccurate because often the conflict exists between the pregnant woman and the health care provider, not the pregnant woman and the fetus. There is no evidence in the cases discussed above that women who have refused obstetrical interventions were valuing their rights above those of the fetuses. For example, Angela Carder was trying to extend her own life and pregnancy so that her fetus would have a greater opportunity for survival.

It is critical that physicians make earnest efforts to fully discuss the reasons for the recommended obstetrical interventions with their patients and attempt to persuade them to comply. Physicians do not have perfect diagnostic tools, and patients are not bereft of reasoned judgment. Should a mentally competent woman refuse to give consent, that refusal should be respected, unless there is overriding evidence that serious damage will be done to the born child and the treatment will be minimally invasive for the woman. Only in extremely rare circumstances, then, should court orders be sought to compel treatment over the objections of the patient. We now turn our attention to another controversial issue involving the courts, an analysis of public policy as it affects pregnant women who use illegal drugs.

Pregnancy, Addiction, and the Law

On the surface, dealing with maternal substance abuse would seem much less ethically complex than dealing with court-ordered obstetrical interventions: pregnant women should not use illegal drugs. All states have child endangerment statutes to protect born children, but do these laws also protect the unborn fetus? In addition, if the fetus is to be aborted, it is unrealistic to argue that it has rights. Born children have rights, not fetuses that will be aborted.

During the 1980s and early 1990s, numerous articles appeared both in the popular press and medical journals about the damaging effects of cocaine and other illegal drugs on the fetus and the born child, and televised investigative reports focused on the "epidemic" of crack babies. Much of this was based on the research of Dr. Ira Chasnoff, professor of pediatrics at the University of Illinois College of Medicine and president of the Children's Research Triangle. He estimated that in 1988, 11 percent of pregnant women used chemical substances (Chasnoff 1989), and his research raised concerns that intrauterine drug exposure could place infants at risk for developmental outcome (Chasnoff et al. 1992, 284). The road initially seemed clear; women who used illegal drugs were condemning their children to poor health and long-term developmental problems, or so we thought.

An argument on behalf of a right to use illegal drugs cannot be supported; if the activity is illegal, there is no right to pursue it, and men and women who possess illegal substances are prosecuted every day for their addictions. But the more complex question is: can a woman be prosecuted for endangering the fetus because of her substance abuse? Prosecutors in about thirty states said "yes" and pursued criminal charges against pregnant addicts. Generally speaking, those prosecutions proved unsuccessful when defendants appealed their convictions; in every state except one, state courts rejected the use of child endangerment statutes as a basis for punishing these women. Specifically, the supreme courts of Ohio (*State v. Gray* 1992), Kentucky (*Commonwealth v. Welch* 1993), and Nevada (*Sheriff v. Encoe* 1994) declined to apply criminal child neglect statutes to maternal substance abuse during pregnancy, and the Florida Supreme Court reversed the conviction of a woman who had been found guilty of delivering a controlled substance (cocaine) to her two children through their umbilical cords during their births, finding that the intent of the state legislature was to treat drug dependent mothers and newborns as public health problems, not as criminal problems. It also found insufficient evidence to prove that delivery of the cocaine had actually occurred during the birth process (*Johnson v. State* 1992).

One state court stood alone as the exception to this nationwide trend. In the late 1980s, South Carolina prosecutors initiated an aggressive policy to arrest, convict, and incarcerate pregnant addicts, and they received strong support from the South Carolina courts. In February 1992, Cornelia Whitner gave birth to a son at Baptist Medical Center in Easley, South Carolina. Shortly thereafter, police and social workers arrived at the hospital and took custody of her newborn, leaving a note for Whitner because she was not in her room. The following day, while still hospitalized, Whitner was handcuffed and arrested. She was charged with criminal child neglect because she had used cocaine during the last trimester of pregnancy. Although cocaine metabolites were identified in her son's system, he was healthy. Like most of the pregnant addicts arrested in South Carolina, she was poor and African American. Whitner pled guilty and was sentenced to eight years in prison. Later she appealed on the grounds of ineffective council because her attorney had not advised her that the child neglect statute applied only to born children, not to a fetus.

In a controversial decision, the South Carolina Supreme Court ruled that "child" as used in the child abuse and endangerment statute included the viable fetus, and citing Chasnoff's research, concluded "there can be no question . . . Whitner endangered the life, health and comfort of her child" *(Whitner v. State* 1997). She appealed to the U.S. Supreme Court, which refused the case, and she continued to serve out her prison sentence while relatives cared for her three children.

A similar set of circumstances arose at the Medical University of South Carolina (MUSC), a public hospital with low-income African Americans constituting a large portion of its patient census. In 1989, hospital staff, police, and the solicitor developed a policy for hospital staff to administer urine tests to selected pregnant patients to screen for illegal drugs without the knowledge or consent of the patient. Those tests could then be turned over to police for possible arrest on a variety of charges, including distribution of an illegal substance to a minor (the fetus) or child neglect, if the patient tested positive during delivery. It is reported that the policy had no provisions for prenatal care or any special treatment for newborns. Lynn Paltrow argues that at the time the policy was initiated, there was not a single residential drug treatment program in the state for pregnant women or new mothers, and even the drug treatment program at

MUSC refused admission to pregnant women (Paltrow 2000; see also Jos, Marshall, and Perlmutter 1995, 124).

It is reported that all but one of the forty-two women arrested at MUSC were African American, and a note in the medical records of the only white woman arrested stated that she lived with her boyfriend, who was black (Paltrow 2000; Miller 1999). In September 1994, the program was suspended after the federal Office of Civil Rights began investigating whether the policy was racially discriminatory (SCAPW 2001; CRLP 1996), and the American Public Health Association (APHA) reported that

> the policy was confined to the overwhelmingly poor and disproportionately non-white group of patients seeking care at a public hospital. These indigent persons had few, if any, other health care providers to turn to. The policy required medical personnel to yield their independence of judgment and ally themselves with the interests of law enforcement officials rather than those of the patients who had come to the hospital seeking prenatal care they could not afford to purchase on the private market. (APHA 2001)

Ten women who received obstetrical care at MUSC and were subsequently arrested filed suit in federal district court against the city of Charleston, law enforcement personnel, and MUSC. The complainants challenged the urine screening policy as unconstitutional because no search warrants were filed and informed consent was not given; the case hinged on the Fourth Amendment protection against unreasonable search and seizure. The U.S. Supreme Court found for the complainants, holding that

> a state hospital's performance of a diagnostic test to obtain evidence of a patient's criminal conduct for law enforcement purposes is an unreasonable search if the patient has not consented to the procedure. The interest in using the threat of criminal sanctions to deter pregnant women from using cocaine cannot justify a departure from the general rule that an official nonconsensual search is unconstitutional if not authorized by a valid warrant. (*Ferguson v. Charleston* 2001, syllabus)

The Court went further by citing the famous *Miranda* decision (1966), which requires that criminal suspects be informed of their rights:

> while state hospital employees, like other citizens, may have a duty to provide the police with evidence of criminal conduct that they inadvertently acquire in the course of routine treatment, when they undertake to obtain such evidence from their patients *for the specific purpose of incriminating those patients* [emphasis in the original], they have a special obligation to make sure that the patients are fully informed about their constitutional rights. (*Ferguson v. Charleston* 2001)

Those who thought the *Ferguson* decision would steer South Carolina prosecutors away from their arrest and incarceration approach were quickly disappointed when on May 21, 2001, jurors in the state's Fifteenth Judicial District (Horry County) found twenty-four-year-old Regina McNight guilty of homicide in the death of her stillborn daughter. McNight fit the profile of South Carolina's typical defendant. She was young, poor, homeless, a high school dropout, and African American. It was reported that she had an intelligence quotient (IQ) of 72 and had attended classes for the "educably mentally handicapped" ("In America" 2001; "S.C. Verdict" 2001). She had not sought prenatal care until the eighth month of her pregnancy, when she went to a county hospital for help, believing something had gone wrong with the pregnancy. She admitted to using cocaine during that month, and traces of cocaine were later found in her stillborn daughter's system. Despite contradictory testimony from physicians about whether McNight's cocaine use had caused the stillbirth, a jury deliberated for only fifteen minutes before finding her guilty of homicide and making her the first woman in the United States to be convicted of a homicide associated with substance abuse during pregnancy. She was sentenced to twelve years in prison without the possibility of parole, and her three children must now be cared for by others.

One must really question why pregnant addicts have been prosecuted and what good comes from such prosecutions. If the societal goal is to punish pregnant women who use drugs—if the intent is punitive—then prosecute. But if the goal is to increase the incidence of healthy babies and reduce the incidence of maternal substance abuse, criminalization is the wrong road to travel for a number of reasons. First, patients need to seek medical care in an environment that encourages trust between the patient and health care provider. Patients need to feel that they can disclose to health care providers the most intimate details of their private lives, including any use of illegal drugs. The health care provider and the patient need to be allies, not adversaries. As the APHA has pointed out, the MUSC policy prompted "care providers to be dishonest in their dealings with patients and to use explicit promises of non-disclosure as well as the trust inherent in their professional relationships to extract private and potentially inculpatory information" (APHA 2001).

Second, the threat of police intervention, the vision of being arrested and led away in handcuffs, and the anxiety associated with potential incarceration and separation from newborn and family will encourage women to hide from a medical system that could help them and their children. Chasnoff, whose early research was cited in *Whitner* as justification for prosecution, spoke against the MUSC policy, stating that it would drive women out of treatment programs and out of prenatal care (APHA 2001), and a retrospective study of the effects of policy at MUSC found that its implementation was accompanied by a decrease in utilization of prenatal care (Tribble et al. 1993, cited in Paltrow 2000). MUSC's own bioethicist expressed concern that it had alienated the patient population (Marshall, Jos, and Perlmutter 1995). A third problem is that arrest and prosecution of pregnant women will interrupt the bonding between mother and newborn since they are physically separated. It may even create an adversarial relationship, as the mother comes to resent the legal difficulties she faces because she brought the pregnancy to term. Some women may terminate pregnancies rather than risk prosecution.

Substance abuse treatment can be successful when the addiction is understood and appropriate psychiatric treatment is followed (Graham and Schultz 2000). If the pregnant addict seeks treatment, however, it is unlikely she will get it because of the shortage of treatment facilities in the United States that admit pregnant women. Even if a pregnant addict is admitted for drug treatment, she faces additional barriers, including the need to find others to care for her children and transportation to the counseling center. The MUSC policy provided neither (Jos, Marshall, and Perlmutter 1995, 126).

Finally, and perhaps most important, despite the research of the 1980s and early 1990s and the sensationalized news reporting

that followed, there is now considerable debate in medical journals about the long-term effects of cocaine and other illegal drugs
on the born child (Hoegerman et al. 1990; Chasnoff and Lowder
1999; Jansson and Velez 1999). Recent research at Albert Einstein
Medical Center shows that children exposed in utero to cocaine
do not differ neurologically from those not exposed (Hurt et al.
2001, "Are There Neurological Correlates . . .") and do not have
lower IQ scores (Hurt et al. 1997). Moreover, differences in neurological development that do exist are based on factors such as
caregiver and home environments rather than in utero cocaine
exposure (Hurt et al. 2001, "A Prospective Comparison . . ."; see
also Little et al. 1996; Woods et al. 1993; and Coles et al. 1992).

Moreover, the evidence is very strong that the use of *legal*
drugs, including alcohol and cigarettes, is more dangerous for
the born child than are cocaine and other illicit drugs
(Hoegerman et al. 1990). Children afflicted with fetal alcohol syndrome (FAS) are subject to facial anomalies and mental retardation, and tobacco use during pregnancy is associated with low
birth weight (DiFranza and Lew 1995, cited in CRLP 1996), a
markedly higher perinatal death rate (Hoegerman et al. 1990,
cited in AIA 2000), and an increased incidence of sudden infant
death syndrome (Lindesmith Center 1996). Despite the fact that
substantially more women use alcohol and tobacco during pregnancy than illicit drugs (NIDA 1994, cited in AIA 2000), women
have rarely been prosecuted for drinking or smoking.

So where does this information leave us? As can be seen
from Table 2.2, in terms of public policy, the Alan Guttmacher
Institute (AGI) reported in September 2002 that one state (South

Table 2.2 State Policies Regarding Substance Abuse during Pregnancy

Criminalize prenatal substance abuse: SC

Terminate parental rights because of prenatal substance abuse: FL, IL, IN, MD, MN, NV, OH, RI, SC, SD, TX, VA, WI

Require reporting or testing by health care professionals for prenatal substance abuse: AZ, IL, IA, MA, MI, MN, UT, VA

Authorize civil commitment of pregnant substance abusers: MN, SD, WI

Give priority access to treatment for substance abuse to pregnant women: AZ, GA, KS, MO, OK, TX, WI

Create or fund substance abuse treatment programs that serve pregnant women: AR, CA, CO, CT, FL, IL, KY, LA, MD, MN, MO, NE, NY, NC, OH, OR, PA, VA, WA

Adapted from the Alan Guttmacher Institute, "Substance Abuse During Pregnancy," *State Policies in Brief*, September 1, 2002. http://www.guttmacher.org. Accessed March 7, 2003.

Carolina) had criminalized prenatal substance abuse, and eight states required health care professionals to report prenatal substance abuse to authorities. Thirteen states had provisions to terminate parental rights in cases of prenatal substance abuse, two authorized commitment of the pregnant woman to inpatient treatment facilities, and one (Wisconsin) allowed detention of the pregnant woman to protect the unborn child.

One cannot condone substance abuse on the part of pregnant women or any behavior that injures the born child, even if that behavior occurs during pregnancy. However, if the goal of reproductive policy is to ensure healthy outcomes for women and children, we are well advised as a nation to use our scarce resources to provide universal prenatal care and appropriate maternal nutrition—both strong predictors of positive pregnancy outcomes—and to provide adequate substance abuse treatment for pregnant addicts. Despite the progress made in approximately one-half the states toward treating addiction rather than criminalizing it, thousands of pregnant addicts still cannot afford the cost of prenatal care, maternal nutrition, or substance abuse treatment. We turn now to the highly controversial issue of fetal and embryo research.

Fetal and Embryo Research

One extension of the debate over reproductive rights and conflict among various interests in human reproduction centers on the utilization of human embryos and fetuses for research or as sources of cells, tissues, and organs. At the center of political controversy over fetal and embryo research is disagreement over the moral and legal status of the embryo. Clearly, the issue of abortion "looms heavily in the background of any discussion of policies regarding research on conceptuses" (Andrews 1993, 26). Because a fetus is unable to consent to being a research subject, there is concern over what type of consent and by whom is sufficient. There are also questions about how to balance research needs with the interests of the pregnant woman and the proper ends of such research. Unlike many other topics discussed here, fetal research has surfaced periodically on the political agenda since the 1980s and has been addressed as an issue by national and presidential commissions, Congress, and many state legislatures.

Although the context of fetal research is complex, resulting in various shadings of support and opposition for particular applications, in general there are two major sides in the debate. The research community and its supporters argue that research using human fetus and embryo materials is critical for progress in many areas of medicine. Prolife groups counter by arguing that research using aborted fetuses will give abortion greater legitimacy and encourage its use in order to aid research or individual patients. They contend that the use of embryos and fetuses for research exploits them as the means to other persons' ends and dehumanizes them. In addition, other interests not fully opposed to such research express concern over potential commercialization and payment questions, the ownership of fetal materials, and the need to delineate boundaries for acceptable uses of fetal material.

One problem in analyzing fetal and embryo research is that it encompasses a broad array of applications. One important distinction is that between investigational research, which cannot benefit the subject fetus, and therapeutic research, which is likely to be beneficial to future fetuses even though it does not benefit the subject fetus. Another key distinction centers on the fetus' stage of development, from pre-implantation to late fetal stages, when research is conducted. The general sources of fetal material include: tissue from dead fetuses; previable or nonviable fetuses in the womb before an elective abortion; nonviable living fetuses outside the womb; and in vitro and preimplantation embryos. Although the variety of potential uses of fetal tissue is virtually unlimited, five critical areas are summarized here (for more details see Blank 2001).

The first category of research deals with investigations of fetal development and physiology. The purpose of this research is to expand scientific knowledge about normal fetal development to provide a basis for identifying and understanding abnormal processes and, ultimately, curing birth deformities. In some instances, this research requires administration of a substance to the woman prior to abortion or delivery by cesarean section, followed by analysis to detect the presence of this substance or its metabolic effects in a sample of umbilical cord blood or in the fetal tissue. This research also focuses on the development of fetal behavior in the womb by monitoring fetal breathing movements, hearing, vision, and taste capabilities.

The second type of research focuses on the development of techniques, like amniocentesis, that are used to diagnose fetal problems. Initial research was conducted on samples of amniotic fluid that were collected during induced abortions to determine the normal values for enzymes known to be affected by a genetic disease. Once it was demonstrated that the particular enzyme was expressed in fetal cells and after normal values were determined, tests were designed to diagnose the abnormal condition in the fetus at risk. Fetal research has also led to expansion of the capacity to diagnose many more diseases, to development of chorionic villus sampling, and to efforts to detect fetal cells in the maternal blood stream.

A third area of research concentrates on the identification of physical defects in the developing fetus. Ultrasound, alpha-fetoprotein tests, tests for fetal lung capacity, and a variety of techniques for monitoring fetal well-being or distress are recent products of this category of fetal research. In each case, following animal studies that indicated the safety and efficacy of the procedure, human fetal research was conducted in a variety of settings. Fetoscopy, for example, because of the potential risk to the fetus, was developed selectively in women undergoing elective abortion. The procedure was performed prior to abortion, and an autopsy was performed afterward to determine its technical success.

A fourth area of fetal research involves efforts to determine the effects of drugs on the developing fetus. These pharmacological studies are largely retrospective in design, involving the examination of the fetus or infant after an accidental exposure. For instance, all studies on the influence of oral contraceptives or other drugs on multiple births or congenital abnormalities have been retrospective, as were most studies of the effects on the fetus of drugs administered to treat maternal illness during pregnancy. In these designs, no fetus was intentionally exposed to the drug for research purposes. However, some pharmacology research involves intentional administration of substances to pregnant women prior to abortion in order to compare quantitative movement of these agents across the placenta as well as absolute levels achieved in fetal tissues.

The availability of human embryos for research purposes followed the development of in vitro fertilization. In 1982, Patrick Steptoe and Robert Edwards, who four years earlier had reported the first birth through IVF, announced plans to freeze "spare" embryos for possible clinical or laboratory use. Theoretically, those spare embryos could be augmented by the deliberate creation of embryos for research, if donors would consent to have their gametes or embryos used in this way. There is considerable hesitancy to move to the deliberate production of embryos for research, even though that might be the only way to satisfy expanding research needs.

Although all assisted reproduction technologies are experimental at some stage and thus might be described as research, there are many nonclinical uses that more clearly fit the research paradigm, such as developing and testing contraceptives, investigating abnormal cell growth, and studying the development of chromosomal abnormalities. Other potential genetic uses of the embryos include attempts at altering gene structures; pre-implantation screening for chromosomal anomalies and genetic diseases; pre-implantation therapy for genetic defects; and development of characteristic selection techniques, including sex preselection.

A final area of fetal research involves the use of fetal cells for transplantation. Unlike other areas of fetal research, in which the tissue is used to develop a treatment that might help future fetuses, in fetal transplantation research the tissue is the treatment used to benefit an identifiable adult patient. Although some persons see no ethical difference between the transplantation of adult organs and of fetal tissues to benefit adult recipients, others contend that the use of fetal tissue for this purpose is ethically questionable because there are no possible benefits to particular fetuses or to future fetuses (Nolan 1988).

Despite the ethical controversy surrounding the use of fetal tissue, many scientists consider it to be especially well-suited for grafting (Lindvall et al. 1990). In contrast to adult tissue, fetal tissue cells replicate rapidly and exhibit tremendous capacity for differentiation into functioning mature cells. This capacity is maximal in the early stages of fetal development and gradually diminishes throughout gestation. Moreover, unlike mature tissue, fetal tissue has been found to have great potential for growth and restoration when transplanted into a host organism.

In animal experiments, fetal tissue has displayed a considerable capacity for survival within the graft recipient. Fetal cells also appear to have increased resistance to oxygen deprivation, which makes them an especially attractive source of transplant material (Mullen 1992, 5). Furthermore, fetal cells are easily cultured in the laboratory, thus allowing development of specific cell lines. They are also amenable to storage via cryopreservation, and because of their immunological immaturity, fetal cells are less likely than adult cells to provoke an immune response leading to rejection by the host organism (OTA 1990, 43).

Although most applications of fetal tissue transplantation are highly experimental, the potential use is significant. The only proven effective treatment to date is the use of fetal thymus transplants for the rare DiGeorge's syndrome. Also, despite less than encouraging success to date, fetal pancreatic tissue transplants for juvenile diabetes are seen as promising. Fetal liver cells have been transplanted in patients with aplastic anemia with reasonable success, although clinical trials and more research are needed to ascertain the mechanism for recovery of these patients. Other potential applications of fetal liver tissue transplants include bone marrow diseases such as severe combined immunodeficiency and acute leukemia in which HLA (human leucocyte antigens)-matched donors are unavailable, an array of inherited metabolic storage disorders, and radiation accidents.

Another concern in fetal research is whether the pregnant woman's medical care can be altered to meet research purposes. Although some observers approve of modifications in the abortion procedure if they pose little risk for the woman and if she is adequately informed and consents, no one has publicly advocated changing abortion procedures that entail a significant increase in the probability of harm or discomfort to the woman. There is general agreement that the means and timing of abortion should be based on the pregnant woman's medical needs and not on research needs.

Furthermore, the difficulty of obtaining cooperation from abortion clinics and obstetricians in making fetal tissue available for research, which is attributed in part to a reluctance to meet the additional time and resource requirements, raises concern over maintaining an adequate supply. In addition, the availability of RU-486 and other abortifacients in the near future will diminish the supply of usable fetal tissue at a time when demand might increase, should fetal tissue prove to be a successful treatment for a common disease. Despite near consensus that fetal tissue procurement should not pose significant risk to the pregnant woman and support for procedural protections, pressure for an expanding supply of usable fetal tissue demands considerable vigilance to minimize abuses that are certain to occur.

Conclusions: Reproductive Technologies and Reproductive Rights

Chapters 1 and 2 have examined a wide range of applications in which traditional notions of reproductive rights are challenged by new capabilities of biomedicine, changing social values, and novel legal trends. Although the concept of rights is well entrenched in U.S. political and legal theory and central to U.S. politics, the issues raised here illustrate how problematic its application to reproduction has become. The cumulative impact of reproductive intervention in the twenty-first century requires a reassessment and clarification of the basic questions regarding rights introduced in Chapter 1. Who has rights? What do they entail? What do we do in cases of conflict? If anything, the topics discussed here have confounded the answers to these questions and demonstrated why reproduction is such an explosive issue within the rights framework.

Although the notion of reproductive rights is intuitively attractive to supporters of women's autonomy in procreative matters, it raises serious problems. Until the 1970s, attention centered on the rights of women not to reproduce, but in the 1980s, the rights concept was increasingly used in reference to rights of the fetus, or, more precisely, the rights of the child, once born to a sound mind and body. To a large extent the debate has shifted from the woman's rights to the rights of the fetus, as U.S. society has debated the right to have children. Also, applications such as contract surrogacy with IVF have pitted the rights of the genetic mother and father against those of the gestational mother. The danger of a rights approach for each party, therefore, is that the balance among rights can easily shift as social values and technological capacities change. Advantages given to one group through rights are fragile and time-bound. Although the shifts may be subtle or overt, the rights approach is a volatile one. There are, then, clear difficulties in using reproductive rights as the framework for analyzing reproductive technologies and risks for all the parties involved. Although rights will always be a critical factor in the United States, the problems raised at all stages of reproduction, from preconception to prenatal to neonatal, suggest a need for a thorough reevaluation of the continued value of rights as the defining factor in specific cases.

Even if we refuse to face difficult questions over societal goals for the future, we are forced to deal with the more immediate question of whether we can afford to define reproductive rights as positive rights. As the range of reproductive interventions widens and the costs escalate, questions of access will intensify. Strong pressures for cost containment in health care and for more explicit allocation and rationing mechanisms will increasingly place reproductive technologies in competition with other areas of health care spending, such as that for acquired immunodeficiency syndrome (AIDS). Unlike most other western nations, the United States largely rejects the notion of a positive right or entitlement to health care and has opted for an individualistic market system.

The economic realities of scarce resources and constrained health budgets, then, make it unlikely that reproduction will be defined as a positive right in terms of access to those technologies that guarantee the individual a capacity to have children and to select for their quality. The right to have children will be defined as a negative right at best. To do so, however, means that many infertile individuals who cannot afford these services or do not have adequate third-party coverage will be denied the means to exercise that right.

New technological capabilities, therefore, have created a paradox regarding reproductive rights. At a time when we are able to give individuals a broad choice of technologies for fertility control, infertility treatment, diagnostics and therapy for fetuses and neonates, and characteristic selection capabilities, we have accompanying problems of access. To provide these services for all persons as a positive right is prohibitively costly and would divert resources from other areas of health care. To deny these services to any individuals who desire them and need them to exercise their reproductive autonomy, however, negates their rights to reproduce in any meaningful sense. Conversely, once the techniques are available in the marketplace, denying their use to people who can afford them would deny even their negative rights to reproduce.

This initial, almost unbridled enthusiasm for reproductive innovation, however, is being moderated by increasingly vocal opposition and the realization that these technologies, like all others, bring with them problems as well as benefits. Given the technological trends, it is becoming clear that we can proceed either toward a world of greater individual choice or a brave new world. The foregoing discussion of issues surrounding the rapid progression of new interventions in human procreation and the burgeoning knowledge of fetal development confirms their importance as matters of public policy. In spite of the benefits these technologies promise for many people, certain applications threaten prevailing values held by many others, thus generating intense opposition from a broad array of interests. This combination of a growing demand for reproductive services and condemnation guarantees that the issues explicated in this book are bound to heighten and that increasingly they will demand public attention.

References

AFS (American Fertility Society). 1988a. "Minimal Standards for Gamete Intrafallopian Transfer (GIFT)." *Fertility and Sterility* 50 (1): 20.

———. 1988b. "Revised New Guidelines for the Use of Semen-Donor Insemination." *Fertility and Sterility* 49 (2): 211.

———. 1993a. "Guidelines for Oocyte Donation." *Fertility and Sterility* 59 (2): 5s–7s.

———. 1993b. "Guidelines for Therapeutic Donor Insemination: Sperm." *Fertility and Sterility* 59 (2): 1s–4s.

———. 1993c. "Minimum Genetic Screening for Gamete Donors." *Fertility and Sterility* 59 (2): 9s.

AIA (Abandoned Infants Assistance Resource Center). 2000. "Perinatal Substance Exposure." http://ist-socrates.berkeley.edu/~aiarc/pubs/perinate.htm. Accessed August 2, 2001.

Andrews, Lori B. 1989. *Between Strangers: Surrogate Mothers, Expectant Fathers, and Brave New Babies.* New York: Harper and Row.

———. 1993. "Regulation of Experimentation on the Unborn." *Journal of Legal Medicine* 14 (1): 25–56.

———.1995. "Beyond Doctrinal Boundaries: A Legal Framework for Surrogate Motherhood." *Virginia Law Review* 81: 2343–2375. http://www.lexisnexis.com/. Accessed September 1, 2002.

APHA (American Public Health Association). Amici Brief in *Ferguson v. Charleston*, 532 U.S. 67 (2001).

Blank, Robert H. 2001. "Fetal Research." In *The Concise Encyclopedia of the Ethics of New Technologies*, Ruth Chapman, ed. San Diego, CA: Academic Press.

Blank, Robert H., and Janna C. Merrick. 1995. *Human Reproduction, Emerging Technologies, and Conflicting Rights.* Washington, DC: Congressional Quarterly Press.

Braverman, Andrea M. 1993. "Survey Results on the Current Practice of Ovum Donation." *Fertility and Sterility* 59 (6): 1216–1220.

Capron, Alexander Morgan. 1998. "At Law: Too Many Parents." *Hastings Center Report* 28 (5): 22–24.

Chasnoff, Ira J. 1989. "Drug Use and Women: Establishing a Standard of Care." *Annals of the New York Academy of Sciences* 562: 208–210.

Chasnoff, Ira J., Dan R. Griffith, Catherine Freier, and James Murray. 1992. "Cocaine/Polydrug Use in Pregnancy: Two-Year Follow-Up." *Pediatrics* 89 (2): 284–289.

Chasnoff, Ira J., Harvey J. Landress, and Mark E. Barrett. 1990. "The Prevalence of Illicit-Drug or Alcohol Use during Pregnancy and Discrepancies in Mandatory Reporting in Pinellas County, Florida." *New England Journal of Medicine* 322 (17): 1202–1206.

Chasnoff, Ira J., and L. Lowder. 1999. "Prenatal Alcohol and Drug Use and Risk for Child Maltreatment: A Timely Approach to Intervention." In *Neglected Children: Research, Practice and Policy,* Howard Dubowitz, ed. Thousand Oaks, CA: Sage Publications.

Coles, Claire D., et al. 1992. "Effects of Cocaine and Alcohol Use in Pregnancy on Neonatal Growth and Neurobehavioral Status." *Neurotoxicology and Teratology* 23 (1): 31–32.

Commonwealth v. Welch, 864 S.W.2d 280 (Ky. 1993).

CRLP (Center for Reproductive Law and Policy). 1996. *Punishing Women for Their Behavior during Pregnancy: An Approach That Undermines Women's Health and Children's Interests.* New York: CRLP.

CSP (Center for Surrogate Parenting). 2001. "Estimated Costs." http://www.creatingfamilies.com. Accessed September 10.

Dailard, Cynthia, and Elizabeth Nash. 2000. "State Responses to Substance Abuse among Pregnant Women." *Guttmacher Report* 3 (6).

D'Alton, Mary E., and Alan H. DeCherney. 1993. "Prenatal Diagnosis." *New England Journal of Medicine* 328 (2): 114–120.

DiFranza, Joseph, and Robert A. Lew. 1995. "Effect of Maternal Cigarette Smoking on Pregnancy Complications and Sudden Infant Death Syndrome." *Journal of Family Practice* 40 (4): 385–394.

Elias, Sherman, and George J. Annas. 1983. "Perspectives on Fetal Surgery." *American Journal of Obstetrics and Gynecology* 145: 807–812.

Epstein, Richard A. 1995. "Surrogacy: The Case for Full Contractual Enforcement." *Virginia Law Review* 81: 2305–2341. Accessed online at http://www.lexisnexis.com/.

Ferguson v. City of Charleston, 532 U.S. 67, 121 S.Ct. 1281, 149 L.Ed.2d 205 (2001).

Graham, Allan W., and Terry K. Schultz, eds. 2000. *Principles of Addiction Medicine.* Chevy Chase, MD: American Society of Addiction Medicine.

Grodin v. Grodin, 102 Mich. App. 396, 301 N.W.2d 869 (1980).

Gurmankin, Andrea D. 2001. "Risk Information Provided to Prospective Oocyte Donors in a Preliminary Phone Call." *American Journal of Bioethics* 1 (4).

Hanafin, Hilary. 1987. "Surrogate Parenting: Reassessing Human Bonding." Paper read at the meeting of the American Psychological Association, New York City.

Harrison, M. R., et al. 1990. "Successful Repair In Utero of a Fetal Diaphragmatic Hernia after Removal of Herniated Viscera from the Left Thorax." *New England Journal of Medicine* 316 (19): 1192–1196.

Healy, Bernadine. 1993. "The Pace of Human Gene Transfer Research Quickens." *Journal of the American Medical Association* 327 (20): 567.

Hoegerman, G., et al. 1990. "Drug-Exposed Neonates: Addiction Medicine and the Primary Care Physician." *Western Journal of Medicine* 152 (5): 546–559.

Hurt, H. Hallam, Joan M. Giannetta, Nancy L. Brodsky, Elsa Malmud, and T. Pelham. 2001. "Are There Neurological Correlates of In Utero Cocaine Exposure at Age 6 Years?" *Journal of Pediatrics* 138 (6): 911–913.

Hurt, H. Hallam, Elsa Malmud, Laura M. Betancourt, Nancy L. Brodsky, and Joan M. Gianetta. 1997. "Children with In Utero Cocaine Exposure Do Not Differ from Control Subjects on Intelligence Testing." *Archives of Pediatric Adolescent Medicine* 151 (12): 1237–1241.

———. 2001. "A Prospective Comparison of Developmental Outcome of Children with In Utero Cocaine Exposure and Controls Using the Battelle Developmental Inventory." *Journal of Developmental and Behavioral Pediatrics* 22 (1): 27–34.

"In America." 2001. Editorial. *New York Times,* May 24.

In re A. C., D.C. Ct. App., April 26, 1990 (en banc. slip op.).

In re Baby M., 525 A.2d 1128 (N.J. Super. Ct. 1987).

In re Marriage of Buzzanca, 61 Cal. App. 4th 1410, 1418 (1998).

In the Matter of Baby M., 537 A.2d 1227 (N.J. 1988).

Ingram, John D. 1993. "Should In Vitro Fertilization Be Covered by Medical Expense Reimbursement Plans?" *American Journal of Family Law* 7 (2): 103–108.

Jansson, L. M., and M. Velez. 1999. "Understanding and Treating Substance Abusers and Their Infants." *Infants and Young Children* 11 (4): 79–89.

Jhordan C. v. Mary K., 179 Cal. App. 3d 386, 224 Cal. Rptr. 530 (1986).

Johnson v. State, 602 So. 2d 1266 (Fla. 1992).

Jos, Philip H., Mary Faith Marshall, and Martin Perlmutter. 1995. "The Charleston Policy on Cocaine Use during Pregnancy: A Cautionary Tale." *Journal of Law, Medicine, and Ethics* 23 (2): 120–128.

Kelliher, Kim. 1999. "Born, but Not Free." *Hospitals and Health Networks* 73 (6): 30.

Kerian, Christine. 1997. "Surrogacy: A Last Resort Alternative for Infertile Women or Commodification of Women's Bodies and Children?" *Wisconsin Women's Law Journal* 12: 113–166. Accessed online at http://www.lexisnexis.com/.

Kinzie v. Physician's Liability Insurance Company, 750P.2d 1140 (Okla. Ct. App. 1987).

Kolder, Veronika, Janet Gallagher, and Michael T. Parsons. 1987. "Court-Ordered Obstetrical Interventions." *New England Journal of Medicine* 316 (19): 1192–1196.

Lindesmith Center Drug Policy Foundation. 1996. "Research Brief: Cocaine and Pregnancy." October.

Lindvall, Olle, et al. 1990. "Grafts of Fetal Dopamine Neurons Survive and Improve Motor Function in Parkinson's Disease." *Science* 247: 574–577.

Little, Bertis B., et al. 1996. "Is There a Cocaine Syndrome? Dysmorphic and Anthropometric Assessment of Infants Exposed to Cocaine." *Teratology* 54 (3): 145–149.

Marshall, Mary Faith, Philip H. Jos, and Martin Perlmutter. 1995. Letters to the Editor. *Journal of Law, Medicine, and Ethics* 23 (3): 299–300.

Miller, Andrea. 1999. South Carolina Advocates for Pregnant Women press release. December 1.

Miranda v. Arizona, 384 U.S. 436 (1966).

Mullen, Michelle A. 1992. *The Use of Human Embryos and Fetal Tissues: A Research Architecture.* Ottawa, Canada: Royal Commission on New Reproductive Technologies.

NIDA (National Institute on Drug Abuse). 1994. National Pregnancy and Health Survey. Rockville, MD: NIDA.

Nolan, Kathleen. 1988. "Genug Ist Genug: A Fetus Is Not a Kidney." *Hastings Center Report* 18 (6): 13–19.

OPTS (Organization of Parents through Surrogacy). 2001. "OPTS State Laws List." September.

OTA (Office of Technology Assessment). 1988. *Infertility: Medical and Social Choices.* Washington, DC: U.S. Government Printing Office.

———. 1990. *Neural Grafting: Repairing the Brain and Spinal Cord.* Washington, DC: U.S. Government Printing Office.

Paltrow, Lynn. 2000. "Background Concerning *Ferguson et al. v. City of Charleston et al.*" National Advocates for Pregnant Women. September 14.

———. 2001. "Statement of Lynn Paltrow, Esq., National Advocates for Pregnant Women, on *Ferguson v. City of Charleston,* 99–936." Press release dated March 21.

Parker, Philip J. 1983. "Motivation of Surrogate Mothers: Initial Findings." *American Journal of Psychiatry* 149 (1): 117–118.

Pergament, Eugene. 1993. "In Utero Treatment: Fetal Surgery." In *Emerging Issues in Biomedical Policy,* Robert H. Blank and Andrea L. Bonnicksen, eds. Vol. 2. New York: Columbia University Press.

Robertson, John A. 1983. "Procreative Liberty and the Control of Conception, Pregnancy, and Childbirth." *Virginia Law Review* 69 (3): 405–464.

Roe v. Wade, 410 U.S. 113 (1973).

Rothman, Barbara Katz. 1986. *The Tentative Pregnancy: Prenatal Diagnosis and the Future of Motherhood.* New York: Viking.

"S.C. Verdict Fuels Debate over Rights of the Unborn." 2001. *Washington Post,* May 27.

SCAPW (South Carolina Advocates for Pregnant Women). 2001. Press Release. March 21.

Sheriff v. Encoe, 110 Nev. 1317, 1319, 885 P.2d 596, 598 (1994).

Spruce, Tracey E. 1998. "The Sound of Silence: Women's Voices in Medicine and Law." *Columbia Journal of Gender and Law* 7: 239–265.

Stallman v. Youngquist, 129 Ill. App. 3d 859 (1984).

State v. Gray, 62 Ohio St.3d 514, 584 N.E.2d 710 (1992).

Surrogate Parenting v. Commonwealth ex rel. Armstrong, 704 S.W.2d 209 (Ky. 1986).

Tribble, L. G., et al. 1993. "Analysis of a Hospital Maternal Cocaine Testing Policy in Association with Prenatal Care Utilization Patterns." National Perinatal Association.

UPA (Uniform Parentage Act). 2000. National Conference of Commissioners on Uniform State Laws.

Webster v. Reproductive Health Services, 492 U.S. 490 (1989).

Whitner v. State, 328 S.C. 1, 492 S.E.2d 777 (1997).

Witcraft v. Sundstrand Health and Disability Group Benefit Plan, 420 N.W.2d 785 (Iowa, 1988).

Woods, Nancy Stewart, et al. 1993. "Cocaine Use during Pregnancy: Maternal Depressive Symptoms and Infant Neurobehavior over the First Month." *Infant Behavior and Development* 16 (1): 83–92.

3

Chronology

1873   Congress passes the Comstock Act, prohibiting the distribution and possession of contraceptive and abortion devices and also outlawing the dissemination of information about contraception and abortion.

1916   The first birth control clinic in the United States is opened in New York City by Margaret Sanger. She is convicted of violating the Comstock Act.

1921   The American Birth Control League is founded by Margaret Sanger. It later merges with other organizations and in 1942 becomes the Planned Parenthood Federation of America.

Congress passes the Sheppard Towner Act to create clinics for women and young children. The American Medical Association objects, fearing socialized medicine, and the program is revised to include only social and educational services. In 1929, under pressure from the AMA, it is discontinued.

1927   *Buck v. Bell*, 274 U.S. 200. The U.S. Supreme Court, in a stinging opinion by Justice Oliver Wendell Holmes, upholds the use of eugenic sterilization. In Holmes's words, "It is better for all the world, if instead of waiting to execute degenerate offspring for the crime, or to let them starve for their imbecility, society can prevent those

1927
(cont.)
who are manifestly unfit from continuing their kind. . . .
Three generations of imbeciles are enough."

1932 Aldous Huxley publishes *Brave New World,* a novel that takes place in a society in which reproductive technologies have reached the stage at which the state is able to centralize control of a human breeding program. To this day, the brave new world analogy represents the political dangers inherent in reproductive technology.

1934 On May 28, the Dionne quintuplets are born in Canada. They are identical (born from a single embryo that divides) and are believed to be the first quintuplets to have survived. All live to adulthood.

1935 Congress enacts Title V of the Social Security Act, providing one of the earliest government programs for maternal and child health services. Beginning in 1981, Title V programs are administered through the Maternal Child Health Services Block Grant.

1942 *Skinner v. Oklahoma,* 316 U.S. 535. In writing for the majority, Justice William O. Douglas asserts that marriage and procreation are basic human rights fundamental to the very existence and survival of the race. The Court holds that Oklahoma's legislation for compulsory sterilization of criminals is not allowable under the equal protection clause of the Fourteenth Amendment. However, this case does not address or overturn the use of eugenic sterilization under *Buck v. Bell* (1927).

1959 The American Law Institute recommends legalization of abortion in cases of rape, fetal deformity, or risk to the woman's physical or mental health.

1960 The Food and Drug Administration (FDA) approves oral contraceptives for sale in the United States.

1962 Sherri Finkbine, a television personality and young mother, requests an abortion after taking the tranquilizer Thalidomide. A media frenzy ensues, the hospital denies her request, and she travels to Sweden for the procedure.

Her trip becomes an agenda-setting event in the move-ment to legalize abortion.

An epidemic of rubella sweeps the nation between 1962 and 1965. More than 15,000 children are born with birth defects, adding momentum to the movement to legalize abortion.

1964   *Raleigh Fitkin–Paul Morgan Memorial Hospital v. Anderson,* 42 N.J. 421, 201 A.2d 537 (*cert. denied,* 377 U.S. 985 [1964]. A New Jersey court orders a Jehovah's Witness to submit to blood transfusions to save her life and that of her unborn child.

1965   *Griswold v. Connecticut,* 381 U.S. 479. In a 7 to 2 decision, the Supreme Court overturns a Connecticut law that made it a crime to sell contraceptive drugs or devices to a married couple. It finds that the Connecticut law vio-lates a married couple's constitutional right to privacy, derived from the "penumbras" and "emanations" of the Bill of Rights. Seven years later, in *Eisenstadt v. Baird,* the Court extends this right to all individuals, regardless of their marital status.

Medicaid is enacted as Title XIX of the Social Security Act. It is jointly funded by the federal and state govern-ments.

1966   The National Organization for Women (NOW) is founded.

1967   Colorado legalizes abortion based on the American Law Institute's model.

1968   The Alan Guttmacher Institute is founded and initially named the Center for Family Planning and Develop-ment. It is a nonprofit research institute devoted to studying reproductive issues.

1969   Attorneys Sarah Weddington and Lynda Coffee per-suade Norma McCorvey to initiate litigation to overturn a Texas statute prohibiting abortion. McCorvey takes the

1969 (cont.)	pseudonym Jane Roe, and litigation culminating in the U.S. Supreme Court decision of *Roe v. Wade* (1973) overturns state statutes prohibiting abortion.

The National Association for the Repeal of Abortion Laws (NARAL) is founded. Later, it changes its name to the National Abortion Rights Action League, in 1994 to the National Abortion and Reproductive Rights Action League, and in 2003 to NARAL Pro-Choice America.

1970 Hawaii, New York, and Alaska legalize abortion.

Congress passes Title X of the Public Health Service Act to provide federal funds to subsidize family planning clinics throughout the United States.

1972 The National Sickle Cell Anemia Control Act becomes law and allocates $85 million over a three-year period to states for screening and counseling programs. One requirement of the act is that to qualify for federal funds, states must administer screening programs on a voluntary basis, instead of a compulsory basis, as was the case in Massachusetts and some other states.

Eisenstadt v. Baird, 405 U.S. 438. The U.S. Supreme Court extends the right to use contraceptives to unmarried couples by applying the equal protection clause of the Fourteenth Amendment.

Congress amends the Social Security Act to require that state Medicaid programs include family planning.

1973 *Roe v. Wade*, 410 U.S. 113. The Supreme Court legalizes elective abortion during the first two trimesters of pregnancy.

The National Right to Life Committee is founded.

Research sponsored by the March of Dimes leads to the first successful in utero treatment for birth defects.

1974 In response to the National Sickle Cell Anemia Control

Act of 1972, Massachusetts amends its earlier compulsory screening program and provides voluntary sickle cell testing to the black population.

1976   The first vote on a Human Life Amendment takes place in the U.S. Senate.

The first Hyde Amendment (named for its sponsor, Representative Henry Hyde, R-IL) restricting use of Medicaid funds for abortion is enacted; it has been reauthorized every year since.

The first birth of a child through a surrogacy arrangement is reported.

1978   The first baby in the world conceived through in vitro fertilization (IVF)—Louise Brown—is born in England in July.

Congress passes the Pregnancy Discrimination Act (Public Law 95–555), which puts discrimination because of pregnancy on a par with other forms of sex discrimination.

1980   In January, after five months of hearings, studies, and close scrutiny by the Virginia Health Department, Norfolk General Hospital obtains governmental approval to make IVF available for the first time in the United States. The Norfolk In Vitro Fertilization Clinic opens its doors for business.

Grodin v. Grodin, 102 Mich. App. 396, 301 N.W.2d 869. A Michigan appellate court upholds the right of a child to be compensated for injuries received in utero.

Prolife groups actively campaign against the reelection of powerful prochoice senators. John Culver (D-IA), Birch Bayh (D-IN), Frank Church (D-ID), and George McGovern (D-SC) are defeated.

1981   *Jefferson v. Griffin Spaulding County Hospital*, 274 S.E. 2d 457 (Ga). After being diagnosed with placenta previa (a condition universally fatal for the fetus and often fatal

1981   for the mother), a Georgia court orders Jessie May Jeffer-
(cont.)   son to submit to a cesarean delivery—which she opposes
          on religious grounds—if she voluntarily admits herself
          to Griffin Spaulding County Hospital. Despite the diag-
          nosis, Jefferson admits herself to a different hospital and
          has an uneventful vaginal delivery and healthy baby.

          The first reported surgery on a fetus in the womb is per-
          formed in San Francisco on a thirty-one-week-old twin
          suffering from a severe urinary tract obstruction. This
          experimental procedure led to other applications, such
          as implanting shunting devices in fetuses diagnosed
          with hydrocephalus, draining collapsed lungs, and per-
          forming heart valve surgery.

          Congress establishes the Maternal Child Health Services
          Block Grant to fund programs originally authorized by
          Title V of the 1935 Social Security Act.

          Congress passes the Adolescent Family Life Act to pro-
          vide federal funds to local programs advocating sexual
          abstinence among teenagers.

          Elizabeth Carr is born on December 28 at Norfolk Gen-
          eral Hospital in Virginia, thus becoming the first baby
          born through IVF in the United States.

1983   The gene for Huntington's disease is discovered and
          leads to the first test for a genetic disease and to the
          search for genetic markers for a host of other diseases.

1984   A report by the National Institutes of Health and the
          FDA finds no clear benefit from routine use of ultra-
          sound, although at least one-third of all pregnant women
          undergo the procedure. The report also concludes that
          the procedure is harmless to the woman and the fetus.

          Stallman v. Youngquist, 129 Ill. App. 3d 859. An Illinois
          appellate court upholds the right of a child to be com-
          pensated by her mother for automobile injuries sus-
          tained in utero.

1985   *In re Jamaica Hospital.* A New York court orders a pregnant woman to submit to a blood transfusion for the benefit of her eighteen-week-old previable fetus.

Conservatorship of Valerie N., S.F.24745, 85 D.A.R. 548 (Ca).
The California Supreme Court invalidates a statute that
had prohibited the sterilization of persons suffering from
mental retardation. The court ruled that by denying the
option of sterilization to an incompetent woman, the
statute deprived her of her only realistic opportunity for
contraception and consequently restricted her chances
for self-fulfillment. According to the court, the statute
"impermissibly deprives developmentally disabled persons of privacy and liberty interests protected by the
Fourteenth Amendment."

Congress passes a law (42 U.S.C. 289) forbidding the federal conduct or funding of research on viable fetuses that
have been aborted, with an exception for therapeutic
research or research that poses no added risk of suffering, injury, or death to the fetus *and* that leads to important knowledge unobtainable by other means. Research
on living fetuses in the womb is still permitted, but
under federal regulations, the standard of risk is to be the
same for fetuses to be aborted as for those that will be
carried to term.

Congress passes legislation (42 U.S.C. 275) creating a Biomedical Ethics Board. It is to be composed of six members from the Senate and six from the House of Representatives, with an equal number from each party. In
August 1987, the board appoints the Biomedical Ethics
Advisory Committee to provide counsel to members of
Congress on ethical issues in medicine and biomedical
research. The committee disbands in September 1989,
having issued no reports.

1986   California passes a law requiring physicians to inform
pregnant patients of the availability of alpha-fetoprotein
tests. These tests are used to detect neural tube defects
such as spina bifida. Although the FDA has approved the

1986   sale of diagnostic kits, controversy arises over high rates
(cont.) of false positives and other problems.

Surrogate Parenting v. Commonwealth ex. rel. Armstrong,
704 S.W.2d 209 (Ky.). The Kentucky Supreme Court
upholds paid surrogacy agreements, if the agreements
are made prior to conception.

In re Madyun, 114 Daily Wash. L. Rptr 2233 (D.C. Super.
Ct.). The Superior Court of the District of Columbia
orders a woman to submit to a cesarean delivery after a
diagnosis of fetal sepsis. Upon delivery, the child shows
no signs of sepsis.

The Center for Surrogate Parenting is founded in Beverly
Hills, California. Initially, it serves as a screening and
matching service for women desiring to become surrogates and couples wanting to contract with surrogates. It
now provides a full range of surrogacy and egg donation
services.

1987   The FDA withdraws approval of Gender Choice sex
selection kits that have been marketed since 1986 by Pro-
Care Industries. The FDA declares that some of the
implied claims on the packages and in the advertising,
particularly about success rates in preselection, have not
been substantiated.

Congress attempts but fails to pass two measures, the
Surrogacy Arrangements Act of 1987 and the Anti-Surro-
gate-Mother Bill of 1987. The Surrogacy Arrangements
Act would have amended Title 18 of the U.S. Code to prohibit surrogate motherhood nationwide and provide for
penalties for anyone brokering a surrogate arrangement.
Also in 1987, 118 bills affecting surrogacy were introduced in state legislatures. Although there was wide variation in content, the clear trend was to prohibit surrogacy.

In re A. C., 533 A.2d 611 (D.C. App.). A District of Columbia trial court orders a cesarean delivery for Angela
Carder, who is twenty-six weeks pregnant and has ter-
minal cancer, and the appellate court quickly affirms the

decision. Both mother and infant die shortly after delivery, but in 1990, the appellate court reverses itself (*In re A. C.*, D.C. Ct. App., April 26, 1990 [en banc., slip op.].

1988   *In the Matter of Baby M*, 537 A.2d 1227 (N.J.). The Supreme Court of New Jersey rules that paid surrogacy contracts are unenforceable because they violate the state's laws against baby selling.

The Office of Human Genome Research is established by the National Institutes of Health to coordinate the Human Genome Initiative. In 1989, the budget proposal for fiscal year 1990 designates $100 million for human genome research, thus justifying it as an independent program. The office becomes the National Center for Human Research.

The American Fertility Society amends its therapeutic donor insemination guidelines, stating that in light of reports of the transmission of human immunodeficiency virus (HIV, the virus that causes AIDS) through donated semen, "the use of fresh semen is no longer warranted." Procedures for screening of semen donation were disseminated to ensure a safe supply free from HIV.

The National Conference of Commissioners of Uniform State Laws adopts the Uniform Status of Children of Assisted Conception Act, which provides two models for state legislative enactment. Virginia enacted the model that regulated surrogacy contracts, and North Dakota adopted the model that voided surrogacy contracts. No other states adopted either version.

Witcraft v. Sunstrand Health and Disability Group Benefit Plan, 420 N.W.2d 785 (Iowa, 1988). The Iowa Supreme Court holds that the dysfunctional reproductive organs of the claimant are an illness and that since claimant's insurance plan covers "expenses related to illness," the claim for in vitro fertilization expenses is valid. This decision is in direct contrast to a 1987 Oklahoma court ruling (*Kinzie v. Physician's Liability Insurance Company*, 750 P.2d 1140 [Okla. Ct. App. 1987]), in which the court denied

1988   recovery on grounds that IVF is elective and is not
(cont.) required to cure or preserve the insured's health.

President Ronald Reagan bans the use of federal funds
for research on fetal tissue transplantation from aborted
fetuses. This decision comes in the aftermath of an
announcement of a plan at the National Institutes of
Health to transplant the tissue into a patient with Parkinson's disease.

President Reagan issues a "gag rule" preventing organizations in the United States from receiving federal funds
if they provide abortion counseling services.

The Human Fetal Tissue Transplantation Research panel
appointed by the Reagan administration recommends
that a moratorium on federal funding of human fetal tissue research be ended. Although the advisory committee
of the National Institutes of Health concurs, no action is
taken to lift the ban.

The abortion pill, RU-486, becomes available in France.

The U.S. Congress Office of Technology Assessment publishes *Infertility: Medical and Social Choices*, the first major
assessment of reproductive technologies in the United
States. The report leads to hearings in Congress to establish a national registry for sperm donors, but no action is
ultimately taken.

1989   In April, the first baby in the world is born following
microinsemination sperm transfer (MIST) in Singapore.
Variations on this technique—in which one selected
sperm is inserted into the egg's outer membrane—are
now widely used to overcome problems with sperm and
are termed intracytoplasmic sperm injection (ICSI).

On November 1, the Bush administration extends the
prohibition of federal funding for fetal tissue transplantation research initiated during the Reagan administration.

York v. Jones, 717 F. Supp. 421 (E.D.Va.). A federal district court holds that a married couple who move from Virginia to California have the right to remove their frozen embryo from the Jones Institute in Norfolk, Virginia. The institute refuses to release the embryo, claiming that the couple have agreed to have it thawed for placement only at their clinic. Because the consent form does not explicitly prohibit transfer, the court rules that the couple retains property interest in the frozen embryo.

Webster v. Reproductive Health Services, 492 U.S. 490. The Supreme Court upholds a Missouri statute that requires fetal viability tests prior to abortion and prohibits the use of public employees and facilities for performing abortions.

The gene for cystic fibrosis is discovered. Cystic fibrosis is the most common fatal hereditary disorder affecting Caucasians in the United States. About 1 in 2,500 Caucasians is affected and 2 to 5 percent carry the cystic fibrosis gene. CF affects the mucus and sweat glands of the body, closing the breathing passages of the lungs. (A.D.A.M. 2002)

Ira Chasnoff, professor of pediatrics at the University of Illinois and president of the Children's Research Triangle, estimates that 11 percent of pregnant women use chemical substances and that such substance abuse puts infants at risk for developmental delays.

1990   *Davis v. Davis,* 842 S.W. 2d 588 (Tenn). In a case in which a divorced couple fights over the fate of seven frozen embryos, the Tennessee Supreme Court rules that the husband's right not to become a parent trumps the wife's right to have the embryos implanted in her uterus.

In September, the first attempt at genetic therapy is conducted at the National Institutes of Health in Bethesda, Maryland. Doctors treat a four-year-old girl suffering from a grave immune deficiency by taking some of her white blood cells, altering them by inserting a gene from the missing enzyme, and returning the altered cells to her body. Although in this case the therapy has no effect

1990
(cont.)
on the disease progression, it leads to approval of further gene therapy studies by the Food and Drug Administration.

The U.S. Food and Drug Administration approves the marketing of the subdermal contraceptive implant Norplant in the United States. It immediately sparks controversy over potential coerced or involuntary applications on teenagers, women on welfare, and black women.

Congress establishes the Maternal and Child Health Bureau to administer the Maternal Child Health Services Block Grant.

1991
The National Institute on Alcohol Abuse and Alcoholism launches the first systematic, multilevel study on the genetics of alcoholism. This study, with a budget of $25 million for the first five years, is designed to better understand the genetic bases of this disease.

International Union, UAW v. Johnson Controls, Inc., 89-1215 (U.S. Sup. Ct.). In a unanimous decision, the Supreme Court rules that Johnson Controls' fetal protection policy, under which women of reproductive age are excluded from jobs in workplaces with high lead concentrations, is discriminatory on its face and thus unacceptable.

Anissa Ayala, suffering from chronic myelogenous leukemia, receives a bone marrow transplant from her younger sister, Marissa, aged fourteen months, who had been conceived for the express purpose of providing the bone marrow transplant.

Arlette Schweitzer gives birth to her twin grandchildren after being implanted with an embryo created through IVF, using her daughter's ova and her son-in-law's sperm.

1992
Congress passes the Fertility Clinic Success Rate and Certification Act (Public Law 102-493) to provide for reporting of pregnancy success rates of fertility pro-

grams and for the certification of embryo laboratories. It also directs the secretary of the Department of Health and Human Services to develop a model program that states can use to certify fertility clinics.

After nearly two decades of controversy, the U.S. Food and Drug Administration approves the general sale and marketing of the injectable contraceptive, Depo-Provera, in the United States. This decision ends a lengthy and costly review process for the drug, which has been used by more than 10 million women in ninety countries. In the United States, it was approved for limited marketing in 1973, but that approval was withdrawn the following year. Later, it was reinstated and again withdrawn.

Planned Parenthood v. Casey, 112 S. Ct. 1791. The Supreme Court rules that states may require that women seeking abortions be provided with information about probable gestational age, that women must then wait twenty-four hours before obtaining the abortion, that parents of young women be notified, and that the abortion provider file a report with the state.

Johnson v. State, 602 So. 2d 1266 (Fla.). The Florida Supreme Court reverses the conviction of Jennifer Johnson for delivery of a controlled substance (cocaine) to minors (her two children) through their umbilical cords during their births.

State v. Gray, 62 Ohio St. 3d 514, 584 N.E.2d 710, 711. The Ohio Supreme Court upholds a trial court's dismissal of an indictment of child endangerment, finding that the statute did not apply to a woman's use of drugs during pregnancy.

1993   On his second day in office, President Clinton issues an executive order removing the ban on the funding for fetal tissue transplantation research.

Dr. David Gunn, an abortion provider in Pensacola, Florida, is murdered outside his clinic. Gunn's murder is

1993
(cont.)
followed by the murders of Dr. John Bayard Britton in Pensacola, Florida, in 1994 and Dr. Barnett Slepian in Amherst, New York, in 1998.

Commonwealth v. Welch, 864 S.W.2d 280 (Ky.). The Kentucky Supreme Court declines to apply criminal child neglect statutes to a woman's substance abuse during pregnancy.

Johnson v. Calvert, 851 P.2d 776 (Cal.1993). The California Supreme Court upholds the validity of a gestational surrogacy contract. The surrogate, who had no biological relationship to the child, had sought custody.

On February 5, President Bill Clinton signs the Family and Medical Leave Act, which includes provisions for unpaid leave for up to twelve weeks for the birth or adoption of a child. His predecessor, President George Bush, had twice vetoed similar legislation.

Scientists at the University of Toronto announce they have cloned a mouse from mouse embryo stem cells.

1994
The National Institutes of Health advocate federally funded embryo research so long as the embryos are not created specifically for research. A major potential source of embryos would be unused embryos being stored at fertility clinics.

Sheriff, Washoe County, Nevada v. Encoe, 110 Nev. 1317; 885 P2d 596 (Nev). The Nevada Supreme Court rules that the state's child endangerment statute does not apply to transmission of illegal substances from the mother to the child during delivery.

1996
President Clinton vetoes legislation that would have banned partial-birth abortions.

Congress appropriates $440 million to assist local sex education programs that oppose sex outside marriage.

Congress enacts the Mothers' and Newborns' Health Protection Act, which guarantees a hospital stay of at least forty-eight hours after delivery. This law is a response to patient and physician protests over insurance company policies of discharging mothers and babies shortly after delivery.

Congress enacts the Abstinence Education Program under Title V of the Social Security Act. In 2000, it has a budget of $50 million.

1997   Congress creates the Children's Health Insurance Program (CHIP) to cover low-income, uninsured children to age eighteen years. Most states administering the CHIP program include reproductive health benefits for teenagers.

On February 23, Dr. Ian Wilmut, a Scottish embryologist, announces the birth of Dolly, a sheep cloned from (and therefore the identical twin to) an adult sheep.

A sixty-three-year-old woman gives birth to a healthy baby after lying to a fertility clinic about her age.

The American Medical Association announces its opposition to partial-birth abortions.

Whitner v. State, 328 S.C. 1,492 S.E.2d 777. The South Carolina Supreme Court rules that the viable fetus is a "person" for purposes of enforcement of criminal child neglect statutes.

The McCaughey septuplets (four boys and three girls) are born in Iowa. They were conceived after their mother took the fertility drug Metrodin. They become the first known surviving set of septuplets.

1998   *In re Marriage of Buzzanca*, 61 Cal. App. 4th 1410, 1418. The California Court of Appeals rules that a child born through gestational surrogacy is legally the child of the intended parents, even though the child is not biologically related to either of them. The California Supreme Court refuses to hear a further appeal.

1998   The World Health Organization reports that the infant
(cont.) mortality rate in the United States is 7 deaths per 1,000
         live births. This rate is higher than that for other indus-
         trialized nations, including Canada, Germany, Australia,
         Japan, and France.

         U.S. scientists isolate human embryonic stem cells.

2000   Adam Nash is born on August 29 in Denver, Colorado.
         On September 26, doctors infuse cells from Adam's
         umbilical cord into his six-year-old sister Molly's circula-
         tory system in an attempt to treat her inherited bone
         marrow deficiency, a condition that is universally fatal
         without a transplant. The case sparks ethical debate
         because the embryo that produced Adam had been
         screened prior to implantation in his mother's womb to
         ensure his cells would be a perfect match to replace his
         sister's faulty bone marrow cells.

         The National Conference of Commissioners of Uniform
         State Laws modifies its 1988 model statute to provide
         that surrogacy agreements be reviewed by the courts in
         a fashion similar to adoption, that agreements not judi-
         cially reviewed be unenforceable, and that intended par-
         ents who refuse to accept the child be subject to child
         support obligations.

         The Children's Health Act creates a National Center on
         Birth Defects and Developmental Disabilities at the Cen-
         ters for Disease Control and Prevention.

2001   On his first day in office, President George W. Bush reim-
         poses the international "gag rule," which prohibits U.S.
         family planning aid from being transferred to foreign
         organizations that provide abortion services or counseling.

         Ferguson v. City of Charleston, 532 U.S. 67, 121 S.Ct. 1281,
         149 L.Ed.2d 205. The U.S. Supreme Court rules 6 to 3 that
         hospitals may not test pregnant women for drug use and
         then give the results to the police without the patient's
         consent or a valid search warrant.

Regina McNight is convicted in South Carolina of killing her unborn child because she used crack cocaine during her eighth month of pregnancy. She is the first woman in the United States to be convicted of homicide caused by substance abuse during pregnancy and is sentenced to twelve years in prison.

The Institute for Reproductive Medicine and Science of St. Barnabas Medical Center in West Orange, New Jersey, announces the birth of the world's first genetically modified babies through a technique called ooplasmic transfer, in which the babies have in effect two mothers. In the technique, doctors take an egg from an infertile woman, an egg from a donor, and sperm from the infertile woman's husband. Using a microscopic needle, they then take cytoplasm from the donor's egg and inject it into the infertile woman's egg along with the sperm.

President George W. Bush announces that he will permit federal funding for embryonic stem cell research, but only for the lines in existence in 2001. Although he argues that there are some sixty lines in existence, many scientists argue that the true number is around thirty.

The use of "comparative genomic hybridization" is announced by in vitro fertilization researchers in Australia. This technique has been developed to reduce the failure rate of IVF by identifying chromosomal abnormalities in embryos before their transfer, but it also raises policy questions regarding the genetic testing of embryos and disposal of those that "fail" the tests.

Stanford University researchers report the first known case of a woman becoming pregnant naturally while undergoing in vitro fertilization. They report that a pair of fraternal twins arose from two transferred embryos and that a pair of identical twins were conceived naturally when the couple had intercourse five days before the woman's eggs were retrieved. Doctors warn that IVF patients should be advised not to have unprotected sex

2001
(cont.)
after ovarian hyperstimulation, especially if they are not willing to undergo embryo reduction if a multiple pregnancy results.

The Massachusetts-based biotechnology company, Advanced Cell Technology, clones a human embryo for the first time. It stresses that it is doing so not to create genetically identical babies but rather to harvest stem cells from the embryos to produce life-saving therapies. The move was criticized widely, however, and some members of the U.S. Senate, where a bill to outlaw all human cloning was under consideration, express alarm at the development.

A major study finds that maternal obesity raises pregnancy risks, including gestational diabetes, significantly. Also, obese women are 50 to 80 percent more likely than nonobese women to need a cesarean delivery. The findings are especially important because maternal obesity in the United States is steadily rising. The study finds that nearly one-quarter of pregnant women are obese in 1999, up from 7 percent in 1980.

On March 21, scientists find links between estrogen and ovarian cancer.

The State of Virginia enacts legislation to prohibit cloning for reproductive purposes. Four states (California in 1997, Michigan and Rhode Island in 1998, and Louisiana in 1999) have previously enacted bans.

A Virginia clinic produces embryonic stem cells from donated ova and sperm.

The New Jersey Supreme Court rules in an embryo custody battle between a divorced couple. It finds that the man cannot have custody of the embryos for purposes of implanting them in a woman other than his former wife, but he can determine whether they will be destroyed or kept permanently in storage. The former wife had sought to have the embryos destroyed.

A lesbian couple living near Washington, D.C., give birth to a deaf son after being impregnated with the sperm of a deaf donor. The couple had contacted several sperm banks requesting a deaf donor but were turned down. A deaf friend, who had provided sperm for the couple's daughter, born five years earlier, provides the sperm for the son.

2002   A National Academy of Sciences panel urges Congress to impose a nationwide prohibition on human cloning. According to the report, experiments to make cloned human babies are too dangerous at present and should be legally banned with "severe penalties" to researchers who proceed with such attempts. This proposed action will not affect the practice of therapeutic cloning for research.

The American Society for Reproductive Medicine issues new ethics guidelines for the provision of reproductive patients with HIV. They do not encourage HIV-infected couples to have children but specify what precautions should be followed if HIV patients request the services of fertility clinics. Precautions discussed include appropriate drug therapy, counseling about consideration of donor sperm, adoption, not having children, and special sperm washing and testing to reduce the risk of transmission.

Researchers at the Reproductive Genetics Institute of Chicago announce that a pre-implantation genetic diagnosis has been used to genetically select an embryo that would be free of the gene for early onset Alzheimer's disease, which the mother has. The daughter is born via IVF from an embryo selected to be free of the mutation. Ethicists raise troublesome issues, including the right of a parent with a disabling disease to have children, given the likelihood that the parent will be unable to care for or even recognize her daughter in a few years.

The New England Journal of Medicine reports test tube babies are more likely to have birth defects than those born naturally.

2002   *In the Matter of the Estate of Marshall G. Gardiner.* The
(cont.)   Kansas Supreme Court rules that a marriage between a
          postoperative male-to-female transsexual and a biologi-
          cal man is invalid because Kansas law recognizes only
          traditional marriages between members of the opposite
          sex.

          President Bush calls on the Senate to outlaw human
          cloning. The House of Representatives has previously
          passed a bill prohibiting it.

          New York becomes the fifteenth state to require health
          insurance plans to cover most infertility treatments, with
          the explicit exclusion of IVF and vasectomy reversal. The
          law also requires that any health insurance plan that pro-
          vides prescription drug coverage must cover the cost of
          drugs for infertility. The law, which takes effect on Sep-
          tember 1, 2002, does not apply to those on Medicaid or to
          people who buy individual policies.

          A survey of pediatricians, family practice doctors, and
          gynecologists finds that 95 percent agree that pregnant
          women have a moral responsibility to ensure that their
          babies will be born healthy. The survey also finds wide-
          spread support for mandatory screening and treatment
          for alcohol and drug abuse for pregnant women. Accord-
          ing to one of the authors of the study, Ernest L. Abel, doc-
          tors are not opposed to viewing alcohol or drug abuse as
          a form of child abuse for the purposes of removing a
          child from custody at birth.

          Swiss citizens vote overwhelmingly (72 percent) to elim-
          inate criminal penalties for performing abortions during
          the first twelve weeks of pregnancy. Prior to the referen-
          dum, abortions were allowed only when the mother's
          physical or mental health was endangered. Despite this
          restriction, 12,000 to 13,000 abortions had been per-
          formed annually before the law was changed, and pros-
          ecutions had been extremely rare.

          In a 6 to 5 vote, the U.S. Court of Appeals for the Ninth
          Circuit rejects a request by a California prison inmate

that he be allowed to mail semen to his wife for artificial insemination, saying that prisoners have no right to procreate. The appeals court decision reverses an earlier ruling in the inmate's favor, but by the slimmest of margins. The court states, "We hold that the right to procreate while in prison is fundamentally inconsistent with incarceration."

On August 5, President George W. Bush signed H.R. 2175, the Born Alive Infants Protection Act, which guarantees that all infants born alive, regardless of their gestation, be given the full benefit of all federal laws.

2003   At six years of age, Dolly was euthanized after suffering various medical problems. The typical life span for a sheep is twelve years.

References

A.D.A.M., Inc., editorial. 2002. "Cystic Fibrosis Causes, Incidence, and Risk Factors." www.1uphealth.com/health/cystic_fibrosis_info.html. Accessed March 24, 2003.

AGI (Alan Guttmacher Institute). 2001. "Bush Okays Some Stem Cell Research Funding; Debate Continues." *Guttmacher Report* 4 (4). http://www.guttmacher.org/pubs/journals/gr040412a.html. Accessed October 11, 2002.

———. 2002a. "Fulfilling the Promise: Public Policy and U.S. Family Planning Clinics." http://www.agi-usa.org/pubs/fulfill.pdf. Accessed October 10, 2002.

———. 2002b. "Issues in Brief. Sex Education Politicians, Parents, Teachers and Teens." http://www.agi-usa.org/pubs/ib_2–01.html. Accessed February 15, 2002.

———. 2002c. "Issues in Brief. Expanding Eligibility and Outreach under CHIP." http://www.agi-usa.org/pubs/ib_4–01.html. Accessed February 15, 2002.

———. 2002d. "Revisiting Public Funding of Abortion for Poor Women." www.agi-usa.org/pubs/ib_funding00.html. Accessed February 15, 2002.

American Society for Reproductive Medicine, Ethics Committee. 2002. "Human Immunodeficiency Virus and Infertility Treatment." *Fertility and Sterility* 77 (2): 218–224.

Barusch, Amanda Smith. 2002. *Foundations of Social Policy.* Itasca, IL: F. E. Peacock Publishers.

Belchak, Alicia Marie. 2000. "Baby Born as Donor Raises Ethical Debate." http://dailynews.yahoo.com/h/nm/20001002/hl/donors_1. html. Accessed October 2, 2002.

Bettelheim, Adriel. 2001. "Embryo Research." *Issues in Health Policy.* Washington, DC: Congressional Quarterly.

Blank, Robert, and Janna C. Merrick. 1995. *Human Reproduction, Emerging Technologies, and Conflicting Rights.* Washington, DC: Congressional Quarterly Press.

Britannica Online Website. 2002. http://search.eb.com/women/articles/ Comstock_Act.html. Accessed June 20, 2002.

Brunner, Borgna. 2001. *Time Almanac 2002.* Boston Information Please Learning Network.

"Case Report: First Natural Conception during IVF." http://dailynews.yahoo.com/h/nm/20011122/hl/ivf_conception_1.html. Accessed November 22, 2001.

Center for Surrogating Parenting. 2002. "History of CSP." http://www. creatingfamilies.com/history.HTML. Accessed April 10, 2002.

Centers for Medicare and Medicaid Services. 2002. "The Newborns' and Mothers' Health Protection Act." http://cms.hhs.gov/hipaa/hipaa1/ content/nmhpa.aspCenters. Accessed October 11, 2002.

Chasnoff, Ira. 1989. "Drug Use and Women: Establishing a Standard of Care." *Annals of the New York Academy of Sciences* 562: 208–210.

City of Hope Department of Hematology and Bone Marrow Transplantation. 2002. "Anissa Ayala Success Story." http://bmt.cityofhope.org/. Accessed April 10, 2002.

CNN.com. 2002. "Swiss Vote to Relax Abortion Law." http://www.cnn. com/2002/WORLD/europe/06/02/swiss.abortion/index. html. Accessed June 2, 2002.

Cohen, Susan A. 2002. "Congress and Reproductive Health: Major Actions in 2001 and a Look Ahead." *Guttmacher Report* 5 (1). http://www. guttmacher.org/pubs/journals/gr050111.html. Accessed October 11, 2002.

"Court Bars Implant of Embryos in Woman." 2001. *Sarasota Herald Tribune,* August 15, p. 3A.

Craig, Barbara Hinkson, and David M. O'Brien. 1993. *Abortion and American Politics.* Chatham, NJ: Chatham House.

Culliton, Barbara J. 1988. "Panel Backs Fetal Tissue Research." *Science* 242: 1625–1626.

Dunham, Will. 2001. "World's First Genetically Altered Babies Born." http://dailynews.yahoo.com/h/nm/20010504/ts/science_babies_genes_dc_2.html. Accessed May 4, 2001.

"Embryo Gene Technique May Raise Fertility." http://dailynews.yahoo.com/h/nm/20011121/hl/fertility_2.html. Accessed November 21, 2001.

Fox, Maggie. 2001. "U.S. Firm Clones Human Embryo for Cells." http://dailynews.yahoo.com/h/nm/20011125/ts/science_clone_dc.html. Accessed November 25, 2001.

———. 2002. "Expert Panel Urges U.S. Ban on Human Cloning." http://dailynews.yahoo.com/20020118/sc/science_cloning_dc_4.html. Accessed January 18, 2002.

Fraser, I. S. 1994. *The Depo-Provera Story: A Continuing Controversy.* New York: CRC Press–Parthenon Publishers.

Healy, Bernadine. 1993. "The Pace of Human Gene Transfer Research Quickens." *Journal of the American Medical Association* 269 (5): 56.

Holden, Constance. 1991. "Probing the Complex Genetics of Alcoholism." *Science* 251: 163–164.

In the Matter of the Estate of Marshall G. Gardiner, 85030 (KS. 2002).

Jansson, Bruce S. 2001. *The Reluctant Welfare State: American Social Welfare Policies—Past, Present, and Future.* Belmont, CA: Brooks/Cole.

Jimenez, Marina. 2002. "Deaf Couple Tailor-Make Child in Their Own Image." *National Post Online,* April 9. http://www.nationalpost.com. Accessed June 30, 2002.

"Kansas Court: Transsexual's Marriage Void." 2002. *St. Petersburg Times,* March 16, p. 7A.

Lu, George C., et al. 2001. "Maternal Obesity and Pregnancy Risk." *American Journal of Obstetrics and Gynecology* 185: 845–849.

March of Dimes. 2002. "March of Dimes Hails Final Passage of Children's Health Act." http://www.marchofdimes.com/printableArticles/791_1876.asp?printable=true. Accessed October 11, 2002.

Maternal and Child Health Bureau. 2002. "MCHB Fact Sheet." www.mchb.hrsa.gov. Accessed October 8, 2002.

Mozes, Alan. 2002. "Docs Favor Drug/Alcohol Testing during Pregnancy."http://story.news.yahoo.com/news/nm/20020517/hl_nm/alcohol_women_dc_1.html. Accessed May 17, 2002.

National Conference of Commissioners of Uniform State Laws. 2000. Uniform Parentage Act.

National Right to Life Committee. 2002. http://www.nrlc.org/. Accessed April 9, 2002.

Office of Technology Assessment. 1988. U.S. Congress. *Infertility: Medical and Social Choices*. Washington, DC: Government Printing Office.

Perez-Pena, Richard. 2002. "State Will Require Coverage of Treatment for Infertility." *New York Times,* May 16, 2002.

Planned Parenthood Federation of America. 2002. "Fact Sheet: A History of Contraceptive Methods." http://www.plannedparenthood.org/library/birthcontrol/020709_bchistory.html. Accessed October 10, 2002.

Tanner, Lindsey. 2002. "Baby Born after Alzheimer Screening." http://story.news.yahoo.comap_on_he_me/prenatal_test_alzheimers_sc_3.html. Accessed February 26, 2002.

Walsh, Denny. 2002. "Inmate's Artificial Insemination Bid Denied." *Sacramento Bee,* June 30. http://www.sacbee.com/.

Wright, John W. 1997. *New York Times 1998 Almanac*. New York: Penguin Reference.

4

Biographical Sketches

Lori B. Andrews

Lori Andrews is an internationally recognized expert on reproductive technologies. Her path-breaking litigation about reproductive and genetic technologies and the disposition of frozen embryos caused the *National Law Journal* to list her as one of the "100 Most Influential Lawyers in America."

Lori Andrews is professor of law at Chicago-Kent College of Law and director of the Institute for Science, Law, and Technology. She holds B.A. and J.D. degrees from Yale University. Andrews served as chair of the Working Group on the Ethical, Legal, and Social Implications of the Human Genome Project. She has been an adviser on genetic and reproductive technology to Congress, the World Health Organization, the National Institutes of Health, the Centers for Disease Control, the Department of Health and Human Services, the Institute of Medicine of the National Academy of Sciences, and several foreign nations including the French National Assembly. She recently served as a consultant to the science ministers of twelve countries on the issues of embryo stem cells, gene patents, and DNA banking.

Andrews is the author of nine books, including *The Clone Age* published in 2000, in which she discusses the motives and methods of a new breed of scientists, and the emerging issues society faces as venture capital funds medical research, technology exceeds legal and ethical ground rules, and people struggle to maintain human dignity and their own emotional balance.

In 2001, Lori Andrews published *Future Perfect: Confronting Decisions About Genetics*, where she outlined the policy models we should consider as we enter an age of increasing knowledge of the human genome. For Andrews, "The lack of systematic policymaking guidelines regarding new genetic technologies in the United States, compounded with the search for financial gains from genetic innovations in our society, has led to inefficient and ineffectual regulations and laws."

Source: Chicago-Kent College of Law: Illinois Institute of Technology. www.kentlaw.edu/faculty/andrews_bio.html. Accessed October 1, 2002.

George Annas

George Annas is the Edward R. Utley professor and chair of the Department of Health Law, Bioethics, and Human Rights of Boston University School of Public Health, and professor in the Boston University School of Medicine and School of Law. He has degrees from Harvard College (A.B., economics 1967), Harvard Law School (J.D. 1970), and Harvard School of Public Health (M.P.H. 1972). Annas has written regularly featured columns for the *Hastings Center Report* (1976–1991), the *American Journal of Public Health* (1982–1992), and since 1991, the *New England Journal of Medicine.* He is the author or editor of twelve books on health law, including *Reproductive Genetics and the Law* (1987), *Judging Medicine* (1987), and *Standard of Care* (1993).

Source: Biographical contributions provided by George Annas.

Marissa-Eve Ayala

Marissa-Eve Ayala was born on April 3, 1990, to Abraham and Mary Ayala, amidst a storm of controversy regarding the reason for her conception. At age sixteen, Marissa's older sister, Anissa, was diagnosed with chronic myelogenous leukemia, a disease typically fatal without a bone marrow transplant. No suitable donor was found either through the National Marrow Donor Program or community drives in California where the Ayalas lived. Abe and Mary Ayala then chose to have another child in hopes of finding a match. At age forty-five, Abe Ayala's seventeen-year-old vasectomy was reversed, and Marissa was conceived. On June 4, 1991, at the age of fourteen months, Marissa became a donor for Anissa, who subsequently recovered. Later, Anissa formed the

Anissa Foundation dedicated to assisting patients suffering from leukemia and other blood related diseases.

Source: Grossmont College. www.grossmont.net/tina.mcduffie/ students/SheryleKazules/index1.html. Accessed September 19, 2002.

Baby M

In 1985, William Stern contracted with Mary Beth Whitehead to serve as a biological surrogate. Whitehead was artificially insem- inated with Stern's sperm in 1985, and "Baby M" was born on March 27, 1986, after an uneventful pregnancy. At the time, Stern was a biochemist, his wife, Elizabeth, was a pediatrician, and Whitehead was a twenty-nine-year-old homemaker who had dropped out of school at age fifteen. She was married to a sani- tation worker and had two older children. The Whiteheads' lifestyle was financially unstable, and at times, Mary Beth received public assistance. A custody battle ensued and culmi- nated in a decision by the New Jersey Supreme Court that iden- tified Stern as the legal father and Whitehead as the legal mother. Custody was awarded to Stern, and visitation was awarded to Whitehead. She divorced Richard Whitehead and remarried, and now goes by the name Mary Beth Whitehead Gould. Baby M goes by the name Melissa Stern. See Chapter 2 for more details.

Andrea L. Bonnicksen

Andrea L. Bonnicksen has published articles in interdisciplinary journals on issues related to human cloning, germ-line gene ther- apy, preimplantation genetic diagnosis, and human embryo freezing. Her work provides sophisticated analyses of the inter- section of philosophical considerations and scientific research. She argues that reproductive technologies are like a train moving forward, and although there will be stops and lurches along the way, that train will continue to move forward. Thus, it is up to policymakers to steer that train and to determine what its even- tual destination will be.

Bonnicksen earned her Ph.D. at Washington State University and is now professor and former chair of the Department of Political Science at Northern Illinois University, where she teaches courses in biomedical and biotechnology policy. She is the author of three books, including *Crafting a Cloning Policy: From Dolly to Stem Cells* (2002) and *In Vitro Fertilization: Building*

Policy from Laboratories to Legislatures (1989). She is the coeditor of three books and the former book review editor for *Politics and the Life Sciences.* Bonnicksen is cochair of the Ethics Committee of the American Society for Reproductive Medicine.

Source: Biographical contributions provided by Andrea L. Bonnicksen.

Louise Joy Brown

Louise Joy Brown, the world's first "test tube baby," was born on July 25, 1978, to Lesley and John Brown of Bristol, England. After failing to conceive naturally, the Browns contacted Dr. Patrick Steptoe, a gynecologist at Oldham General Hospital near Manchester, England, and Dr. Robert Edwards, a physiologist at Cambridge University. Lesley's egg was fertilized in vitro with John's sperm and placed in her womb. The pregnancy progressed normally, and Louise Brown was born healthy and was the subject of much news media coverage. The Browns had a second daughter, also conceived through in vitro fertilization. Prior to Louise Brown's conception, Steptoe and Edwards had attempted in vitro fertilization more than eighty times without a successful pregnancy.

Source: http://history1900s.about.com. Accessed September 12, 2002.

Keith Campbell

Keith Campbell, a cell biologist, worked in collaboration with Ian Wilmut to develop the adult stem cell transfer technology that resulted in the cloned birth of Dolly, the sheep. The research was conducted at the Roslin Institute in Midlothian, England. Prior to joining the Roslin Institute in 1991, Dr. Campbell studied microbiology at Queen Elizabeth College, London, and obtained a Doctorate of Philosophy from the University of Sussex.

Source: Wilmut, Ian, Keith Campbell, and Colin Tudge. 2000. "The Second Creation: Dolly and the Age of Biological Control." http://www.fsbassociates.com/fsg/secondcreation.htm#author. Accessed March 31, 2003.

Arthur Leonard Caplan

Arthur Leonard Caplan is the Emmanuel and Robert Hart professor of Bioethics, chair of the Department of Medical Ethics, and the director of the Center for Bioethics at the University of Pennsylvania in Philadelphia.

Caplan is the author or editor of more than twenty books including *Beyond Baby M: Ethical Issues in New Reproductive Techniques* (1989) and *Due Consideration in the Age of Medical Miracles* (1998). He is also the author of more than 500 papers in refereed journals of medicine, science, philosophy, bioethics, and health policy including "Does Ethics Make a Difference?—The Debate over Human Cloning" in G. McGee, ed., *The Human Cloning Debate* (1998); "Human Rights and Maternal-Fetal HIV Transmission Prevention Trials in Africa" in the *American Journal of Public Health* (1998); "What Is Wrong with Eugenics?" in the *British Medical Journal* (with McGee and Magnus, 1999), and "Cloning Human Embryos" in the *Western Journal of Medicine* (with McGee, 2002). He has written a weekly newspaper column for the Hearst/King Features syndicate on bioethics and currently writes a regular column on bioethics for MSNBC.com. In one of Caplan's recent online articles, he asserts that although the Bush administration opposes cloning based on their prolife stance, cloning should not be considered unethical when it may find cures for diseases.

Source: Biographical contributions provided by Arthur Leonard Caplan.

Alexander Morgan Capron

Alexander Capron is a commissioner on the National Bioethics Advisory Commission and often testifies before Congress as the expert on legal issues in bioethics. On June 19, 2001, he presented the Commission's Report, *Cloning Human Beings*, to the U.S. House Judiciary Committee. Capron has also served as chairman of the Biomedical Ethics Advisory Committee of the U.S. Congress (1987–1990), the Advisory Panel to the Joint Committee on Surrogate Parenting of the California Legislature (1989–1990), and the National Institutes for Health's Recombinant DNA Advisory Committee (1984–1992). He has written and edited eight books, including *Law, Science, and Medicine* and the *Treatise on Health Care Law.* Capron is the director of Ethics and Health at the World Health Organization, Geneva, Switzerland, on leave from the University of Southern California where he is professor and codirector of the Pacific Center for Health Policy and Ethics. He earned his LL.B. at Yale University and now specializes in health policy and medical ethics.

Source: Biographical contributions provided by Alexander Morgan Capron.

Angela Carder

At age thirteen, Angela Carder was diagnosed with cancer, and during the next fourteen years, she underwent many treatments including surgery, chemotherapy, radiation, and a leg amputation. In 1986, she married Rick Carder and became pregnant. At twenty-six weeks gestation, doctors at George Washington University Hospital (GWUH) in Washington, D.C., discovered a tumor and advised Carder that her death was imminent. On June 16, 1987, GWUH obtained a court order to deliver the fetus by cesarean section over the objections of her family and attending obstetricians. Carder did not testify at the hearing because she was heavily sedated, but when informed of the trial judge's decision later in the day when she was more lucid, she clearly stated that she did not want the cesarean delivery and did not give consent. Three judges of the Court of Appeals for the District of Columbia conferred via conference call and were informed that the hospital had scheduled the cesarean to begin within sixteen minutes. The three-judge panel then upheld the decision of the trial judge, and the cesarean was performed. The infant daughter died shortly after delivery from prematurity, and Angela Carder died two days later on June 18, 1987. In 1988, the Court of Appeals sitting *en banc* reversed the decision of the three-judge panel, and in 1990, it reversed the decision of the trial judge. Carder's parents subsequently reached an out-of-court settlement with GWUH that included the adoption of a policy recognizing the right of a pregnant patient to determine treatment for herself and her fetus.

Source: Settlement Agreement between Nettie and Daniel Stoner and the George Washington University Hospital; Amended Brief on the Merits. Filed September 8, 1988. *In the Matter of A.C.* No. 87–609. District of Columbia Court of Appeals.

R. Alta Charo

Attorney R. Alta Charo is the author of over seventy-five articles, book chapters, and government reports on topics including family planning and abortion law, medical genetics law, and reproductive technology policy. Charo's publications emphasize the intersection between the ethics and politics of older reproductive rights debates, such as those over abortion and family planning, with new debates surrounding surrogacy, in vitro fertilization, cloning, and stem cell research. Her publications include "Children by Choice: Reproductive Technologies and the Boundaries of Personal Autonomy" in *Nature/Cell Biology* (2002) and *Nature/Medicine* (2002); "The Ethics of Control," *Yale Journal of Health Law and Policy* (2002); "Cloning, Ethics, and Public Policy," *Hofstra Law Review* (1999); "Family Planning Policies and the Politics of New Reproductive Technologies," in K. Petersen ed., *Intersections: Women on Law, Medicine, and Technology* (1997); and "The Hunting of the Snark: The Moral Status of Embryos, Right-to-Lifers, and Third World Women," *Stanford Law and Policy Review* (1995).

Source: Biographical contributions provided by R. Alta Charo.

Ira J. Chasnoff

Chasnoff is president of the Children's Research Triangle (CRT) and a professor of Clinical Pediatrics at the University of Illinois College of Medicine in Chicago. He is one of the nation's leading researchers in the field of maternal drug use during pregnancy and the effects on the newborn infant and child. His research includes a study of the long-term cognitive, behavioral, and educational developmental effects of prenatal exposure to alcohol, cocaine, and other drugs; the effects on birth outcome of prenatal treatment and counseling for pregnant drug abusers; and the effectiveness of both outpatient and residential treatment programs for pregnant drug abusers. Chasnoff and the team at CRT opened and operated a laboratory preschool classroom to develop specific interventions for children prenatally exposed to alcohol and other drugs and developed a model Head Start Family Service Center for children and their families at risk from drugs and the drug-seeking environment. In addition, Chasnoff and the CRT research team ran one of five national sites conducting research into the integration of behavioral health interventions into primary health care services for high-risk children and their families, and through this project they studied the impact of concurrent planning on permanency placement for children in the foster care system. In 2002, CRT, under Chasnoff's leadership, was selected by the Centers for Disease Control as one of five national centers for research into innovative treatment for children with fetal alcohol syndrome. Chasnoff's current work focuses on community approaches to the integration of behavioral health services into primary health care for women and children.

The recipient of several awards for his work with high-risk women, children, and families, Chasnoff for several years has been selected by a poll of physicians across the nation for listing in *America's Best Doctors*, cited for his ability to translate complex medical and psychosocial issues into relevant policy that guides the delivery of quality services. Chasnoff has been active in establishing comprehensive family intervention programs for children in Australia, Denmark, Portugal, the former Soviet Union, and across the United States. Chasnoff is also the author of several books and numerous articles on the effects of drug use on pregnancy and on the long-term cognitive, behavioral, and learning outcomes of prenatally exposed children. His book, *Drugs, Alcohol, Pregnancy, and Parenting*, received the Book of the Year Award from the *American Journal of Nursing*. Chasnoff's most recent book, *The Nature of Nurture: Biology, Environment, and the Drug-Exposed Child*, explores the biological and environmental factors that affect the ultimate development of alcohol- and drug-exposed children and presents practical strategies for helping children reach their full potential at home and in the classroom.

Source: Biographical contributions provided by Ira J. Chasnoff.

Wendy Chavkin

Wendy Chavkin, M.D., M.P.H. has been active on a host of reproductive health issues, particularly on issues related to substance abuse during pregnancy. She published a major study on prenatal substance abuse in New York City that found that infant mortality rates of children born to substance abusers was nearly 2.5 times the citywide rate and that three-fourths of HIV-positive newborns were born to intravenous drug users (Chavkin, Driver, Forman 1989).

Chavkin directed the Bureau of Maternity Services and Family Planning at the New York City Department of Health from 1984 to 1988. She developed the Perinatal Addiction Research and Policy Unit within the Chemical Dependency Institute at Beth Israel Medical Center. She is now professor of Clinical Public Health and Obstetrics and Gynecology at Columbia University's School of Public Health. Chavkin has been editor-in-chief of the *Journal of the American Medical Women's Association* since 1994. She chairs the Board of Directors of the Society of Physicians for Reproductive Choice and Health. She has written extensively about women's reproductive health issues. Her current research focuses on welfare reform policies and the health consequences for women and children around the world.

Source: Biographical contributions provided by Wendy Chavkin. See also Wendy Chavkin, Cynthia R. Driver, and Pat Forman. 1989. "The Crisis in New York City's Perinatal Services." New York State Journal of Medicine 89 (12):658–663.

Carl Djerassi

Carl Djerassi is generally credited with the invention of the birth control pill. He is emeritus professor of chemistry at Stanford University and is one of the few American scientists to have been awarded both the National Medal of Science (for the first synthesis of a steroid oral contraceptive) and the National Medal of Technology (for aiding in the development or commercialization of a technology beneficial to the United States). A member of the U.S. National Academy of Sciences and the American Academy of Arts and Sciences as well as many foreign academies, Djerassi has received nineteen honorary doctorates together with numerous other honors, such as the first Wolf Prize in Chemistry, the first Award for the Industrial Application of Science from the National Academy of Sciences, and the American Chemical Society's highest award, the Priestley Medal.

According to Djerassi, his emphasis is on "policy research in the area of human fertility control and extends way beyond my initial involvement in developing new contraceptive 'hardware' (e.g., steroid oral contraceptives) to the complex issues and sociocultural elements of human fertility control. I have also chosen the most recent advances in male reproductive biology dealing with male infertility and erectile dysfunction as the subjects of my 'science-in-fiction' novels Menachem's Seed and NO respectively, while my science-in-theatre play, An Immaculate Misconception, performed in London, San Francisco, and Vienna in 1999 and New York in 2001, examines the societal implications of the latest assisted reproduction techniques."

Source: Stanford University. www.stanford.edu/dept/chemistry/faculty/djerassi.html. Accessed March 23, 2003.

Robert Edwards

Robert Edwards is one of the leading scientists to develop techniques for in vitro fertilization and "test tube babies." He attended the Universities of Wales and Edinburgh and earned a Ph.D. in 1957 from the Institute of Animal Genetics in Edinburgh. He became a medical researcher in the area of physiology, and in 1968, he successfully fertilized a human egg outside of the womb through in vitro fertilization (IVF). That same year, he began collaborative work at the Centre for Human Reproduction in Oldham, England, with Patrick Steptoe, a gynecologist and obstetrician. After more than 100 unsuccessful attempts with previous patients, their joint efforts led to the 1978 birth of Louise Brown, the world's first "test tube baby." Between 1978 and 2002, more than 1 million babies were born through IVF.

Sources: "Steptoe, Patrick, and Edwards, Robert." *Encyclopedia Britannica.* http://search.eb.com/eb/articl?eu=1303. Accessed September 13, 2002; IVFOnline. www.ivfonline.com/HTML/Newsstand/ResPapers/Bob.htm. Accessed September 13, 2002.

John C. Fletcher

John C. Fletcher is well known for his work with sociologist Dorothy C. Wertz on medical geneticists' approaches to ethical problems in screening, testing, and counseling. This research was based on an international survey of geneticists in nineteen nations and is presented in the book *Ethics and Human Genetics: A Cross-Cultural Perspective* (1989).

Fletcher has also published or coedited seven books, including *Fetal Diagnosis and Therapy: Science, Ethics Consultation in Health Care* (1989), and written more than 250 articles and chapters in professional literature. Fletcher earned his Ph.D. at Union Theological Seminary in 1969 and is currently professor emeritus of Biomedical Ethics and Internal Medicine at the University of Virginia School of Medicine where he founded its Center for Biomedical Ethics.

Source: Biographical contributions provided by John C. Fletcher.

Helen Bequaert Holmes

Helen Bequaert Holmes, a strong feminist critic of reproductive and genetic technologies, believes that such technologies reinforce childbearing as the major role for women and enhance society's control over product quality under the guise of offering "choice." She is an independent scholar and coordinator of the

Research Archive of the Center for Genetics, Ethics, and Women, in Amherst, Massachusetts. She has a doctorate in population genetics from the University of Massachusetts (1970) and now specializes in feminist analysis of reproductive technologies and the Human Genome Project, with special emphases on sex selection, risks of in vitro fertilization (IVF), and the impact of the new genetics on women. She edited four books including *Issues in Reproductive Technology* (1992), in which thirty authors from six countries analyze new contraceptives, human embryo freezing, psychosocial dimensions to IVF, and contract pregnancy. In this volume, she argues "that freezing eggs would be disastrous for women. It would be another tooth in the saw that dismembers women into body parts, another spoke in the wheel that requires reproduction as validation of a true woman."

Source: Biographical contributions provided by Helen Bequaert Holmes.

Ruth Hubbard

Ruth Hubbard, an internationally known biochemist, has written and lectured on the politics of health care and on reproductive health issues, especially as they relate to women. One of the early scholars in the area of reproductive health, she has published more than 150 articles and nine books, including *Genes and Gender II: Pitfalls in Research on Sex and Gender,* with Marian Lowe (1979), *The Politics of Women's Biology* (1990), and *Exploding the Gene Myth,* with Elijah Wald (1993). Hubbard is professor emerita of biology at Harvard University. She was born in Vienna, Austria, and graduated from Radcliffe College in 1944, with an A.B. in biochemical sciences; then in 1950, she earned a Ph.D. in biology, also from Radcliffe. She serves on the boards of the Council for Responsible Genetics and the Boston Women's Health Book Collective.

Source: Cameron University. www.cameron.edu/festival/speakers/ hubbard-bio.html. Accessed March 23, 2003.

Marcia C. Inhorn

As a medical anthropologist, Marcia C. Inhorn specializes in studies of infertility and new reproductive technologies among Middle Eastern populations. She is associate professor of health behavior and health education and anthropology at the University of Michigan, where she also serves as associate director of the Center for Middle Eastern and North African Studies. She has written and coedited five books, including *Quest for Conception: Gender, Infertility, and Egyptian Medical Traditions*, which was awarded the Society for Medical Anthropology's Eileen Basker Prize for Outstanding Research in Gender and Health (1995). Her most recent book, *Local Babies, Global Science: Gender, Religion, and In Vitro Fertilization in Egypt*, explores moral decision making surrounding the uses of in vitro fertilization in a Muslim society.

Source: Biographical contributions provided by Marcia C. Inhorn.

Leon R. Kass

For over thirty years Leon Kass has been involved in analyzing the ethical and philosophical issues raised by biomedical advances. Two of his articles published in *The Public Interest*—"Making Babies—The New Biology and the 'Old' Morality" in 1972 and "Making Babies Revisited" in 1979—laid much of the groundwork for the discussion of emerging reproductive technologies. He also authored "Determining Death and Viability in Fetuses and Abortuses," in *Research on the Fetus, Appendix* for The National Commission for the Protection of Human Subjects of Biomedical and Behavioral Research in 1975. In 1998, he and political scientist James Q. Wilson analyzed the ethics of human cloning and other reproductive technologies in *The Ethics of Human Cloning*. Kass was selected to chair President George W. Bush's Council on Bioethics in 2001, and in the same year he published "Preventing a Brave New World: Why We Must Ban Human Cloning Now" in *The New Republic*.

Source: The John Olin Center for Inquiry into the Theory and Practice of Democracy. http://olincenter.uchicago.edu/kass_cv.html. Accessed March 23, 2003.

Patricia A. King

Georgetown Law Professor Patricia A. King has been at the forefront of national and international discussions in the area of reproductive rights. She has published extensively in this field including "Embryo Research: The Challenge for Public Policy" in the *Journal of Philosophy and Medicine* (1997); "Special Considerations for Minority Participation in Prenatal Diagnosis" in the *Journal of the American Medical Association* (1980); and "Harms of Excluding Pregnant Women from Clinical Research: The Case of HIV-Infected Pregnant Women" in the *Journal of Law, Medicine, and Ethics* (with N. Kass and H. Taylor, 1996). She is also the coauthor, with Judith C. Areen, of *Cases and Materials on Law, Science, and Medicine* (1996).

Source: "A Celebration of Black Alumni: Harvard Law School." http://www.law.harvard.edu/alumni/celebration/king.shtml. Accessed September 27, 2002.

Bartha Maria Knoppers

Bartha Maria Knoppers, O.C., Canada Research Chair in Law and Medicine, is the current chair of the International Ethics Committee of the Human Genome Organization (HUGO) and was a member of the International Bioethics Committee of the United Nations Educational, Scientific, and Cultural Organization (UNESCO), which drafted the Universal Declaration on the Human Genome and Human Rights (1993–1997), a UNESCO policy statement regarding protocols for human genome research. She was a commissioner on the Royal Commission on New Reproductive Technologies (1990–1993) and is cofounder of the International Institute of Research in Ethics and Biomedicine (IREB) and codirector of the Quebec Network of Applied Genetic Medicine. In 1999, she became a member of the Canadian Biotechnology Advisory Committee, and in the year 2000 of the Board of Genome Canada.

She is professor at the faculty of law, Université de Montréal. She is a graduate of McMaster University (B.A.), University of Alberta (M.A.), McGill University (LL.B., B.C.L.), Cambridge University, U.K. (D.L.S.), Sorbonne (Paris I) (Ph.D.) and was admitted to the Bar of Quebec in 1985. In October 2001, she received a Doctor of Law *Honoris Causa* from the University of Waterloo and in December 2002, she received a Doctor of Medicine *Honoris Causa* from Université de Paris V (René Descartes). Her major publications include *Human DNA: Law and Policy— International and Comparative Perspectives* (1997), in which she argues in favor of a careful socioethical and legal international framework for DNA sampling and biobanking.

Source: Biographical contributions provided by Bartha Maria Knoppers.

Mary B. Mahowald

Mary B. Mahowald, Ph.D., a leading philosopher in the field of reproductive ethics from a feminist perspective, is "opposed not only to sexism but also to racism, classism, heterosexism, and ableism." Currently, she is working on a book that examines non-reproductive as well as reproductive health issues from that standpoint. Her recent books include *Women and Children in Health Care: An Unequal Majority* (1996); *Disability, Difference, Discrimination: Perspectives on Justice in Bioethics and Public Policy* (1998), with Anita Silvers and David Wasserman; *Philosophy of Woman: Classical to Current Concepts* (1994); *Genes, Women, Equality* (2000); and *Genetics in the Clinic: Clinical, Ethical, and Social Implications for Primary Care* (2001), coedited with Victor McKusick, Angela Scheuerle, and Timothy Aspinwall. She has served on review panels for the U. S. Office of Technology Assessment and the Department of Defense Breast Cancer Research Program, and as a consultant or reviewer for various journals and governmental or private programs.

Mahowald is professor emerita in the Department of Obstetrics and Gynecology, the MacLean Center for Clinical Medical Ethics, and the College and Committee on Genetics, all at the University of Chicago. She taught in the philosophy departments of Villanova University and Indiana University at Indianapolis for twelve years before moving to a medical school and hospital setting in 1982.

Source: Biographical contributions provided by Mary Mahowald.

Deborah Mathieu

Political scientist Deborah Mathieu, the author of *Preventing Prenatal Harm* (1991), explores in depth the controversy over whether the state should have the power to intervene in the lives of pregnant women in order to prevent serious prenatal harm, a subject that raises some of the most basic issues about rights, duties, the moral limits of the law, and the scope of legitimate state action. Mathieu earned an M.A. in religion at Yale University and a Ph.D. in philosophy at Georgetown University and is now associate professor in the Department of Political Science at the University of Arizona where she teaches political theory and jurisprudence. Among her other publications in biomedical ethics and health policy are *Organ Substitution Technology* (1988) and *Ethics and Emergency Medicine* (1995).

Source: Biographical contributions provided by Deborah Mathieu.

Norma McCorvey

Norma McCorvey (a.k.a. Jane Roe) was the lead plaintiff in *Roe v. Wade* (1973). At age twenty-one, with two young children being raised by family members, McCorvey became pregnant for a third time. She was a high school dropout and a drifter. She had attempted to obtain an abortion but was denied. Attorneys Sarah Weddington and Lynda Coffee persuaded her to initiate litigation to overturn the Texas statute prohibiting abortion. She did not abort her third pregnancy and her newborn was given up for adoption. In the mid 1990s, in a philosophical about-face, McCorvey joined the antiabortion group, Operation Rescue, and condemned legalized abortion. McCorvey is the author of several books including, *Our Choices: Women's Personal Decisions about Abortion* (1993), *I Am Roe: My Life,* Roe v. Wade, *and Freedom of Choice* (1994), and *Won by Love* (1998). She also heads a ministry entitled "Roe No More."

Frances H. Miller

Frances Miller writes "considering the dizzying pace at which genetic testing science currently progresses, one can easily imagine prospective parents to be the modern day equivalent of Diogenes, continually moving on in the search for the perfect fetus" (Miller 2002). She is professor of law, School of Law, professor of public health, School of Public Health, and professor of health care management, School of Management, all at Boston University. She earned her law degree at Boston University and specializes in biotechnology and genetics, the economics of health care delivery systems, and comparative health systems. Miller is faculty editor of the *American Journal of Law and Medicine* and serves on numerous hospital and other boards.

Source: Biographical contributions provided by Frances Miller. *See also* Miller, Frances H. "Phase II of the Genetics Revolution: Sophisticated Issues for Home and Abroad." 2002. *American Journal of Law and Medicine.*

Christine Overall

Christine Overall was one of the first scholars to write about the impact of new reproductive technologies on women. Currently, she is professor of philosophy and an associate dean in the Faculty of Arts and Science at Queen's University, Kingston, Ontario. She earned her Ph.D. in philosophy from the University of Toronto in 1980. Her academic areas of research include biomedical ethics, feminist theory, and philosophy of religion. She is the editor of three books, including *The Future of Human Reproduction* (1989), and the author of five books, including *Ethics and Human Reproduction: A Feminist Analysis* (1987), *Human Reproduction: Principles, Practices, Policies* (1993), *A Feminist I: Reflections from Academia* (1998), and *Aging, Death, and Human Longevity: A Philosophical Inquiry* (2003). Overall is also the author of a weekly feminist column entitled "In Other Words," which appears in the *Kingston Whig-Standard*. She writes her column from the perspective of the importance of family and family histories and the ongoing struggle for control of women's bodies and reproductive rights. Her columns touch on personal and social morality, religious beliefs, parenting and raising children, sexual orientation, and gender equality in the workplace. Many of these columns were collected in a book, *Thinking Like a Woman*, that appeared in 2001.

Source: Biographical contributions provided by Christine Overall.

Lynn Paltrow

A graduate of Cornell University and the New York University School of Law, Lynn Paltrow is a civil-liberties, civil-rights attorney who specializes in cases involving reproductive freedom and health issues. Paltrow worked on cases each of which involved women who used illegal drugs during pregnancy. In *Ferguson v. Charleston,* Paltrow filed the first affirmative federal civil rights challenge against a hospital policy that required selected pregnant women to be screened for substance abuse without their knowledge and to have the results of those screens turned over to police. Also among her cases are *California v. Pamela Rae Stewart, Johnson v. Florida,* and *Whitner v. South Carolina.* Ms. Paltrow has been Director of Special Litigation for the Center for Reproductive Law and Policy. In addition to her extensive litigation and organization background, Paltrow is the first legal director for the National Abortion and Reproductive Rights Action

League and Vice President for Public Affairs for Planned Parenthood of New York City. She is also the founder of National Advocates for Pregnant Women, an organization advocating the idea that pregnant women's drug and health problems are health and public welfare issues instead of criminal justice matters. Her publications include "Punishing Women for Their Behavior during Pregnancy: An Approach That Undermines the Health of Women and Children," in *Drug Addiction Research and the Health of Women* (1998).

Source: South Carolina Advocates for Pregnant Women. www.scapw. org/napw/. Accessed March 23, 2003.

Laura M. Purdy

Laura Purdy is particularly interested in the philosophical question of whether it could ever be wrong to reproduce. In her book *Reproducing Persons: Issues in Feminist Bioethics* (1996), she considers the right to reproduce, abortion, and issues connected with surrogacy and the new reproductive technologies. She earned her Ph.D. in philosophy at Stanford University (1974) and has been writing on reproductive issues ever since. She is author or coeditor of six books, including *In Their Best Interest? The Case against Equal Rights for Children* (1992). She was a clinical bioethicist at the University Health Network and the University of Toronto from 1997 to 2000, where she was a member of the Ob-Gyn Ethics Committee. She serves on the editorial boards of *Bioethics,* which focuses on a wide range of ethical issues in medicine, and *Hypatia,* a scholarly journal focusing on feminist philosophy. Purdy has been active in the IAB network *Feminist Approaches to Bioethics* (FAB), an international association focusing on women's bioethical issues around the globe.

Source: Biographical contributions provided by Laura M. Purdy.

John A. Robertson

John A. Robertson is widely known for his analysis of procreative liberty as an important value in devising public policy about the use of reproductive technologies. This view is comprehensively presented in his 1994 book *Children of Choice: Freedom and the New Reproductive Technologies.* His framework also provides a productive way for dealing with the many challenges in human reproduction that will come with increased knowledge of the human genome. He is currently working on the ethical, legal, and social impacts of human genomics.

Robertson holds the Vinson and Elkins chair at the University of Texas School of Law at Austin. A graduate of Dartmouth College and Harvard Law School, he has written and lectured widely on law and bioethical issues including numerous articles on reproductive rights, genetics, organ transplantation, treatment of newborns with disabilities, and human experimentation. He has served on or been a consultant to many national bioethics advisory bodies, including advisory bodies on organ transplantation, assisted reproduction, and fetal tissue and stem cell transplantation. He is chair of the ethics committee of the American Society for Reproductive Medicine.

Source: Biographical contributions provided by John A. Robertson.

Barbara Katz Rothman

Barbara Katz Rothman, an internationally known sociologist specializing in human reproductive issues, is best known for her arguments regarding the primacy of social relationships rather than genetic ties in establishing parenthood. She holds a Ph.D. and is professor of Sociology at the City University of New York. Her books, published in the United States, Great Britain, Germany, Finland, and Japan, include: *In Labor* (1982); *The Tentative Pregnancy* (1986); *Recreating Motherhood* (1989); *Centuries of Solace: Expressions of Maternal Grief in Popular Literature,* with Wendy Simonds (1992); *The Encyclopedia of Childbearing* (1993), and most recently, *The Book of Life: A Personal and Ethical Guide to Race, Normality, and the Implications of the Human Genome Project* (2001) in which she writes "that genetics is more than a science, it is an ideology . . . the single best explanation, the most comprehensive theory since God." Katz Rothman is past president of two national sociological professional associations, Sociologists for Women in Society and the Society for the Study of Social Problems.

Source: Biographical contributions provided by Barbara Katz Rothman.

Margaret Sanger

Margaret Sanger (1879–1966) was a nurse who worked among the immigrant poor in New York City during the Progressive Era and

is considered the founder of the birth control movement in the
United States. Sanger was a strong supporter of contraception
despite public policies such as the Comstock Acts, which prohibited both contraception and informing people about contraception. In 1916, she opened the first birth control clinic in the United
States in New York City and was incarcerated for a short time for
violating the first Comstock Act. In 1921, she founded the American Birth Control League, which later became the Planned Parenthood Federation of America; and in 1930, she opened a family
planning clinic in Harlem. She published the journal, *Birth Control
Review,* which appeared for the first time while she was incarcerated, and several books including *What Every Mother Should Know*
(1917) and *My Fight for Birth Control* (1930).

Source: Planned Parenthood Federation of America. http://www.
plannedparenthood.org/about/thisispp/sanger.html. Accessed March
23, 2003; Britannica Online Website: http://search.eb.com/women/
articles/Sanger_Margaret_Higgins.html. Accessed March 23, 2003.

Thomas C. Shevory

Thomas C. Shevory, associate professor of politics at Ithaca College, argues that advanced reproductive and other technologies
of body manipulation and control have multiple, complex social
interactions: although these technologies foster political oppres-
sion and economic inequality, they represent possible freedoms.
He is a political scientist who specializes in health, reproductive
and environmental politics, and media studies. Shevory has published three books, including *Body/Politics: Studies in Production,
Reproduction, and (Re)Construction* (2000). He earned his Ph.D.
from the University of Iowa in 1983 and now serves on the editorial board of *Pop-Comm: A Journal of Popular Communication.*

Source: Biographical contributions provided by Thomas C. Shevory.

Peter Singer

Philosopher Peter Singer is one of the earliest and most controversial writers in the area of reproductive rights. He and coauthor Helga Kuhse state in the preface to *Should the Baby Live? The
Problem of Handicapped Infants* (1985) that "some infants with
severe disabilities should be killed." His other books, *Test-Tube
Babies* (1982), *The Reproduction Revolution: New Ways of Making*

Babies (1984, with Deane Wells), *Embryo Experimentation* (1993, et al.), and *Animal Liberation* (1977) were equally controversial and created a debate among academics, ethicists, and the news media.

Singer was born in Melbourne, Australia, and was educated at the University of Melbourne (Australia) and the University of Oxford. In 1977, he was appointed to a chair of philosophy at Monash University in Melbourne and subsequently was the founding director of that university's Centre for Human Bioethics. In 1999 he became the Ira W. DeCamp Professor of Bioethics in the University Center for Human Values at Princeton University. Singer was the founding president of the International Association of Bioethics, and with Helga Kuhse, founding coeditor of the journal, *Bioethics*.

Source: Princeton University Center for Human Values. http://www.princeton.edu/~uchv/index.html. Accessed March 23, 2003.

Bonnie Steinbock

Philosopher and bioethicist Bonnie Steinbock specializes in the areas of reproductive ethics and genetics. In the field of reproductive ethics, she has consistently defended women's rights to make their own decisions about pregnancy, while insisting that this prochoice stance is consistent with recognizing the obligation to protect children from prenatal harm. Steinbock is the area editor for "Fertility and Reproduction" in the third edition of the *Encyclopedia of Bioethics* (forthcoming 2003); the author of *Life before Birth: The Moral and Legal Status of Embryos and Fetuses* (1992); the coeditor, with Dan Beauchamp, of *New Ethics for the Public's Health* (1999); the editor of *Legal and Ethical Issues in Human Reproduction* (2002); and the coeditor, with John Arras and Alex London, of *Ethical Issues in Modern Medicine,* sixth edition (2002). She received her Ph.D. in philosophy from the University of California at Berkeley and is now professor of philosophy at the State University of New York at Albany, with joint appointments in public policy and public health.

Source: Biographical contributions provided by Bonnie Steinbock.

William Stern

See "Baby M"

Patrick Steptoe

Patrick Steptoe was a leading scientist in the development of in vitro fertilization technology. In 1968 he began collaborating on research with physiologist Robert Edwards at the Centre for Human Reproduction in the United Kingdom that led to the birth of the first "test tube baby," Louise Brown, in 1978. Since that time, more than 1 million children have been born via in vitro techniques.

Dr. Steptoe was born in Witney, Oxfordshire, England. He graduated from St. George Hospital Medical School in London and specialized in obstetrics and gynecology. In 1951, he joined the medical staff at Oldham Hospital in Oldham, England. In 1967, he published a major work, *Laparoscopy in Gynaecology.*

Source: "Steptoe, Patrick, and Edwards, Robert" *Encyclopedia Britannica.* http://search.eb.com/eb/articl?eu=1303; IVFOnline www.ivfonline.com/HTML/Newsstand/ResPapers/Bob.htm. Accessed September 13, 2002.

Laurence H. Tribe

Constitutional scholar Laurence H. Tribe is the author of *Abortion: The Clash of Absolutes* (1990), a ground-breaking analysis of the struggle between prochoice and prolife interest groups, who can find no common ground. Tribe is the Tyler Professor of Constitutional Law at Harvard. Born in China of Russian Jewish parents, Tribe came to the United States at age six, attended public schools in San Francisco, entered Harvard College at age sixteen, and received his Harvard A.B. *summa cum laude* in mathematics in 1962 and his Harvard Law School J.D. *magna cum laude* in 1966. Tenured at age twenty-eight, Tribe was thirty-five when *Time Magazine* named him one of the nation's ten most outstanding law professors.

Source: Biographical contributions provided by Laurence H. Tribe.

Sarah Weddington

In 1973, Sarah Weddington, a recent law school graduate, was the lead attorney representing Norma McCorvey (a.k.a. Jane Roe) in the landmark U.S. Supreme Court case of *Roe v. Wade* (1973), which legalized elective abortion in the United States. It is believed that at the time, Weddington was the youngest person, at the age of twenty-six, to have argued before the U.S. Supreme Court. Together, she and McCorvey changed the landscape of abortion policy and threw the nation into a very public debate about the ethics of elective abortion.

At present, Weddington is an adjunct professor at the University of Texas at Austin, teaching "Gender-Based Discrimination" and "Leadership in America." She received her J.D. degree from the University of Texas School of Law (1967). Weddington is the founder of The Weddington Center for Leadership and Life Skills. She was the first woman from Travis County elected to the Texas House of Representatives (1973) and served three terms. She served as assistant to President Jimmy Carter (1978–1981), specializing in women's issues and leadership outreach. In 1992, Weddington published *A Question of Choice*, which chronicles the history of her experience with *Roe v. Wade*.

Source: Biographical contributions provided by Sarah Weddington.

Mary Beth Whitehead

See "Baby M"

Ian Wilmut

Ian Wilmut, Head of the Department at Roslin Institute, Midlothian, U.K., was the leader of the research team that produced Dolly, the first cloned animal to develop after nuclear transfer from an adult cell, the results of which are published in the journal *Nature* (1997). He obtained a B.Sc. in agricultural science at the University of Nottingham. His Ph.D. degree was awarded in 1971 for research on the deep freeze preservation of boar semen. His subsequent research led to the birth of the first calf, Frosty, from a frozen embryo in 1973. His more recent research focused on the factors regulating embryo development after nuclear transfer, which led to the first birth of cloned lambs from embryo-derived cells and then to the birth of cloned lambs derived from fetal and adult cells. This research has been recognized by the award of an Officer of the British Empire in the queen's birthday honours of 1999. Wilmut is editor of the journal *Cloning and Stem Cells* and has also published a book, with Keith Campbell and Colin Tudge, *The Second Creation: Dolly and the Age of Control* (2000).

Source: Biographical contributions provided by Ian Wilmut.

Laura R. Woliver

Political scientist Laura R. Woliver is the author of the recently published book, *The Political Geographies of Pregnancy* (2002) in which she explores the gender politics of abortion, surrogacy, the Human Genome Project, adoption, and state surveillance of pregnant women. She concludes that many policies aimed at controlling pregnant women actually erode the dignity and bodily autonomy of women and ignore the social class, race, and sexuality context for the reproductive decisions pregnant women make. She is also the author of many articles and book chapters on reproductive politics and grassroots group dynamics including *From Outrage to Action: The Politics of Grassroots Dissent* (1993), about ad hoc grassroots interest groups.

Woliver is professor of political science in the Department of Government and International Studies and associate director of the women's studies program at the University of South Carolina. She serves on the editorial boards of several nationally and internationally recognized journals, including *Women and Politics* and *Asian Women.* She earned her doctorate in political science at the University of Wisconsin–Madison (1986) and now specializes in women and politics, social movements, and interest groups.

Source: Biographical contributions provided by Laura R. Woliver.

5

Facts and Statistics

G iven the breadth of the issues and the rapid advancement in reproductive technologies and their many applications, it should not be surprising that there is a massive amount of documents, statistics, and events surrounding reproduction. This chapter, therefore, makes no attempt to be comprehensive but instead attempts to give the reader a taste of the variety of facts, events, and statistics available. It offers examples of state statutes, court cases, scientific and policy reports, databases, and relevant statistics toward that end.

Abortion

Abortion Statistics

- Forty-eight percent of pregnancies among women in the United States are unintended; one-half of them are terminated by abortion.
- In 1997, 1.33 million abortions took place, down from an estimated 1.61 million in 1990.
- From 1973 through 1997, more than 35 million legal abortions occurred.
- Each year, 2 out of every 100 women aged fifteen to forty-four have an abortion; 47 percent of them have had at least one previous abortion, and 55 percent have had a previous birth.
- Fifty-two percent of U.S. women obtaining abortions are younger than twenty-five: women aged twenty to

twenty-four obtain 32 percent of all abortions, and teenagers obtain 20 percent.
- Black women are more than three times as likely as white women to have an abortion, and Hispanic women are roughly two times as likely.
- Catholic women are 29 percent more likely than Protestants to have an abortion but are about as likely as all women nationally to do so.
- Two-thirds of all abortions are among never-married women. About 13,000 women have abortions each year following rape or incest.
- Of those women having abortions in 1995, 58 percent had used a contraceptive method during the month they became pregnant. Eleven percent of women having abortions have never used a method of birth control; nonuse is greatest among those who are young, unmarried, poor, black, Hispanic, or poorly educated. Nine in ten women at risk of unintended pregnancy are using a contraceptive method.

Source: Alan Guttmacher Institute. 2002. "Facts in Brief: Induced Abortion." http://www.agi-usa.org/pubs/fb_induced_abortion.html. Accessed September 29.

Abortion Providers and Services

In the United States, 93 percent of abortions are performed in clinics or doctors' offices. The number of abortion providers declined by 14 percent between 1992 and 1996 (from 2,380 to 2,042). Eighty-six percent of all U.S. counties lacked an abortion provider in 1996, although they were home to 32 percent of all fifteen- to forty-four-year-old women. Among all abortion facilities, 43 percent provide services only through the twelfth week of pregnancy.

Clinics seem to be providing abortions to women earlier in their pregnancies: 42 percent of nonhospital facilities provided abortions to women less than six weeks pregnant in 1996, a 27 percent increase since 1992, when only one-third provided such early abortions. In 1997, the cost of a nonhospital abortion with local anesthesia at ten weeks of gestation ranged from $150 to $1,535, and the average amount paid was $316.

Source: Alan Guttmacher Institute. 2002. "Facts in Brief: Induced Abortion." http://www.agi-usa.org/pubs/fb_induced_abortion.html. Accessed September 29.

Abortion Funding

Through the Hyde Amendment, the U.S. Congress has barred the use of federal Medicaid funds to pay for abortion, except in cases of rape or incest, or when the woman's life is in danger because of the pregnancy. Despite this restriction, about 14 percent of all abortions in the United States are paid for with public funds, virtually all of which come from state funds. The following states pay for abortions for some poor women: Alabama, California, Connecticut, Hawaii, Idaho, Illinois, Massachusetts, Maryland, Minnesota, Montana, New Jersey, New Mexico, New York, Oregon, Vermont, Washington, and West Virginia.

Source: Alan Guttmacher Institute. 2002. "Facts in Brief: Induced Abortion." http://www..agi-usa.org/pubs/fb_induced_abortion.html. Accessed September 29.

Public Opinion regarding Abortion

The nation continues to be divided over abortion policy and under what circumstances it should be legal. Gallup Polls conducted in 2002 showed that approximately 25 percent of adults in the United States support legalized abortion under "any circumstances," and an additional 51 percent under "certain circumstances." On the issue of late-term, "partial birth" abortions, 52 percent thought this procedure should be legal. An overwhelming majority (80 percent) of respondents felt "strongly" about abortion, but they were evenly divided in identifying themselves as "prochoice" or "prolife." A Harris Poll, also conducted in 2002, showed that only 1 percent of respondents identified abortion as one of the two most important issues facing government. Terrorism and the economy were identified as the two most important issues.

Sources: Gallup Polls conducted from May 6, 2002, to May 9, 2002, and from July 5, 2002, to July 8, 2002; Harris Poll conducted from June 14, 2002, to July 17, 2002. http://http://www..lexisnexis.com. Accessed on October 1, 2002.

Born-Alive Infants Protection Act of 2002

(Enrolled as Agreed to or Passed by Both House and Senate.) H.R.2175. Begun and held at the City of Washington on Wednesday, the twenty-third day of January, two thousand and two.

An Act to protect infants who are born alive.
Be it enacted by the Senate and House of Representatives of the United States of America in Congress assembled,
SECTION 1. SHORT TITLE.
This Act may be cited as the "Born-Alive Infants Protection Act of 2002."
SEC. 2. DEFINITION OF BORN-ALIVE INFANT.
(a) IN GENERAL- Chapter 1 of title 1, United States Code, is amended by adding at the end the following:
"Sec. 8. "Person," "human being," "child," and "individual" as including born-alive infant
"(a) In determining the meaning of any Act of Congress, or of any ruling, regulation, or interpretation of the various administrative bureaus and agencies of the United States, the words "person," "human being," "child," and "individual," shall include every infant member of the species homo sapiens who is born alive at any stage of development.
"(b) As used in this section, the term "born alive," with respect to a member of the species homo sapiens, means the complete expulsion or extraction from his or her mother of that member, at any stage of development, who after such expulsion or extraction breathes or has a beating heart, pulsation of the umbilical cord, or definite movement of voluntary muscles, regardless of whether the umbilical cord has been cut, and regardless of whether the expulsion or extraction occurs as a result of natural or induced labor, cesarean section, or induced abortion.
"(c) Nothing in this section shall be construed to affirm, deny, expand, or contract any legal status or legal right applicable to any member of the species homo sapiens at any point prior to being "born alive" as defined in this section."
(b) CLERICAL AMENDMENT- The table of sections at the beginning of chapter 1 of title 1, United States Code, is amended by adding at the end the following new item:
"8. "Person," "human being," "child," and "individual" as including born-alive infant."
Signed into law by President George W. Bush on August 5, 2002.

Assisted Reproduction

Uniform Parentage Act (2000)

Abridged

Article 7: Child of Assisted Reproduction
National Conference of Commissioners on Uniform State Laws
Prefatory Comment
Medical science has developed a wide range of assisted reproductive technologies, often referred to as ARTS, which enable childless couples to become parents. Thousands of children are born in the United States each year as the result of ARTS. If a married couple uses their own eggs and sperm to conceive a child born by the wife, the parentage of the child is straightforward. The wife is the mother—by gestation and genetics, the husband is the father—by genetics and presumption, and, insofar as UPA (2000) is concerned, neither fits the definition of a "donor."

If, using assisted reproduction, a wife gives birth to a child conceived using sperm from a man other than her husband, she is the mother and her husband is the presumed father. However, the man providing the sperm might assert his biological paternity, or the husband might seek to rebut the martial presumption of paternity by proving through genetic testing that he is not the genetic father. As was the case in UPA (1973), it is necessary for UPA (2000) to establish the parentage of a child born under these circumstances.

Similarly, assisted reproduction may involve the eggs from a woman other than the wife—perhaps using the husband's sperm, perhaps not. In either event, the Act must clearly exclude the egg donor from claiming maternity. Theoretically, it is even possible that absent legislation the wife could attempt to deny maternity based on her lack of genetic relationship.

Finally, a very common ARTS procedure mixes sperm and eggs to form a prezygote that is then frozen for future use. If the couple later divorce or one of them dies, the disposition of these prezygotes can be a potential problem on which courts need guidance.

SECTION 701. SCOPE OF ARTICLE. This [article] does not apply to the birth of a child conceived by means of sexual intercourse [, or as the result of a gestational agreement as provided in (Article) 8].

SECTION 702. PARENTAL STATUS OF DONOR. A donor is not a parent of a child conceived by means of assisted reproduction.

SECTION 703. HUSBAND'S PATERNITY OF CHILD OF ASSISTED REPRODUCTION. If a husband provides sperm for, or consents to, assisted reproduction by his wife as provided in Section 704, he is the father of a resulting child.

SECTION 704. CONSENT TO ASSISTED REPRODUCTION.

(a) Consent by a married woman to assisted reproduction must be in a record signed by the woman and her husband. This requirement does not apply to the donation of eggs by a married woman for assisted reproduction by another woman.

(b) Failure of the husband to sign a consent required by subsection (a), before or after birth of the child, does not preclude a finding that the husband is the father of a child born to his wife if the wife and husband openly treated the child as their own.

SECTION 705. LIMITATION ON HUSBAND'S DISPUTE OF PATERNITY.

(a) Except as otherwise provided in subsection (b), the husband of a wife who gives birth to a child by means of assisted reproduction may not challenge his paternity of the child unless:

(1) within two years after learning of the birth of the child he commences a proceeding to adjudicate his paternity; and

(2) the court finds that he did not consent to the assisted reproduction, before or after birth of the child.

(b) A proceeding to adjudicate paternity may be maintained at any time if the court determines that:

(1) the husband did not provide sperm for, or before or after the birth of the child consent to, assisted reproduction by his wife;

(2) the husband and the mother of the child have not cohabited since the probable time of assisted reproduction; and

(3) the husband never openly treated the child as his own.

(c) The limitation provided in this section applies to a marriage declared invalid after assisted reproduction.

SECTION 706. EFFECT OF DISSOLUTION OF MARRIAGE.

(a) If a marriage is dissolved before placement of eggs, sperm, or embryos, the former spouse is not a parent of the resulting child unless the former spouse consented in a record that if assisted reproduction were to occur after a divorce, the former spouse would be a parent of the child.

(b) The consent of a former spouse to assisted reproduction may be withdrawn by that individual in a record at any time before placement of eggs, sperm, or embryos.

SECTION 707. PARENTAL STATUS OF DECEASED SPOUSE. If a spouse dies before placement of eggs, sperm, or embryos, the deceased spouse is not a parent of the resulting child unless the deceased spouse consented in a record that if assisted reproduction were to occur after death, the deceased spouse would be a parent of the child.

Source: "Uniform Parentage Act." 2000. Drafted by the National Conference of Commissioners on Uniform State Laws.

Contested Surrogacy Cases

In Chapter 2, we discussed surrogate motherhood and the law. Although most surrogacy arrangements go smoothly, there are notable exceptions that deserve our attention. For example, in 1987, Alejandra Munoz, a non–English-speaking citizen of Mexico with a second-grade education, was reportedly brought to the United States illegally to assist her infertile cousin, Hatie Haro. She was inseminated at home with the sperm of Hatie's husband, and she believed that the embryo would be transferred to Hatie for gestation. She later claimed that once pregnant, she was told the transfer could not be completed and she would have to bear the child. Although unable to read, she signed a handwritten agreement saying she would accept a fee of $1,500, an amount well below the typical surrogacy fee. Several months after the birth, she demanded a higher fee, and a custody battle ensued. Ultimately, the father gained custody, and Munoz was allowed visitation (Blank and Merrick 1995, 122; Arditti 1987, 44–45; U.S. House 1987, 37–43).

Another case involved biological surrogate Patty Nowakowski of Michigan, who became pregnant with twins. Shortly before the birth, the intended father (who was also the biological father) stated that he wanted only a girl and would refuse to accept a male child; if both twins were male, he would refuse them both. When a boy and girl were born, he took the female home, but the male twin was initially placed in foster care and then in the Nowakowski home, where he was named after Patty's husband. Subsequently, the Nowakowskis won custody of the twin girl as well (Andrews 1989, 250).

A similar situation arose in 2001, when a young British woman entered into a surrogacy agreement with a California couple. Helen Beasley met the couple via the Internet and became pregnant with twins through in vitro fertilization, using the intended father's sperm and donated eggs. It is reported that Beasley was aware that the intended parents wanted only one child and that she notified them in the eighth week that there were two fetuses. According to Beasley, the intended parents did not request an abortion until the thirteenth week, and when she refused because of the lateness of the request, the intended parents notified her they were unwilling to accept two infants. At that time, Beasley had received about $1,000 of her $19,000 fee. She then filed suit, seeking damages for medical expenses and emo-

tional suffering, and sought to make arrangements for the placement of the unborn twins with another couple. As of this writing,
the case had not been resolved ("Surrogate Mother" 2001).

Uncertainty about the intended parents' commitment is
increased when birth defects are involved. In 1983, Judith Stiver
agreed to serve as a biological surrogate for Alexander Malahoff.
The child was born with microcephaly (an indicator of mental
retardation) and a life-threatening streptococcus infection. It is
reported that Malahoff refused permission to treat the infection,
and the hospital obtained a court order. Subsequently, a paternity
test indicated that the biological father was Stiver's husband, but
at the time of the birth, neither Malahoff nor the Stivers knew
that, and both denied responsibility for the child (Capron 1987,
691; Corea 1985, 219). In another case reported in the *New England Journal of Medicine*, a couple refused to accept custody of an
infant after it tested positive for the human immunodeficiency
virus (HIV) (Frederick et al. 1987, 1352).

Sources: Andrews, Lori B. 1989. *Between Strangers: Surrogate Mothers,
Expectant Fathers, and Brave New Babies.* New York: Harper and Row.

Arditti, Rita. 1987. "The Surrogacy Business." *Social Policy* 18 (2):
42–46.

Blank, Robert, and Janna C. Merrick. 1995. *Human Reproduction,
Emerging Technologies, and Conflicting Rights.* Washington, DC: Congressional Quarterly Press.

Capron, Alexander Morgan. 1987. "Alternative Birth Technologies:
Legal Challenges." *University of California, Davis, Law Review* 20: 679–704.

Corea, Gena. 1985. *The Mother Machine: Reproductive Technologies from
Artificial Insemination to Artificial Wombs.* New York: Harper and Row.

Frederick, Winston, et al. 1987. "HIV Testing of Surrogate Mothers."
New England Journal of Medicine 317 (21): 1351–1352.

"Surrogate Mother Suing Calif. Couple." 2001. *Yahoo News.* August 10.
http://dailynews.yahoo.com. Accessed August 13, 2001.

U.S. House of Representatives. 1987. *Hearing before the Subcommittee on
Transportation, Tourism, and Hazardous Materials of the Committee on Energy
and Commerce, "Surrogacy Arrangements Act of 1987."* 100th Cong., 1st
sess. October 15.

American Society of Reproductive Medicine Ethics Statements

Embryo Splitting for Infertility Treatment

Because early embryonic cells are totipotent (capable of developing into
complete organisms), the possibility of splitting or separating the blas-

tomeres of early preimplantation embryos to increase the number of embryos that are available for IVF treatment of infertility is being discussed. Because embryo splitting could lead to two or more embryos with the same genome, the term "cloning" has been used to describe this practice. Embryo splitting, however, does not involve any direct manipulation, transfer, or substitution of the entire genome, as occurs in conventional understanding of cloning by nuclear substitution.

Splitting one embryo into two or more embryos could serve the needs of infertile couples in several ways. For couples who can produce only one or two embryos, splitting embryos could increase the number of embryos available for transfer in a single IVF cycle. Because the IVF pregnancy rate increases with the number of embryos transferred, it is thought that embryo splitting when only one or two embryos are produced may result in a pregnancy that would not otherwise have occurred. For couples who produce more than enough embryos for one cycle of transfer, splitting one or more embryos may provide sufficient embryos for subsequent transfers without having to go through another retrieval cycle, thus lessening the physical burdens and costs of IVF treatment for infertility. In addition, this technique may have application in preimplantation genetic diagnosis.

Whether embryo splitting is clinically feasible, and whether the expected benefits to infertile couples will outweigh its risks and possible misapplication is unknown at the present time and cannot be determined without further research. However, a number of ethical objections have been raised against the practice. One ethical objection is that embryos will be manipulated and destroyed in the process of research and application. Another objection is that identical twins may be deliberately created, and might be born several years apart. Some commentators also raised the possibility that the technical ability to split embryos could lead couples to have embryos split, not as part of a treatment for infertility, but to provide "back up" embryos in case an existing child with the same genome needs a tissue or organ transplant, or dies. Fears also have been voiced that embryo splitting and storage could lead to a market in stored embryos based on the desirability of the genetic trait of children born with that genome.

Whereas these ethical concerns raise important issues, neither alone nor together do they offer sufficient reasons for not proceeding with research into embryo splitting and blastomere separation. Several of the concerns—such as the use of split embryos as a source of organs or tissues for an existing child, or the sale of stored embryos with desirable genomes based on the appearance of characteristics of existing children—are speculative and hypothetical. It is unclear whether such practices would occur at all or to any significant extent, even if embryo splitting were clinically feasible and successful. Although some of these applications may be unethical, they could be prohibited without also prohibiting embryo splitting designed to produce sufficient embryos for successful IVF treatment or other medical applications.

Concerns that embryo splitting could lead to more than one child born with identical genomes is a more realistic possibility if embryo splitting is clinically successful, but still is not a sufficient reason to discourage research in the technique. Since identical twins often are born independent of assisted reproduction and do well, the birth of twins as a result of embryo splitting should not be a major concern. Indeed, such an event usually will be the byproduct of an attempt to have one child, and not the result of the intention to create twins. As long as a couple is fully informed of the risk of such an outcome, there would appear to be no major ethical objection to placing two or more embryos with the same genome in the uterus with the hope of producing a single pregnancy.

Of greater concern is the possibility that embryo splitting could lead to offspring with identical genomes being born at different times—twins or triplets (if that is the proper term) whose births are separated in time. This could arise because splitting embryos or blastomere separation could produce more embryos than are transferred to the uterus in a single cycle, with the remainder cryopreserved and transferred at a later time. If such later transfers occur, they most likely would be transferred within a few years of the birth of the first child with that genome, but also subsequent transfers and births could occur several years later. Transfer in these cases raise philosophical and psychological questions about personal identity and the meaning of being a twin that require further investigation before it can be determined that such transfers are ethical. Such a possibility could be eliminated entirely by transferring all genetically identical embryos in the same cycle.

In sum, since embryo splitting has the potential to improve the efficacy of IVF treatments for infertility, research to investigate the technique is ethically acceptable. Persons asked to donate gametes or embryos for such research should be fully informed that research in embryo splitting is intended or planned as a result of their donation. The fears of possible future abuses of the technique are not sufficient to stop valid research in use of embryo splitting as a treatment for infertility.

This statement was developed by the American Society for Reproductive Medicine's Ethics Committee and accepted by the Board of Directors on December 8, 1995.

Source: Reprinted by permission from the American Society of Reproductive Medicine. 1997. "Embryo Splitting for Infertility Treatment." *Fertility and Sterility* 67: 4–5.

Informed Consent and the Use of Gametes and Embryos for Research

The ethical acceptability of research involving human gametes and embryos has been affirmed by national commissions and committees and published in their respective reports.[1] In view of the public concern about human embryo research, the ASRM advises that the investigator bear the burden of demonstrating the worthiness of studies involving human embryos and that embryos be studied only when there is no adequate alternative, the study is likely to yield important clinical data, and the number of embryos is kept to a minimum.

A critical component of ethical research is the clinician's obligation to obtain Institutional Review Board (IRB) approval and to secure informed consent from the donors of oocytes, spermatozoa, and embryos.

In general, patients must give consent for any research use of their cells or tissues. In the field of assisted reproduction, the following cells and tissues might be studied: oocytes, spermatozoa, normal but spare fresh or frozen embryos not needed by couples in IVF programs, nonviable or abnormal embryos, abnormally fertilized eggs that will not be transferred to the uterus, and eggs and sperm used to generate embryos intended for research but not transfer. Although informed consent should be obtained before any of these cells or tissues are studied, the most sensitive issues arise for research in which viable embryos are studied or generated for study and then discarded. Informed consent protects donors and investigators and it encourages clarity in the clinic's prospective research plans. Precise statements about intended benefits and methods are also desirable to help address misconceptions patients and members of the public may have about embryo research.

Prospective donors in assisted reproductive programs must be assured that nonparticipation will not adversely affect their status in the program. They should have access to material that informs them of the goals and benefits of the research and, if they request, articles that raise and address ethical concerns about embryo research. They should be apprised if the cells or tissues they donate will yield an expected commercial value for the investigators. It is imperative that couples not feel pressured to donate. Gamete and embryo donation for research must not be induced by financial payment, although donors may be compensated for expenses associated with donation.

Clinicians should be aware that couples may change their minds and decide not to donate their gametes or embryos for study. Couples should be informed that it is possible to change their minds without prejudice at any time until the experiment actually begins, and clinicians should inform couples about the mechanisms to be used if the prospective donors decide not to participate. Investigators should make clear that once embryos are donated for research and not for transfer, and experimental manipulations begin, the embryos cannot be transferred for possible pregnancy.

To secure informed consent, clinicians must provide enough information for prospective donors (those part of an assisted reproductive program or anonymous gamete donors) to make an informed choice about whether to participate. This includes informing potential donors of the purpose, nature, and risks and benefits of the research. The research purpose is important because prospective donors may be willing to donate for some purposes, such as studies designed to improve success rates in assisted reproduction, but not for others, such as inquiries into cancer or contraceptive research. Other donors will have no such preferences. The nature of the research is important because prospective donors may be willing to donate for some types of studies, such as those involving passive observation of embryos, but not for others, such as those involving active manipulation of embryos. Whether the embryos to be studied are normal and viable or abnormal and nonviable may also be important for the donors. Anonymous oocyte and sperm donors must consent to have their gametes used to generate embryos for research purposes. Investigators should obtain consent to discard or donate embryos or gametes that cannot be used in ways stipulated by the donor. They should obtain reapproval by the IRB if significant changes are made in the purpose or nature of the research, and they should generate a new consent form for the donors after a discussion of the changes.

Regarding the benefits and risks, couples who donate spare embryos for research should be informed that the benefit will take the form of advanced knowledge and that they will not directly benefit from the study. Donors should also be aware that any discoveries in their gametes or embryos such as the presence of a genetic mutation will not be conveyed to them. They should be advised that one risk is that they may later regret not having saved the embryos for their infertility treatment or for donation to other couples.

Consent forms should receive prior approval from the IRB or equivalent oversight committee. Consent to study gametes should be sought before the collection of a semen sample or oocyte recovery, when potential donors have time to consider consent forms and other material. Physicians should secure consent with a witness present and then place the consent form in a confidential file.

In summary, a carefully specified procedure for obtaining informed consent is vital for the ethical implementation of studies involving human gametes and embryos. In order to preserve the interests of the infertile population, all research activities must be performed with strict attention to ethical standards. Informed consent, along with active IRB involvement and confidentiality, remain the best vehicles for assuring this protection.

1. National Institutes of Health. 1994. "Report of the Human Embryo Research Panel: Final Draft." September 27, 1994.

Source: Reprinted by permission from the American Society of Reproductive Medicine. 1997. "Informed Consent and the Use of Gametes and Embryos for Research." *Fertility and Sterility* 68: 780–781.

Cloning and Stem Cell Research

In 2002, a Gallup Poll was conducted to measure support in the United States for cloning. Fifty-nine percent of respondents favored cloning of human organs or body parts for medical transplants, and 37 percent opposed it. Four percent had no opinion. However, when asked about cloning adult human cells for use in medical research, the favorable response dropped to 51 percent, and opposition rose to 44 percent. Favorable responses dipped even lower when asked about cloning human embryos for use in medical research, with only 34 percent of respondents responding affirmatively and 61 percent responding negatively. Finally, when asked about cloning designed to result in the birth of a human being, an overwhelming 90 percent of respondents were opposed, 8 percent were supportive, and 2 percent had no opinion.

Source: Public Opinion Online. Roper Center at the University of Connecticut. 2002. Accessed on September 30, 2002, via LexisNexis.

Remarks by President George W. Bush on Stem Cell Research

Abridged

August 9, 2001

Good evening. I appreciate you giving me a few minutes of your time tonight so I can discuss with you a complex and difficult issue, an issue that is one of the most profound of our time.

The issue of research involving stem cells derived from human embryos is increasingly the subject of a national debate and dinner table discussions. The issue is confronted every day in laboratories as scientists ponder the ethical ramifications of their work. It is agonized over by parents and many couples as they try to have children, or to save children already born. . . .

Based on preliminary work that has been privately funded, scientists believe further research using stem cells offers great promise that could help improve the lives of those who suffer from many terrible diseases—from juvenile diabetes to Alzheimer's, from Parkinson's to spinal cord injuries. And while scientists admit they are not yet certain, they believe stem cells derived from embryos have unique potential.

You should also know that stem cells can be derived from sources other than embryos—from adult cells, from umbilical cords that are discarded after babies are born, from human placenta. And many scientists feel research on these type of stem cells is also promising. Many patients suffering from a range of diseases are already being helped with treatments developed from adult stem cells.

However, most scientists, at least today, believe that research on embryonic stem cells offer the most promise because these cells have the potential to develop in all of the tissues in the body.

Scientists further believe that rapid progress in this research will come only with federal funds. Federal dollars help attract the best and brightest scientists. They ensure new discoveries are widely shared at the largest number of research facilities and that the research is directed toward the greatest public good. . . .

As I thought through this issue, I kept returning to two fundamental questions: First, are these frozen embryos human life, and therefore, something precious to be protected? And second, if they're going to be destroyed anyway, shouldn't they be used for a greater good, for research that has the potential to save and improve other lives. . . .

On the first issue, are these embryos human life—well, one researcher told me he believes this five-day-old cluster of cells is not an embryo, not yet an individual, but a pre-embryo. He argued that it has the potential for life, but it is not a life because it cannot develop on its own.

An ethicist dismissed that as a callous attempt at rationalization. Make no mistake, he told me, that cluster of cells is the same way you and I, and all the rest of us, started our lives. One goes with a heavy heart if we use these, he said, because we are dealing with the seeds of the next generation.

And to the other crucial question, if these are going to be destroyed anyway, why not use them for good purpose—I also found different answers. Many argue these embryos are byproducts of a process that helps create life, and we should allow couples to donate them to science so they can be used for good purpose instead of wasting their potential. Others will argue there's no such thing as excess life, and the fact that a living being is going to die does not justify experimenting on it or exploiting it as a natural resource. . . .

In recent weeks, we learned that scientists have created human embryos in test tubes solely to experiment on them. This is deeply troubling, and a warning sign that should prompt all of us to think through these issues very carefully. . . .

I strongly oppose human cloning, as do most Americans. We recoil at the idea of growing human beings for spare body parts, or creating life for our convenience. And while we must devote enormous energy to conquering disease, it is equally important that we pay attention to the moral concerns raised by the new frontier of human embryo stem cell research. Even the most noble ends do not justify any means. . . .

I also believe human life is a sacred gift from our Creator. I worry about a culture that devalues life, and believe as your President I have an important obligation to foster and encourage respect for life in America and throughout the world. And while we're all hopeful about the potential of this research, no one can be certain that the science will live up to the hope it has generated. . . .

As a result of private research, more than 60 genetically diverse stem cell lines already exist. They were created from embryos that have already been destroyed, and they have the ability to regenerate themselves indefinitely, creating ongoing opportunities for research. I have concluded that we should allow federal funds to be used for research on these existing stem cell lines, where the life and death decision has already been made. . . .

I also believe that great scientific progress can be made through aggressive federal funding of research on umbilical cord placenta, adult, and animal stem cells which do not involve the same moral dilemma. This year, your government will spend $250 million on this important research.

I will also name a President's council to monitor stem cell research, to recommend appropriate guidelines and regulations, and to consider all of the medical and ethical ramifications of biomedical innovation. This council will consist of leading scientists, doctors, ethicists, lawyers, theologians, and others, and will be chaired by Dr. Leon Kass, a leading biomedical ethicist from the University of Chicago.

I have made this decision with great care, and I pray it is the right one.

Thank you for listening. Good night, and God bless America.

Source: The White House. 2002. "Remarks by President George W. Bush on Stem Cell Research." http://www.whitehouse.gov/news/releases/2001/08/20010809–2.html. Accessed on October 1.

Culturing Human Embryonic Stem Cells

Stem cells are cells that have the ability to divide for indefinite periods in culture and to give rise to specialized cells. There are many sources for stem cells, including umbilical cords, fetal tissue, and adults, but the most controversial, and arguably the most promising, source is through the process of culturing human embryonic stem cells. As illustrated in Figure 5.1, this process requires retrieval of eggs that have been fertilized in vitro. After reaching the blastocyst stage at about five to seven days, the nuclei from each of the hundreds of individual cells are removed and placed in a cultural medium where unlimited numbers of undifferentiated stem cells can be produced from each original cell. These new cells are termed pluripotent, which means they can be manipulated to give rise to most types of cells (blood, neural, muscle) except for cells necessary for fetal development. Some researchers believe that these stem cells hold the promise of revolutionizing medicine and treating all manner of diseases and injuries.

Figure 5.1

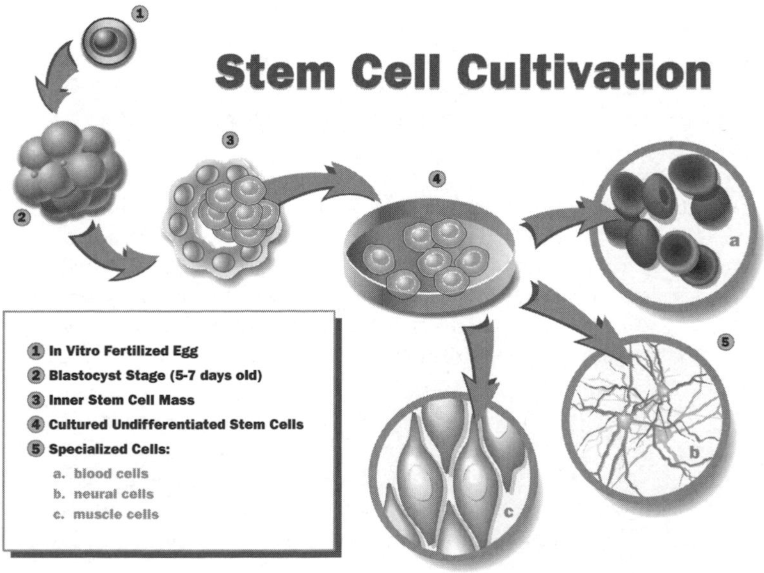

Stem Cell Cultivation

1. In Vitro Fertilized Egg
2. Blastocyst Stage (5-7 days old)
3. Inner Stem Cell Mass
4. Cultured Undifferentiated Stem Cells
5. Specialized Cells:
   a. blood cells
   b. neural cells
   c. muscle cells

Source: University of Wisconsin Board of Regents. "Embryonic Stem Cultivation." http://www.news.wisc.edu/packages/stemcells. Accessed March 23, 2003.

Coerced Obstetrical Intervention

In Chapter 2, we discussed the issue of court-ordered obstetrical interventions and the Angela Carder case. There are additional cases that also merit our attention. One of the earliest such cases occurred when a New Jersey court ordered a Jehovah's Witness to submit to a blood transfusion to save her life and the life of the fetus (*Raleigh Fitkin–Paul Morgan Memorial Hospital v. Anderson* 1964). Two decades later, a New York court ordered a blood transfusion for the benefit of an eighteen-week-old previable fetus (*In re Jamaica Hospital* 1985).

Similar decisions were reached in cases in which women refused consent for cesarean sections. A Georgia court ordered Jessie May Jefferson to submit to cesarean delivery because her doctor had diagnosed her with placenta previa and the court believed there was a 99 percent chance that the infant would die and a 50 percent chance she would die (*Jefferson v. Griffin Spaulding Co. Hosp.* 1981). Jefferson refused consent on religious grounds and subsequently delivered a healthy boy in an uneventful vaginal delivery. This pattern was repeated in several additional cases, including the 1982 case of a Michigan woman, also diagnosed with placenta previa, who refused consent for the cesarean based on religious beliefs. It is reported that she went into hiding and police were authorized to search for her. They did not succeed, and she later had an uneventful vaginal delivery at another hospital (Rhoden 1986, 2009). St. Vincent's Hospital in New York unsuccessfully sought a court order when a fetus was diagnosed as having the umbilical cord wrapped around its neck. Several hours after the judge refused to issue the order, a healthy baby was born through vaginal delivery ("Court-Ordered Caesareans" 1988).

A court order was obtained, however, in the 1986 case of Ayesha Madyun, when her physician at Georgetown University Hospital recommended a cesarean delivery because of the possibility of fetal infection. Already in labor and disagreeing with the diagnosis, Madyun attended the hearing that had been quickly convened at the hospital. The Superior Court of the District of Columbia ordered the surgery, finding that parents may not make a martyr of their unborn infant (*In re Madyun* 1986), and the decision was upheld by a late-night call to two appellate justices. A healthy son was delivered surgically but showed no signs of infection.

In 1990, Chao Lee, a Hmong immigrant in Wisconsin, was diagnosed with placenta previa but refused to consent to a cesarean delivery. It is believed that her refusal resulted from cultural values that oppose surgery, pressure from her clan, and a disagreement regarding the diagnosis. The hospital sought a court order, and shortly before the hearing, a public defender was appointed to represent her. Because the situation was believed to be an emergency, he did not have adequate time to prepare and never even spoke with Chao Lee. He did not know the facts of the case, and the issues were outside his normal practice of law. An order was issued requiring Chao Lee to submit to the cesarean section if she arrived voluntarily at the hospital and the surgery was necessary to save her life (Perlich 1992). Chao Lee then consulted another physician who testified at a subsequent hearing that vaginal delivery could be safely accomplished, the order was rescinded, and a healthy baby was delivered vaginally.

In 1993, Tabita Bricci, a Pentecostal, refused to submit to a cesarean delivery at St. Joseph's Hospital in Chicago. The court denied St. Joseph's request for a court order, and Bricci delivered a healthy child vaginally at another hospital. The following year, both the Illinois trial and appellate courts refused to order a woman to submit to a cesarean after she would not consent based on religious grounds. Doctors predicted that the fetus would die without the cesarean because of insufficient oxygen coming through the placenta (*In re Baby Boy Doe* 1994; Levy 1999, 174). Contrary to the diagnosis, a healthy but somewhat underweight boy was born through vaginal delivery.

Despite the rulings in *Baby Boy Doe,* the Circuit Court of Cook County, Illinois (1996), ordered Darlene Brown, thirty-four weeks into her pregnancy, to submit to a blood transfusion after heavy bleeding occurred during surgery to remove a urethral mass. Brown had not anticipated the need for blood and had not discussed her religious objections to blood transfusions with her doctor prior to the surgery. When unexpected bleeding began and the doctor ordered the blood, Brown refused and was not transfused. She continued to bleed after the surgery, and the doctor determined that without a blood transfusion, the chance of either her or the fetus surviving was less than 5 percent. The hospital filed for custody of the fetus under the Illinois Juvenile Act of 1987, and a hearing was held the same day. The Circuit Court awarded temporary custody of the fetus to the hospital administrator and authorized him to compel the blood transfusion. Brown attempted to physically resist and was overpowered, forcibly restrained, and sedated during the transfusion. Shortly after the birth of a healthy baby, Brown filed an appeal, and the Court of Appeal of Illinois reversed the lower court decision, finding that the fetus was not a minor within the purview of the Juvenile Act. It also held that

> the State may not override a pregnant woman's competent treatment decision, including refusal of recommended invasive medical procedures, to potentially save the life of the viable fetus . . . a blood transfusion is an invasive medical procedure that interrupts a competent adult's bodily integrity. We thus determine that the circuit court erred in ordering Brown to undergo the transfusion on behalf of the viable fetus. (*In re Fetus Brown* 1997)

Sources: "Court-Ordered Caesareans: Judges Deciding Parent's Can't Be Indulged at Risk of Unborn Infants." 1988. *St. Petersburg Times* (online), January 20. http://www.sptimes.com. Accessed August 27, 2001.

In re Baby Boy Doe, 632 N.E.2d 326 (Ill.App.Ct. 1994).

In re Fetus Brown, 689 N.E. 2d 397 (Ill.App.Ct. 1997).

In re Jamaica Hospital, 128 Misc. 2d 1006, 491 N.Y.S.2d 898 (Sup. Ct. 1985).

In re Madyun, 114 Daily Wash. L. Rptr. 2233 (D.C. Super. Ct. July 26, 1986).

Jefferson v. Griffin Spaulding County Hospital, 247 Ga. 86, 274 S.E.2d 457 (1981).

Levy, Joelyn Knopf. 1999. "Jehovah's Witnesses, Pregnancy, and Blood Transfusions: A Paradigm for the Autonomy Rights of All Pregnant Women." *Journal of Law, Medicine and Ethics* 27 (2): 171–189.

Perlich, John J. 1992. Circuit Judge, Branch 4, LaCrosse, Wisconsin. Presiding judge in *Unborn Child of Chao Lee*, Case number: 90 JV 210, LaCrosse County, Wisconsin. Personal correspondence, September 22.

Raleigh Fitkin–Paul Morgan Memorial Hospital v. Anderson, 42 N.J. 421, 201 A.2d 537 cert. denied, 377 U.S. 985 (1964).

Rhoden, Nancy. 1986. "The Judge in the Delivery Room: The Emergence of Court Ordered Cesareans." *California Law Review* 74 (6): 951–2030.

Decision-Making by Pregnant Women

In Chapter 2, we discussed in detail the 1987 case of Angela Carder who, at twenty-six weeks gestation, was hospitalized at the George Washington University Hospital (GWUH) in Washington, D.C., because, in addition to her pregnancy, she was critically ill with cancer. Hospital staff there obtained a court order mandating delivery of the fetus by cesarean section, and both mother and daughter died. Subsequently, her parents, Daniel and Nettie Stoner, reached an out-of-court settlement with GWUH that provided, among other things, that the hospital would create a policy on decision making by pregnant patients. That policy follows.

Policy on Decision-Making by Pregnant Patients at the George Washington University Hospital[1]

Decision-Making with Adult Patients Generally:

Health care decision-making is a joint enterprise between patient(s) or surrogate(s) on the one hand and caregiver(s) on the other. Ethics, law and sound medical practice emphasize both patient autonomy and professional standards. No party should be the mere instrument of another. In shared decision making, the act of informed consent or informed refusal affirms and protects patient autonomy while acknowledging the physician's commitment to professional standards.[2]

We base our policies regarding decision making on this hospital's (and the medical profession's) strong commitment to respecting the autonomy of all patients with capacity. Respect for autonomy does not end because an adult patient with capacity refuses a course of action strongly recommended by an attending physician. Nor do professional standards require that patients comply with every physician recommendation or that physicians agree to comply with every patient's request. From this respect for both patient autonomy and for professional standards flows our strong preference for maintaining decision-making within the physician-patient relationship rather than having outsiders (e.g., courts) impose health care decisions on unwilling patients.

Some patients are not capable of consenting to or refusing treatment in an informed fashion, either because they have lost capacity (such as an adult who becomes comatose)[3] or because they never had capacity (such as infants and children, or adults who have been mentally disabled from birth). These patients' preferences as to health care decisions should be determined through the doctrine of "substituted judgment." Under this doctrine, the surrogate decision-maker attempts to determine what the patient would have decided if capable, based upon the surrogate's knowledge of the patient's value system, expressed wishes or other reasonably reliable evidence of the patient's desires.

When no reasonably reliable evidence exists from which a surrogate and the care-giver can determine an incompetent patient's desires relevant to a particular treatment decision, the surrogate and the care-giver together must consider what would be in the patient's "best interest."

Decision-Making with Pregnant Patients:

These ethical, legal and medical standards also govern the decision-making process with a pregnant patient. But the uniqueness of the maternal-fetal relationship may occasionally create special considerations in the application of these principles.

The American College of Obstetricians and Gynecologists ("ACOG") and the American Academy of Pediatrics ("AAP") both recognize that a pregnant woman and her fetus comprise "two patients." Both organizations recognize as well that the unique characteristic of this situation is that one patient (the fetus) is dependent upon and accessible only through the other (the woman). ACOG advises that the "obstetrician should be concerned with the health care of both the pregnant woman and the fetus within her, assessing the attendant risks and benefits to each during the course of care."[4] AAP similarly suggests that pediatricians "formulate treatment recommendations that balance the best interests of the fetus and the potential risks to the woman."[5]

Consistent with the ACOG and AAP statements, it is the policy of this hospital that obstetricians must consider the health of the pregnant patient and her fetus in assessing the range of medically reasonable treatment options, and must communicate this information about the risks and benefits to each to enable the pregnant patient to make informed health care decisions. The difficulty in evaluating a degree of benefit or risk to the fetus requires great care in presenting such information. That evaluation often will be enhanced by input from pediatric and other appropriate specialists.

For the vast majority of women, the welfare of the fetus is of enormous if not primary, importance, and conflicts between a pregnant woman's medical treatment decisions and fetal well-being are unusual. Both the obstetrician and the pregnant woman work together for the well-being of both the woman and fetus. When the decision serves both maternal and fetal welfare, ordinarily there is no need to question the basis for the patient's decision.

When a pregnant patient with capacity is properly counseled by her attending physician about the risks and benefits to her and her fetus of a particular course of care, the decision of the pregnant patient to consent or to refuse that care may be inconsistent with the welfare of the patient or her fetus. When a pregnant patient's decision appears unnecessarily to disserve her own or fetal welfare, great care should be taken to verify that her decision is both informed and authentic. Our usual expectation is that a pregnant patient usually wants to give birth to the healthiest possible baby and will take prudent steps to promote that goal. When a patient's choice appears to conflict with her own values or when her decision conflicts with our usual expectation, special attention to the decision and process of decision-making is warranted.

In such a situation, the attending physician should explore the reasoning behind the pregnant patients' decision. Such a decision may result from the patient's inadequate understanding or misconstruing of the relative risks and benefits to herself and to her fetus of available treatment alternatives.[6] It may result from pressures by family members, who in turn may have an inadequate understanding of these risks and benefits.

Additional counseling by obstetrician and by pediatric and other appropriate specialists may correct inadequacy of information or misunderstandings. The attending physician may suspect, however, that the pregnant patient's decision, like that of any other patient, stems from emotional or psychological difficulties. In such circumstances, a psychiatric consultation should be requested since treating impaired mental functioning may restore the patient's decision-making capacity. Discussions with family members also may be appropriate.[7] The attending physician is encouraged to bring such matters to the attention of the hospital ethics committee, which is available to consult with the attending physician, the pregnant patient, family members and other interested parties.[8]

When a fully informed and competent pregnant patient persists in a decision which may disserve her own or fetal welfare, this hospital's policy is to accede to the pregnant patient's preference whenever possible (see paragraphs on "Withdrawal from Participation by an Individual Care-giver" and "Withdrawal from Participation by an Institution"). As noted earlier, our respect for autonomous adult patients' decisions is not altered simply on the basis of disagreement between the patient and her care-givers regarding the appropriate course of treatment.

Assessing Decision-Making by a Pregnant Patient's Surrogate:

When a pregnant patient is not capable of consenting to or refusing treatment in an informed fashion, her preferences should be determined through the doctrine of "substituted judgment." When a properly-selected or legally-recognized surrogate insists that the pregnant patient, if capable, would have decided to act in a fashion which appears unnecessarily to disserve the welfare of the mother or her fetus, the care-giver must scrutinize each element of the surrogate's participation to evaluate, for example (a) the possibility of conflict of interest (b) the reliability of the evidence of the patient's desires upon which the surrogate purportedly is relying (c) the surrogate's knowledge of the patient's value system and (d) the surrogate's responsible commitment to the decision-making process.

The care-giver should enlist the assistance of appropriate consultants, including the hospital Ethics Committee, in undertaking this evaluation. This policy contemplates that a surrogate's decision to act in a fashion which appears unnecessarily to disserve the welfare of the pregnant patient or her fetus will be honored only if the care-giver and the hospital are convinced that the surrogate's decision is well-founded under the criteria articulated above. The hospital will accede to a well-founded surrogate's decision whenever possible (see paragraphs on "Withdrawal from Participation by an Individual Care-giver" and "Withdrawal from Participation by an Institution").

Withdrawal from Participation by an Individual Care-Giver:

This policy also recognizes that professional standards do not require individual care-givers to comply with every patient decision. When an individual care-giver believes that compliance with a pregnant patient's refusal of or request for treatment would cause that care-giver to violate his/her professional standards, it may be appropriate for the care-giver to withdraw from the relationship with the pregnant patient. As in any other treatment situation, withdrawal from the care of a pregnant patient is appropriate only where that patient is given adequate notice and assistance in obtaining competent substitute care.

Withdrawal from Participation by an Institution:

Wherever a conflict in such cases arises which cannot be resolved within the care-giver/patient relationship, all other intrainstitutional resources, including the Ethics Committee, must be utilized. The remote case may still ensue that a pregnant patient's decision continues to appear to disserve fetal welfare and is so ethically unsettling that it may justify an institutional decision to withdraw from the case. Such justification normally would exist when there was unanimity or overwhelming consensus among the attending physician and assisting members of the health care team that:

- There is near certainty of substantial and imminent harm to the fetal patient absent the proposed treatment; and
- The proposed procedure has a very high possibility of reversing or preventing the anticipated harm to the fetus; and
- Risk to the pregnant patient is minimal; and
- Withdrawal from the case is not likely to cause the pregnant patient to abandon medical care for herself and her fetus or otherwise to cause harm to herself.

Seeking Judicial Intervention:

Courts are an inappropriate forum for resolving ethical issues. We recognize there may be legal motivations to seeking judicial intervention in such situations. Resort to the courts should rarely occur.

When Time Is Short:

The activities encouraged by this policy presume the availability of time: for a care-giver to explain his/her professional standards to the pregnant patient; for a care-giver to engage in a substantive and meaningful dialogue with the pregnant patient calculated to enable that patient to consent to or refuse treatment in an informed fashion; for the pregnant patient to contemplate the reasonable medical options and to consult with the care-giver and family members; for the care-giver to enlist the assistance of appropriate consultants, when necessary.

Every effort should be made to address treatment decisions as early as possible. We recognize, however, that there will be times when decisions need to be made under emergent circumstances. In those cases, as in other emergency situations, the principle of therapeutic privilege ought to apply. Therapeutic privilege should only be invoked when it is virtually impossible to apply the process outlined earlier in this document.

Conclusion:

1. Health care decision-making is a joint enterprise between patients (or their surrogates) and their care-givers with patient autonomy and professional standards respects [sic] complementary values.
2. Respect for patient autonomy compels us to accede to the treatment decisions of a pregnant patient whenever possible. When a pregnant patient persists in a decision which unnecessarily disserves maternal or fetal welfare, care-givers must undertake to ensure that the decision is not the result of inadequate information or a correctable misunderstanding before either acceding to the decision or if the care-giver feels compelled by professional standards, withdrawing from the case.
3. Respect for patient autonomy and professional standards engenders a strong commitment to keeping health care decision-making within the patient-physician relationship. When a care-giver's question about a patient's treatment decision requires input from outside the immediate relationship, that input should be solicited from other elements of the hospital community, including individual consultants in appropriate specialties and the Ethics Committee. It may occasionally, for ethical reasons, be appropriate to seek judicial intervention to assess or override a pregnant patient's decision.

Notes:

1. This policy relates to treatment decisions of pregnant patients but does not alter, restrict or encumber the right of a woman, adult or minor, to choose to terminate a pregnancy to the extent permitted by law.

2. President's Commission for the Study of Ethical Problems in Medicine and Biomedical and Behavior Research, *Decisions to Forego Life Sustaining Treatment,* U.S. Government Printing Office, Washington, 1983.

3. See D. C. Mun. Regs. Tit 22 * 600.7(a) (1986) providing that "a minor of any age may consent to health services which he or she requests for the prevention, diagnosis, or treatment of (certain) medical situations" including "pregnancy or its lawful termination."

4. ACOG Committee Opinion Number 55, October 1987, "Patient Choice: Maternal-Fetal Conflict."

5. AAP Committee on Bioethics, "Fetal Therapy: Ethical Considerations."

6. Brock, D. W., Ph.D: Wartman, S. A., PhD: 1995. "Sounding Board: When Competent Patients Make Irrational Choices." *New England Journal of Medicine* 332: 1595–1599.

7. *See* The George Washington University Hospital Ethics Committee, *Ethics Committee Structure,* recognizing the patient's right to confidentiality.

8. *ID* identifying "interested parties."

Contraception and Sterilization

Emergency Contraception

Emergency contraception (i.e., contraception after intercourse) can reduce the likelihood of conception. There are two methods of emergency contraception. The "morning after" pill utilizes increased doses of certain oral contraceptives administered under a physician's supervision. It works best if taken within seventy-two hours of intercourse. A second method of emergency contraception is the insertion of a copper intrauterine device (IUD) within five to seven days after intercourse.

Source: Planned Parenthood Federation of America. "Emergency Contraception." http://www.plannedparenthood.org/ec/index.html. Accessed September 1, 2002.

Sterilization

Vermont Statutes

Title 18: Health

> Chapter 204: Sterilization
>
> Sections 8706 to 8710

It is the policy of the state of Vermont to allow voluntary and involuntary sterilizations of mentally retarded adults under circumstances which will ensure that the best interests and rights of such persons are fully protected. In accordance with this policy, no mentally retarded person, as defined by section 7101(12) of this title, may be sterilized without his or her consent unless there is a prior hearing in the superior court as provided in this chapter. No mentally retarded person under the age of eighteen may be sterilized. Sterilization is defined to mean a surgical procedure, the purpose of which is to render an individual incapable of procreating.

8706. Voluntary sterilization

Any mentally retarded person over the age of eighteen, who does not have either a guardian or protective services worker with the power to consent to nonemergency surgery, may obtain a voluntary sterilization subject to all of the following preconditions:

(1) the mentally retarded person has freely, voluntarily and without coercion, personally requested a physician to perform a sterilization; and

(2) the mentally retarded person has given informed consent to the sterilization in that:

(A) the physician has provided a complete explanation concerning: (i) the nature and irreversible consequences of a sterilization procedure, and (ii) the availability of alternative contraceptive measures;

(B) the physician is satisfied that the consent is based upon an understanding of that information and that before the operation is undertaken the physician personally obtains evidence of the person's retention of that understanding, not less than 10 days following the original explanation;

(C) the consent is in writing and signed by the mentally retarded person;

(3) the mentally retarded person has been informed and is aware that his consent may be withdrawn at any time prior to the operation;

(4) the physician has reviewed medical records and psychological assessments of the mentally retarded person.

8707. Competency to consent; procedure

(1) If the physician from whom the sterilization has been sought refuses to perform the sterilization because he is not satisfied that the mentally retarded person has the ability to give the informed consent

required by section 8706 of this title, the mentally retarded person may file a petition in superior court for a determination of the person's competency to consent to the sterilization.

(2) The petition shall set forth the information required by section 8709(b).

(3) Upon filing of the petition the court shall appoint a qualified mental retardation professional as defined in section 8821(8) of this title to examine the mentally retarded person and present evidence to the court as to that person's ability to give informed consent.

(4) The hearing shall be limited to a determination of the mentally retarded person's competency to consent to a sterilization, and shall be conducted in accordance with sections 8709(c), 8710, and 8711(a) and (b) of this title.

(5) If, after the hearing, the court determines on the basis of clear and convincing proof that the mentally retarded person is competent to consent and has given the required consent, it shall order that a voluntary sterilization may be performed.

(6) If the court determines that the mentally retarded person is not competent to give consent it shall inform the person that he has the right to petition the court for an involuntary sterilization pursuant to the requirements of section 8708 of this title.

8708. Involuntary sterilization

(a) Any sterilization sought on behalf of a mentally retarded person or requested by any person denied a voluntary sterilization by section 8707 of this title shall be considered an involuntary sterilization.

(b) Involuntary sterilizations may be performed only after a hearing in the superior court pursuant to sections 8709–8712 of this title. For the purposes of involuntary sterilization proceedings under this chapter, the mentally retarded person subject to a petition for sterilization shall be defined as the respondent.

8709. Petition and notice of hearing

(a) Any mentally retarded adult, his or her parent, private guardian, near relative, as defined in section 8821 of this title, or physician, may file a petition in the superior court alleging that the person is mentally retarded and in need of sterilization.

(b) The petition shall set forth:

(1) the name, age and residence of the person to be sterilized;

(2) the names and addresses of the petitioner and parents, guardians, spouse and nearest relative of said person;

(3) the mental condition of said person;

(4) a statement of said person's ability to give informed consent to the sterilization;

(5) said person's ability to pay for legal counsel;

(6) the relation of said person to the petitioner;

(7) the reasons and supporting facts why sterilization is in the best interest of said person.

(c) Upon filing of the petition the court shall fix a time and place for the hearing not more than 45 days from the receipt of the petition. Not less than 20 days prior to the date set for the hearing, the court shall cause petitioner to serve respondent with the petition and notice of hearing. The court shall also mail a copy of the petition and notice of the hearing to respondent's counsel, his legal guardian and nearest relative.

8710. Appointment of counsel

The respondent shall be represented by counsel throughout the proceeding. Upon filing of the petition the court shall notify the respondent that he shall be afforded the right to counsel. If the petition states that the respondent is unable to pay for counsel, the court shall appoint counsel to be paid by the state or set a hearing for a determination of respondent's ability to pay for counsel. The court may also require appointment of a guardian ad litem to represent the interest of the respondent. Counsel shall receive copies of the comprehensive evaluations required by section 8711(d) of this title and such other documents as may be received and issued by the court.

HIV and Pregnancy

The spread of the human immunodeficiency virus (HIV), the virus that causes acquired immune deficiency syndrome (AIDS), continues to be of major concern in the United States. HIV may be spread from mother to the fetus in utero, during delivery, and through breast milk. Table 5.1 provides information on the characteristics of HIV-infected women who gave birth in 1993, 1995, and 1996.

Sex Education

A nationwide public opinion poll released in October 2002 by the Sexuality Information and Education Council of the United States (SIECUS) found that lower-income parents overwhelmingly support classroom and home sex education instruction. Eighty-one percent of respondents favored sex education programs that teach young people about all aspects of sexuality,

Table 5.1 Characteristics of HIV-Infected Women Who Gave Birth[a]—
Selected States, 1993, 1995, and 1996

State	No.	(%)
Colorado	35	(2.9)
Indiana	47	(3.8)
Louisiana	301	(24.6)
Michigan	146	(11.9)
Missouri	103	(8.4)
New Jersey	368	(30.1)
South Carolina	222	(18.2)
Race/ethnicity		
Black	934	(76.4)
White	207	(16.9)
Hispanic	73	(6.0)
Asian/Pacific Islander	3	(0.2)
American Indian/Alaska Native	1	(0.1)
Unknown	4	(0.3)
Mode of exposure		
Heterosexual contact	619	(50.7)
Injection-drug use	345	(28.2)
Hemophilia/Transfusion	11	(0.9)
No risk reported	247	(20.2)
Age at delivery (yrs)		
Younger than 20	113	(9.2)
20–29	765	(62.7)
30–39	329	(26.9)
Older than 40	14	(1.1)
Clinical status before or during pregnancy		
HIV positive	945	(77.3)
AIDS: CD4 less than 200	145	(11.9)
AIDS: opportunistic illness	38	(3.1)
Unknown	94	(7.7)

Note: a. A total of 1,222 HIV-infected women accounted for 1,321 births. For women with more than one pregnancy, data reflect earliest pregnancy.

Source: Centers for Disease Control. May 11, 2001. *Mortality and Morbidity Weekly Report.* "Successful Implementation of Perinatal HIV Prevention Guidelines."

including birth control and protection against sexually transmitted diseases, over programs that are solely abstinence-based. There was some variation in responses by race, with African Americans responding slightly more favorably (85 percent), compared to whites (80 percent) and Hispanics (80 percent). Parents overwhelmingly acknowledged the importance of their own roles in discussing reproductive issues with their children, but 20 percent of parents with children aged thirteen to fourteen years and 11 percent of parents with children aged fifteen to eighteen years acknowledged that they had not discussed sexual issues with their children.

Source: SIECUS. "SIECUS Launches Ad-Campaign to Encourage Parents to Talk with Their Kids about Sex." http://www.siecus.org/media/press/press0029.html. Accessed on September 1, 2002.

Alcohol Use among Pregnant Women and Nonpregnant Women

Alcohol use among pregnant women may cause serious harm to the born child, including facial anomalies and mental retardation. Table 5.2 provides data on alcohol use by pregnant women and nonpregnant women, and Table 5.3 provides data on fetal alcohol syndrome.

Table 5.2 Estimated percentage[a] of pregnant and nonpregnant women aged 18–44 years who reported alcohol use, by selected characteristics—United States, 1995–1999

Characteristic	Any use						Binge drinking[b]						Frequent drinking[c]					
	Pregnant[d]			Nonpregnant[e]			Pregnant			Nonpregnant			Pregnant			Nonpregnant		
	%	OR[f]	CI[g]	%	OR	CI	%	OR	CI	%	OR	CI	%	OR	CI	%	OR	CI
Age (yrs)																		
18–30	11.8	0.6	(0.5–0.7)	54.1	1.1	(1.0–1.1)	2.2	0.6	(0.4–1.0)	15.5	1.7	(1.6–1.8)	2.7	0.6	(0.4–1.0)	17.3	1.4	(1.4–1.5)
31–44	16.8	1.0	Referent	52.3	1.0	Referent	3.0	1.0	Referent	8.1	1.0	Referent	3.5	1.0	Referent	10.8	1.0	Referent
Race																		
White	12.8	0.9	(0.7.1.1)	57.9	1.9	(1.8–1.9)	2.4	1.1	(0.6–2.2)	13.1	2.2	(2.0–2.4)	2.7	0.9	(0.5–1.7)	15.5	2.1	(1.9–2.2)
Nonwhite[h]	14.8	1.0	Referent	41.8	1.0	Referent	2.6	1.0	Referent	7.4	1.0	Referent	3.5	1.0	Referent	9.2	1.0	Referent
Education																		
<High school	9.8	1.0	Referent	33.6	1.0	Referent	2.2	1.0	Referent	9.3	1.0	Referent	2.8	1.0	Referent	10.3	1.0	Referent
≥High school	14.0	1.5	(1.0–2.3)	55.3	2.0	(1.8–2.1)	2.5	0.9	(0.4–2.0)	11.6	1.1	(1.0–1.2)	3.0	0.9	(0.5–1.9)	14.1	1.2	(1.1–1.4)
Employed																		
Yes	15.5	1.5	(1.1–1.9)	57.1	1.5	(1.5–1.6)	3.3	2.7	(1.4–5.3)	12.2	1.3	(1.2–1.4)	3.8	2.3	(1.3–4.1)	14.7	1.3	(1.2–1.4)
No	10.7	1.0	Referent	44.4	1.0	Referent	1.3	1.0	Referent	9.7	1.0	Referent	1.8	1.0	Referent	11.5	1.0	Referent
Married																		
Yes	11.2	1.0	Referent	50.3	1.0	Referent	1.7	1.0	Referent	7.3	1.0	Referent	2.0	1.0	Referent	9.3	1.0	Referent
No	20.1	2.3	(1.8–3.0)	56.6	1.4	(1.4–1.5)	4.8	3.7	(2.0–6.6)	16.5	2.3	(2.2–2.5)	5.9	3.6	(2.1–6.1)	19.1	2.3	(2.1–2.4)

a. Adjusted for age, race, education, employment, and marital status.
b. ≥ 5 drinks on one occasion.
c. ≥ 7 drinks/week or binge.
d. 1996 = 1,378, 1997 = 1,429, 1999 = 1,888.
e. 1996 = 29,149, 1997 = 33,694, 1999 = 38.603.
f. Odds ratio.
g. Confidence interval.
h. Includes Asian/Pacific Islander, American Indian/Alaska Native, black, and Hispanic.

Source: Centers for Disease Control. April 5, 2002. Morbidity and Mortality Weekly Report 51 (13): 273–276.

Table 5.3 Number and prevalence rate[a] of fetal alcohol syndrome cases, by race/ethnicity—Alaska, Arizona, Colorado[b], and New York[c], Fetal Alcohol Syndrome Surveillance Network, 1995–1997

Race/ethnicity[d]	Alaska			Arizona			Colorado			New York			Total		
	No. births	No. cases	Rate	No. births	No. cases	Rate	No. births	No. cases	Rate	No. births	No. cases	Rate	No. births	No. cases	Rate
White, non-Hispanic	19,007	6	0.3	114,851	15	0.1	63,653	11	0.2	68,932	18	0.3	266,443	49	0.2
Black	1,341	0	—	7,054	4	—[e]	5,508	5	0.9	13,455	21	1.6	27,358	30	1.1
Hispanic	1,287	0	—	80,626	16	0.2	21,579	8	0.4	3,635	0	—[e]	107,127	24	0.2
Asian/Pacific Islander	1,493	0	—	4,371	1	—[e]	2,556	0	—[e]	1,693	0	—	10,113	1	—[e]
AI/AN[f]	7,117	40	5.6	15,685	39	2.5	1,744	1	—[e]	627	1	—[e]	25,173	81	3.2
Other/unknown[g]	39	0	—	456	0	—	96	0	—	447	0	—	1,038	0	—
Total	30,284	45	1.5	223,043	75	0.3	95,136	25	0.3	88,789	40	0.4	437,252	185	0.4

a. Per 1,000 population.
b. Denver-Boulder Consolidated Metropolitan Statistical Area.
c. Nine counties in western New York.
d. Black includes black Hispanic and non-Hispanic; Hispanic excludes black Hispanic.
e. Rates were not calculated when the number of cases was < 5.
f. American Indian/Alaska Native.
g. Other non-Hispanic and unknown.

Source: Centers for Disease Control. May 24, 2002. Morbidity and Mortality Weekly Report 51 (20): 433–435.

6

Organizations and Governmental Agencies

This chapter provides information about organizations that are making important contributions to clinical research and policy development in the area of reproductive issues. In order to ensure accuracy, the entries were provided directly by the organizations or derived from their websites.

Alan Guttmacher Institute
120 Wall Street, 21st Floor
New York, NY 10005
(212) 248-1111
http://www.agi-usa.org

The Alan Guttmacher Institute (AGI) was founded in 1963 as the Center for Family Planning Program Development, a semiautonomous division of the Planned Parenthood Federation of America, and then was renamed in honor of Dr. Alan F. Guttmacher, an eminent obstetrician and gynecologist who served for more than a decade as president of Planned Parenthood. AGI became an independent, not-for-profit corporation in 1977. It seeks to advance sexual and reproductive health and rights in the United States and worldwide by conducting social science research, policy analysis, and public education to encourage enlightened public debate, promote sound policy and program development, and inform individual decision making. The institute works to ensure access to information and services that will enable people to avoid unplanned pregnancies; prevent sexually transmitted diseases, including human immunodeficiency virus (HIV); exercise their right to have an abortion; achieve healthy pregnancies and give birth; balance parenting with other roles; and have healthy, satisfying sexual relationships. It publishes several journals, including *Family Planning Perspectives, International Family Planning Perspectives,* and *The Guttmacher Report on Public Policy.*

American Association of Tissue Banks
1350 Beverly Road, Suite 220-A
McLean, VA 22101
(703) 827-9582; fax (703) 356-2198
http://www.aatb.org

The American Association of Tissue Banks (AATB) is a scientific, not-for-profit organization founded in 1976 to make available transplantable cells and tissues in quantities sufficient to meet national needs. The association publishes standards to help ensure that the conduct of tissue banks meets acceptable norms of technical and ethical performance, and specifies procedures to foster responsible approaches to recovery, processing, preservation, and distribution of transplantable tissue.

To maintain tissue banking at the highest level of quality, AATB works closely with officials of the U.S. Food and Drug Administration, engaging in an ongoing program of information exchange by sponsoring meetings, seminars, and workshops and publishing proceedings from these meetings, newsletters, and other educational material relevant to tissue banking. In addition, AATB supports promotional and educational programs that stimulate tissue donation and encourage efficiency and professionalism of tissue banking worldwide. It is designed to serve as a source of information and advice to individuals and organizations wishing to establish or expand banking activities and to speak for the industry as a whole.

American College of Obstetricians and Gynecologists
409 12th Street, SW
P.O. Box 96920
Washington, DC 20090-6920
(202) 863-5400
http://www.acog.org

Founded in 1951 in Chicago, Illinois, the American College of Obstetricians and Gynecologists (ACOG) today has over 41,000 members and is the nation's leading group of professionals providing health care for women. Now based in Washington, D.C., it is a private, voluntary, nonprofit membership organization. In 1951, ACOG created the specialty's first nationwide professional organization that was open to all qualified applicants. Today, board certification in obstetrics-gynecology is a requirement to become an ACOG fellow, and about 95 percent of obstetrician-gynecologists in the United States are affiliated with ACOG. Women comprise 36 percent of ACOG's total fellowship, and 64 percent of the junior fellows are women. ACOG members include both generalists and subspecialists, including maternal-fetal medicine specialists, gynecologic oncologists, and reproductive endocrinologists. A new subspecialty, urogynecology, was recently officially recognized.

ACOG currently advocates for quality health care for women, strives to maintain the highest standards of clinical practice and continuing education for its members, promotes patient education, stimulates patient understanding of and involvement in medical care, and increases awareness among its members and the public of the changing issues facing women's health care. It supports an extensive continuing medical educational program so that its fellows are current on the latest developments in the field.

The college also keeps its members informed about current medical care standards and its professional recommendations through publications including educational bulletins, committee opinions, and practice bulletins. ACOG also publishes *Obstetrics and Gynecology*, a monthly peer-reviewed scientific journal, *ACOG Clinical Review*, and *ACOG Today*, a monthly newsletter. To promote public education, ACOG publishes a variety of materials, including *Planning Your Pregnancy and Birth*, *Encyclopedia of Women's Health*, and *Managing Menopause Magazine*, in addition to more than 200 patient education pamphlets on aspects of women's health.

American Life League
P.O. Box 1350
Stafford, VA 22555
(540) 659-4171
http://www.all.org

The American Life League (ALL) seeks to serve God by building a society that protects innocent human life from fertilization to natural death. As a reflection of its association with the Catholic Church, ALL believes that, from a medical position, abortion can never be necessary to save the life of the mother. Both the mother and her baby are to be respected as human beings of inestimable worth and deserve equal protection. ALL opposes all forms of abortion and does not make exceptions for rape, incest, fetal deformity, or saving the life of the mother. It opposes sex education except for programs that lead children toward the practice of virtue while avoiding the subject of sex in any concrete, detailed, or descriptive way. ALL also opposes artificial birth control and stem cell research.

American Social Health Association
P.O. Box 13827
Research Triangle Park, NC 27709
(919) 361-8400; fax (919) 361-8425
http://www.ashastd.org
http://www.iwannaknow.org (for teens)

The American Social Health Association (ASHA) was founded in 1914 by Edward L. Keyes, Jr. He was recruited by Prince A. Morrow, then known as the father of social hygiene of New York, to serve as the secretary of Morrow's Society for Sanitary and Moral Prophylaxis. Morrow defined the movement and brought the problem of venereal disease into full public view in New York. As ASHA evolved and expanded, in 1960 staff decided to change the name to the American Social Health Association to reflect its expanded vision in the arena of sexually transmitted diseases (STDs). ASHA's mission is to communicate about the risks, prevention, screening, and treatment of STDs and their impact on community and family health. It advocates social change to promote responsible sexual behavior and improve public health. Today, ASHA delivers accurate, reliable sexual health information to millions of people worldwide via six national hotlines (STDs, HIV, immunization, cardiopulmonary resuscitation, herpes, and human papilloma virus), informative websites, responsive e-mail services, and a variety of educational programs.
    Summary provided by ASHA.

American Society for Reproductive Medicine
1209 Montgomery Highway
Birmingham, AL 35216-2809

(205) 978-5000; fax (205) 978-5005
http://www.asrm.org

The American Society for Reproductive Medicine (ASRM) is a voluntary, nonprofit organization devoted to advancing knowledge and expertise in reproductive medicine and biology. Members must demonstrate the high ethical principles of the medical profession, evince an interest in reproductive medicine and biology, and adhere to the objectives of the society. ASRM was founded by a small group of fertility experts who met in Chicago in 1944. Today, ASRM members reside in all 50 of the United States and in more than 100 other countries. The society is multidisciplinary, with members including obstetrician-gynecologists, urologists, reproductive endocrinologists, embryologists, mental health professionals, internists, nurses, practice administrators, laboratory technicians, pediatricians, research scientists, and veterinarians. The ASRM has an administrative office in Birmingham, Alabama, and a public affairs office in Washington, D.C.

Since 1950, ASRM has published *Fertility and Sterility*, as well as two newsletters, *ASRM News* and *Menopausal Medicine*. Ethical statements are published regularly by the society's Ethics Committee, and the ASRM Practice Committee has produced many reports in the form of guidelines, minimal standards, committee opinions, and technical and educational bulletins. Legislation and public policy are addressed by its Washington, D.C., Public Affairs Office.

Center for Reproductive Law and Policy
120 Wall Street
New York, NY 10005
(212) 637-3600; fax (212) 637-3666
http://www.crlp.org

The Center for Reproductive Law and Policy (CRLP) was founded in 1992 by nationally recognized reproductive rights attorneys and activists. It is a nonprofit legal advocacy organization dedicated to promoting and defending women's reproductive rights worldwide. To further that end, it supports laws and policies that allow women the freedom to decide whether and when to have children and to obtain access to basic health services, including contraception, abortion, education, and safe pregnancy care. CRLP is involved with legislation, litigation, public education, and research and policy analysis and has published an extensive list of books and reports. It is fully funded by supporters and accepts no government funding.

Center for Surrogate Parenting and Egg Donation
15821 Ventura Boulevard, Suite 675
Encino, CA 91436
(818) 788-8288; fax (818) 981-8287
http://www.creatingfamilies.com

The Center for Surrogate Parenting and Egg Donation (CSP) was founded in Beverly Hills, California, in 1986 as the Center for Surrogate Parenting by attorney William Handel. In 1994, it changed its name to the Center for Surrogate Parenting and Egg Donation. By 2002, CSP had closed its Beverly Hills office but had offices in Encino, California, and in Maryland. CSP offers four programs in assisted reproduction, including traditional surrogacy, in which the surrogate is artificially inseminated with the sperm of the intended father; gestational surrogacy, in which an embryo created from the sperm and egg of the biological parents is implanted in a surrogate; in vitro fertilization with egg donation, in which the sperm of the intended father is combined with the egg of a donor and then implanted in the uterus of a surrogate; and egg donation, in which the egg from a donor is fertilized by the intended father and implanted in the uterus of the intended mother. Fees in 2002 were as follows: traditional surrogacy, $61,975; gestational surrogacy, $66,975; in vitro fertilization and egg donation, $75,425; and egg donation, $8,450.

Council on Contemporary Families
208 East 51st Street, Suite 315
New York, NY 10022
(212) 969-8571; fax (212) 634-0376
http://www.contemporaryfamilies.org

The Council on Contemporary Families (CCF) was founded in 1997 as a nonprofit, nonpartisan organization of family researchers and practitioners desiring to promote informed discussion about changing families in the United States. Membership is open to specialists in family issues only. CCF seeks to educate the press and the general public about the complexities and nuances of contemporary family life and to get past simplistic generalizations about what family forms or values are "better" or "worse." In its view, a more appropriate research question at this time is, "what do we know about the strengths and weaknesses of today's families and their social support networks, and how can we help all types of families build on their strengths and minimize their weaknesses?" CCF holds an annual conference each spring in New York, where both researchers and practitioners exchange information and present recent findings in their fields of expertise. CCF also maintains a listserve for members and regularly provides reporters and policymakers with updates and briefings on family issues.

Summary provided by the Council on Contemporary Families.

EngenderHealth
440 Ninth Avenue
New York, NY 10001
(212) 561-8000; fax (212) 561-8067
www.engenderhealth.org

Founded in 1943, EngenderHealth (formerly the Association for Voluntary Surgical Contraception International) is an international nonprofit agency that works worldwide to support and strengthen reproductive health services for women and men and provides technical assistance, training, and information in the areas of family planning; maternal and child health; sexually transmitted infections, HIV, and acquired immunodeficiency syndrome (AIDS); quality improvement; infection prevention; and men as partners. EngenderHealth publishes a wide range of materials, including training curricula, clinical guidelines, instructional videos, brochures, working papers, articles, and online information. The publications provide guidance to field programs and are frequently cited as authoritative sources.

Family Care International
588 Broadway, Suite 503
New York, NY 10012
(212) 941-5300; fax (212) 941-5563
http://www.familycareintl.org

Family Care International (FCI) was founded in 1986 as an independent nonprofit organization that strives to improve women's sexual and reproductive health and rights, with a special emphasis on making pregnancy and childbirth safer. FCI works to advance a comprehensive, women-centered approach to reproductive health, which has been endorsed by almost every country in the world at United Nations conferences since the early 1990s. FCI addresses a range of urgent health issues, including maternal health, adolescent sexual and reproductive health, family planning, unsafe abortion, and violence against women. FCI conducts global advocacy and information sharing; provides technical assistance in Africa (in both English- and French-speaking countries), Latin America, and the Caribbean; and develops guidelines, training materials, and other information tools.

FCI has published more than forty documents in print, CD-ROM, and video formats, including manuals for health education and behavioral change communication and resources for sexual and reproductive health and rights advocacy. FCI also serves as the global secretariat for the Inter-Agency Group for Safe Motherhood (IAG), a consortium of United Nations agencies and nongovernmental organizations working to improve maternal and newborn survival and well-being by promoting and supporting the implementation of cost-effective safe motherhood interventions in the developing world. The IAG carries out policy support and disseminates best practices and other information among policymakers, program managers, and other stakeholders worldwide. IAG's website can be viewed at www.safemotherhood.org.

Feminist Majority Foundation
1600 Wilson Boulevard, Suite 801
Arlington, VA 22209
(703) 522-2214; fax (703) 522-2219
http://www.feminist.org

The Feminist Majority Foundation (FMF), founded in 1987, is dedicated to fostering women's equality, reproductive health, and nonviolence. Its goal is to advance the legal, social, and political equality of women and to train young feminists for future leadership roles in the feminist movement in the United States. To carry out these aims, FMF engages in research and public policy development, develops public educationand leadership training programs, and organizes grassroots projects and forums on issues of women's equality and empowerment. Its sister organization, the Feminist Majority, engages in lobbying and other direct political action, pursuing equality between women and men through legislative avenues. FMF maintains a comprehensive website devoted to women's issues, especially reproductive issues, and provides excellent web links to other organizations.

Feminists for Life
733 15th Street, NW, Suite 1100
Washington, DC 20005
(202) 737-3352; fax (202) 737-0414
http://www.feministsforlife.org

Established in 1972, Feminists for Life (FFL) is a nonprofit, nonsectarian, nonpartisan, grassroots organization that seeks equality for all human beings and champions the needs of women. It opposes all forms of violence, including abortion, infanticide, child abuse, domestic violence, assisted suicide, euthanasia, and capital punishment, and the exploitation of women and children, because they are inconsistent with the core feminist principles of justice, nonviolence, and nondiscrimination. FFL's efforts focus on facilitating practical resources and support for women in need, as well as sharing its prowoman, prolife legacy. Its publications include the quarterly journal, *The American Feminist* (formerly called *Sisterlife*), and several brochures.

Ford Foundation
210 East 43rd Street
New York, NY 10017
(212) 573-5000; fax (212) 351-3677
http://www.fordfound.org

An independent, nonprofit, nongovernmental organization, the Ford Foundation was founded in 1936 as a local philanthropical agency in Michigan and has operated for more than fifty years as a national and international foundation. It works to strengthen democratic values, reduce poverty and injustice, enhance international cooperation, and advance human achievement. Twelve of the foundation's fourteen offices in the United States and overseas support work in sexuality and reproductive health. The foundation publishes a quarterly magazine, *Ford Foundation Report*, and other publications related to individual programs and areas of grant making.

Global Reproductive Health Forum
Harvard School of Public Health
Department of Population and International Health

665 Huntington Avenue
Boston, MA 02115
(617) 432-4619
http://www.hsph.harvard.edu/organizations/healthnet

Begun in 1998, the Global Reproductive Health Forum at Harvard encourages the proliferation of critical discussions about reproductive health, reproductive technologies, reproductive rights, and gender. It offers interactive electronic forums, worldwide Internet discussions, and access to reproductive health and rights materials through an extensive collection of online information as well as an up-to-date research library. The site was specifically designed to involve and meet the needs of underserved groups globally, the reproductive health community internationally, academics, and all people who are interested in the field of reproductive health. The site is currently available in English and Spanish.

Human Cloning Foundation
1100 Hammond Drive, Suite 410A
Atlanta, GA 30328
(404) 255-1439
http://www.humancloning.org

The Human Cloning Foundation (HCF) was established in February 1998 as a volunteer nonprofit organization whose sole purpose is to promote all aspects of human cloning and other forms of biotechnology. Members of HCF have confidence that blood and organs can be cloned and that infertility and cancer can be cured with the use of this new technology. HCF currently distributes information over the Internet only, via its website, message boards, and chat rooms. Access to published essays and a variety of educational programs about human cloning and other forms of biotechnology is available through a complimentary resource exchange. HCF also operates a subscription Internet mailing list at no cost that contains a summary of the most recent developments and information regarding human cloning. Any donations to the Human Cloning Foundation are currently focused on funding research into reproductive human cloning for therapeutic purposes, in the hope of someday allowing infertile couples to conceive a genetically related child. Upcoming organizational plans include an annual international conference on human cloning technology.

International Confederation of Midwives
Eisenhowerlaan 138
2517 KN The Hague
The Netherlands
+31-070-3060520; fax +31-070-3555651
http://www.internationalmidwives.org

The International Confederation of Midwives (ICM), founded in 1919, advances globally the aims and aspirations of midwives in the attainment of improved outcomes for women in their child-bearing years, their newborns, and their families wherever they reside, with a specific goal of reducing rates of maternal and neonatal mortality and morbidity. Its goal is to develop the role of the midwife as a practitioner in her own right, and it also supports and advises associations of midwives in liaison with their governments. It represents midwifery to international bodies and agencies in meetings, consultations, and direct relationships with heads or governing bodies of such organizations. ICM is currently based in Africa, Asia-Pacific, the Americas, and Europe and is the only international midwifery organization with an official relationship with the United Nations. All members of the confederation are either independent organizations of midwives or midwives' groups within other organizations, providing that the group is autonomous.

Position statements are available on topics of clinical and professional interest to midwives, as are full reports on the proceedings and outcomes of international meetings. The ICM's newsletter, *International Midwifery*, is sent free of charge to all member associations. Individual subscriptions are welcomed.

International Federation of Gynecology and Obstetrics
70 Wimpole Street
London W1G 8AX, United Kingdom
+44-20-7224-3279; fax +44-20-7935-0736
http://www.figo.org

Established in Switzerland in 1954 as the Fédération Internationale de Gynécologie et d'Obstétrique (FIGO), the International Federation of Gynecology and Obstetrics is the only global organization of obstetricians and gynecologists. FIGO's mission is to promote the well-being of women and to raise the standard of practice in obstetrics and gynecology. With affiliates in more than 102 countries, FIGO is uniquely capable of linking highly skilled professionals in the developed world with their less experienced counterparts in other countries.

As part of its ongoing commitment to improving the health and well-being of women and their children around the world, the federation organizes the triennial World Congress of Gynecology and Obstetrics, international workshops, fellowships, and visiting professorship programs. FIGO also publishes the monthly peer-reviewed *International Journal of Gynecology and Obstetrics* and the triennial *Report on Gynecological Cancer*, which provides comparability between therapeutic statistics to offer a reliable evaluation of the different methods of treatment used.

Summary provided by FIGO.

International Women's Health Coalition
24 East 21st Street
New York, NY 10010
(212) 979-8500; fax (212) 979-9009
http://www.iwhc.org

Founded in 1984 by Joan Dunlop and Adrienne Germain, the nonprofit organization International Women's Health Coalition (IWHC) bases its activities on the principle that global well-being and social and economic justice can only be achieved by ensuring women's rights. IWHC is committed to three main goals: comprehensive sexuality education and services for adolescents, worldwide access to safe abortion, and expansion of sexual rights for women and girls. IWHC provides technical and financial support to local organizations and networks in Africa, Asia, and Latin America that work to promote these rights. As a result of IWHC's support, many of these organizations have become strong forces in their communities and influential players in regional and international policymaking. IWHC also advocates directly for women's health and rights on an international level. First, it informs public debate in the United States and abroad through its multilingual publications, media involvement, website, and videos. Second, it collaborates with UN agencies, donor governments, and private foundations on health sector reform and global health initiatives. And third, it participates in major UN conferences on health, population, women, and children. IWHC publishes articles, reports, fact sheets, and bibliographies on a variety of topics related to women's and girls' health and rights. For a complete list of

IWHC's publications, visit http://www.iwhc.org/index.cfm?
fuseaction=page&pageID=4.

March of Dimes
1275 Mamaroneck Avenue
White Plains, NY 10605
(888) 663-4637; fax (914) 997-4763
http://www.modimes.org

The March of Dimes was originally established as the National
Foundation for Infantile Paralysis in 1938 by President Franklin
Delano Roosevelt for the purpose of fighting polio, a disease that
afflicted the president. As part of an early fundraiser, the public
was asked to send dimes to the White House, and later, the foundation changed its name to the March of Dimes. It initially
focused on the eradication of polio by funding the research of Dr.
Jonas Salk, who by 1955 had developed the first vaccine against
polio. Having conquered polio, the March of Dimes began a crusade to prevent birth defects. Its current mission is to improve the
health of babies by preventing birth defects and infant mortality
through programs of research, community services, education,
and advocacy. In 2001, it provided more than $26.5 million to
fund scientific research to prevent birth defects.

NARAL Pro-Choice America
1156 15th Street, NW, Suite 700
Washington, DC 20005
(202) 973-3000; fax (202) 973-3030
http://www.naral.org; http://www.fight4choice.com

NARAL (National Abortion and Reproductive Rights Action
League) Pro-Choice America was originally founded in 1969 as
the National Association for the Repeal of Abortion Laws. The
name was changed in 1973 to the National Abortion Rights
Action League to reflect the Supreme Court's historic decision
legalizing abortion in *Roe v. Wade*. The name was again changed
in 1996 to the National Abortion and Reproductive Rights Action
League (still with the same acronym, NARAL) to reflect its
expanded mission that all women must have the right to make
personal decisions regarding the full range of reproductive
choices. NARAL Pro-Choice America also works to elect prochoice candidates to ensure that the right to choose is protected
for future generations.

NARAL Pro-Choice America's work is divided among three organizations: NARAL, Inc., a nonprofit organization whose mission is to develop and sustain a constituency that uses the political process to guarantee every woman the right to make personal decisions regarding the full range of reproductive choices, including preventing unintended pregnancy, bearing healthy children, and choosing legal abortion; NARAL-PAC, a political action committee that works to elect prochoice officials; and the NARAL Foundation, a charitable organization that has the same goals as NARAL, Inc. NARAL Pro-Choice America also produces several publications, including the annual *Who Decides? A State-by-State Review of Abortion and Reproductive Rights,* and countless fact sheets discussing issues pertaining to reproductive rights.

National Abortion Federation
1755 Massachusetts Avenue, NW, Suite 600
Washington, DC 20036
(202) 667-5881; fax (202) 667-5890
http://www.prochoice.org; http://www.earlyoptions.org;
http//www.supremecourtwatch.org; http://www.cliniciansforchoice.org

The National Abortion Federation (NAF), founded in 1977, is the professional association for abortion providers in the United States and Canada and is a nonprofit organization whose mission is to keep abortion safe, legal, and accessible. NAF serves those who make reproductive choice a reality: the physicians, nurses, counselors, administrators, and other staff members at nonprofit, proprietary, independent, and Planned Parenthood clinics, and private physicians' offices providing abortion services. It provides a full range of membership services to support abortion clinics, their staffs, and their patients and is North America's only fully accredited continuing medical education resource for abortion-specific programs in both medical and surgical abortion. Its programs include a national toll-free abortion information and referral hotline; Clinicians for Choice, a grassroots program for prochoice midwives, nurse practitioners, and physician assistants; a residency training initiative to encourage abortion training in medical residency programs throughout the United States; active state and federal public policy advocacy for abortion rights; and clinic defense and security programs. NAF offers many clinical, professional, and consumer education publications on the topic of abortion, including *A Clinician's Guide to Medical and Surgical Abortion,* a textbook published in 1999.

National Advocates for Pregnant Women
45 West 10th Street, 3F
New York, NY 10011
(212) 921-7421
http://www.advocatesforpregnantwomen.org

National Advocates for Pregnant Women (NAPW) is a nonprofit organization dedicated to protecting the rights of pregnant women and mothers. It opposes the prosecution and incarceration of women who use illegal drugs during pregnancy and believes that substance abuse among pregnant women and mothers be viewed as a public health issue. Treating substance abuse during pregnancy as a crime undermines the health of both women and children and targets vulnerable, low-income women of color. NAPW works through litigation, public education, grassroots organizing, and direct support to affected women. Its website includes valuable information on the status of current and past litigation.

National Center for HIV, STD, and TB Prevention
Centers for Disease Control and Prevention
1600 Clifton Road, NE
Atlanta, GA 30333
(888) CDC-FACT (FAXBACK)
http://www.cdc.gov/nchstp/od/nchstp.html

The National Center for HIV, STD, and TB Prevention (NCHSTP) was established in 1995 as part of the Centers for Disease Control and Prevention (CDC), under the agency of the U.S. Department of Health and Human Services. NCHSTP assumes responsibility for public health surveillance, prevention research, and programs to prevent and control human immunodeficiency virus (HIV) infection and acquired immunodeficiency syndrome (AIDS), other sexually transmitted diseases (STDs), and tuberculosis (TB). The NCHSTP staff work in collaboration with international and domestic governmental and nongovernmental partners, as well as the general public, in all areas of research, surveillance, technical assistance, and evaluation. The CDC National Prevention Information Network (NPIN) is available through the NCHSTP website as a reference, referral, and distribution service for information on HIV/AIDS, STDs, and tuberculosis (TB). To accomplish its mission, NPIN offers searchable databases, reference and referral services, resource and training centers, free fax services, and a resource service for business and labor groups. A list of consumer health information fact sheets is available online, some in more than thirty languages, and most may be viewed in both PDF and HTML formats.

National Center on Birth Defects and Developmental Disabilities
Centers for Disease Control and Prevention
1600 Clifton Road
Atlanta, GA 30333
(404) 488-7150
http://www.cdc.gov/ncbddd/default.htm

The National Center on Birth Defects and Developmental Disabilities at the Centers for Disease Control and Prevention seeks to promote optimal fetal, infant, and child development; prevent birth defects and childhood developmental disabilities; and enhance the quality of life and prevent secondary conditions among children, adolescents, and adults who are living with a disability. The Centers for Birth Defects Research and Prevention are conducting the largest study of the causes of birth defects ever undertaken, the National Birth Defects Prevention Study (NBDPS). The collaborative study, currently in its fifth year, is being conducted by each of the seven centers, using the same protocol so that the data can be combined. The National Birth Defects Prevention Network, an independent organization formed and supported by NCBDDD, continues to expand its ability to influence both the quality and quantity of birth defects monitoring data. During fiscal year 2001, the network finalized the *Congenital Malformations Surveillance Report* for 2000, a state-based surveillance report with birth defects data from thirty states. The center also administers the Fetal Alcohol Syndrome Program.

National Coalition of Abortion Providers
206 King Street
Alexandria, VA 22314
(703) 684-0055; fax (703) 684-5051
http://www.ncap.com

The National Coalition of Abortion Providers (NCAP) is a non-profit organization founded in 1990 to represent abortion providers. In 2002, it represented more than 150 providers. It was originally formed to lobby in Washington, D.C., and now has expanded its services to include trade association functions such as negotiation of supplies, malpractice insurance, pathology services, and advertising. It has published a number of position papers, and its website provides a list of abortion providers as well as a pregnancy options workbook to assist women in their decision making regarding abortion.

National Human Genome Research Institute
9 Memorial Drive, Room B1E10
Bethesda, MD 20892
(301) 402-1770
http://www.nhgri.nih.gov/

The National Human Genome Research Institute (NHGRI) was originally established in 1989 as the National Center for Human Genome Research. Its mission is to head the Human Genome Project, a research project to identify and map the genes in human DNA, for the National Institutes of Health (NIH). NHGRI is one of twenty-four institutes, centers, or divisions that make up the National Institutes of Health, the federal government's primary agency for the support of biomedical research. The collective research components of the NIH, which is part of the U.S. Department of Health and Human Services, make up the largest biomedical research facility in the world.

National Right to Life Committee
512 10th Street, NW
Washington, DC 20004
(202) 626-8800
http://www.nrlc.org

The National Right to Life Committee (NRLC) was founded in 1973 in response to *Roe v. Wade.* It is a nonsectarian, nonpartisan organization with more than 3,000 chapters in all fifty states and the District of Columbia. The NRLC Board of Directors consists of a director from each state, an internally elected nine-member executive committee and officers, and three at-large board positions. NRLC publishes a monthly newspaper, the *National Right to Life News,* and has a political action committee and educational trust fund.

The NRLC aims to restore legal protection to innocent human life. The primary interest of the committee and its members has been the abortion controversy; however, it is also concerned about other matters of medical ethics relating to the right to life, including euthanasia and infanticide. In addition to maintaining a lobbying presence at the federal level, NRLC serves as a clearinghouse of information for its state and local chapters, its individual members, the press, and the public.

Pacific Institute for Women's Health
3450 Wilshire Blvd., Suite 1000
Los Angeles, CA 90010
(213) 386-2600; fax (213) 386-2664
http://www.piwh.org

The Pacific Institute for Women's Health was founded in 1993 under the umbrella of the Western Consortium for Public Health and became an independent nonprofit organization in 1999. The institute works to improve the sexual and reproductive health of women and girls, locally and globally, by emphasizing access to contraception and safe abortion and reduction of unsafe abortion; prevention of sexually transmitted infections, including HIV/AIDS; and reduction of gender-based violence. The institute fosters collaboration and coalition building among activists, practitioners, researchers, and policymakers, both in the United States and internationally. In addition, the institute strives to enhance the organizational capacity of women's nongovernmental organizations internationally by making small grants to its partners. Programs are currently in operation throughout Latin America, Southeast Asia, sub-Saharan Africa, and California. All the institute's work is based on the conviction that women's health is a human right.

Planned Parenthood Federation of America
810 Seventh Avenue
New York, NY 10019
(212) 541-7800; fax (212) 245-1845
http://www.plannedparenthood.org

The Planned Parenthood Federation of America (PPFA) is a not-for-profit organization founded by Margaret Sanger in 1916 as the first birth control clinic in the United States. It provides comprehensive reproductive health care services, advocates for public policies that guarantee reproductive rights and access to reproductive services, provides educational programs on human sexuality, and promotes research in reproductive health care. PPFA also addresses family planning needs in developing countries through a variety of international programs and through its membership in the International Planned Parenthood Federation. PPFA has offices in New York, San Francisco, Chicago, and Washington, D.C., and has affiliations with 875 health centers in forty-eight states and the District of Columbia. Its website offers a wealth of information on the history and current status of reproductive policy in the United States, provides contraception and abortion information, including locations of providers, and has a special page for teenagers.

Population Action International
1300 19th Street, NW, 2nd Floor
Washington, DC 20036
(202) 557-3400; fax (202) 728-4177
http://www.populationaction.org

Population Action International (PAI) is an independent policy advocacy group working to strengthen political and financial support worldwide for population programs grounded in individual rights. It was established in 1965 as the Population Crisis Committee and changed its name in 1993. A nonprofit organization that accepts no government funds, PAI is committed to advancing universal access to family planning and related health services and to educational and economic opportunities, especially for girls and women. PAI fosters the development of U.S. and international policy on population and reproductive health issues through an integrated program of research. Serving as a bridge between the academic and policymaking communities, PAI seeks to make clear the linkages between population, reproductive health, the environment, and development. PAI shares its findings through the dissemination of publications, participation in and sponsoring of events, and other efforts to educate and inform policymakers and the general public about population issues. PAI publications include fact sheets, wall charts, brochures, and small books on such topics as strategies for improving the quality of and access to reproductive health care, financial resource flows for reproductive health programs, the impacts of population growth and consumption patterns on the environment, and other aspects of human security and sustainable economic development.

Population Council
1 Dag Hammarskjold Plaza
New York, NY 10017-2201
(212) 339-0500; fax (212) 755-6052
http://www.popcouncil.org

The Population Council is an international, nonprofit institution that conducts biomedical, social science, and public health research. It was established in 1952 by John D. Rockefeller III to improve the world's understanding of problems relating to population.

The Population Council researches services and products to meet people's reproductive health needs, designs interventions to treat and prevent HIV/AIDS and other sexually transmitted diseases, studies the effects of population factors on a country's ability to provide a better life for its citizens, and investigates the influence of education and job opportunities on young girls and women. It is also concerned with the reproductive health and well-being of the 1 billion adolescents in the developing world who are about to enter their reproductive years and whose behavior will shape their countries' futures.

The council's headquarters and Center for Biomedical Research (CBR) are both located in New York City. It also has an office in Washington, D.C., that manages global programs to improve reproductive health and prevent the spread of sexually transmitted infections. Half the staff of nearly 600 people is based in developing countries. The council has five regional offices and nineteen country offices and does work in more than fifty countries.

Program for Appropriate Technology in Health
1455 NW Leary Way
Seattle, WA 98107
(206) 285-3500; fax (206) 285-6619
http://www.path.org

The Program for Appropriate Technology in Health (PATH) is an international, nonprofit organization dedicated to creating new technologies and interventions to improve health, especially the health of women and children. Since 1977, PATH has managed more than 1,000 projects in 120 countries, directly benefiting people, communities, and countries with limited health resources. PATH's programs cover the following areas: reproductive health; HIV/AIDS; adolescent health; gender, violence, and human rights; technology solutions; maternal and child health and nutrition; a children's vaccine program; a malaria vaccine initiative; and the meningitis vaccine project. The staff for these programs work in partnership with PATH's country programs, which are based in Cambodia, France, India, Indonesia, Kenya, Latin America and the Caribbean, Philippines, Senegal, Thailand, Uganda, Ukraine, and Vietnam. PATH also has its headquarters in Seattle and an office in Washington, D.C.

PATH produces a range of publications and websites that provide information for readers in developing countries and low-resource settings. PATH's Reproductive Health Outlook (RHO) website (http://www.rho.org), for example, covers twelve reproductive health topics. *Outlook,* PATH's quarterly reproductive health publication, is currently in its twentieth year of publication and is produced in up to seven languages. *Outlook* and additional materials produced by PATH can be accessed from the PATH website and from PATH's Children's Vaccine Project website (http://www.childrensvaccine.org).

Sexuality Information and Education Council of the United States
130 West 42nd Street, Suite 350
New York, NY 10036
(212) 819-9770; fax (212) 819-9776
http://www.siecus.org

Founded in 1964, the Sexuality Information and Education Council of the United States (SIECUS) is an independent not-for-profit organization that promotes comprehensive sexuality education for people of all ages and seeks to protect the rights of individuals to make responsible choices about their sex lives and reproduction. Because it holds that sexuality is a natural and healthy part of living, SIECUS develops, collects, and disseminates information; promotes comprehensive education about sexuality; and advocates for the right of individuals to make responsible sexual choices.

SIECUS's programs include the State and Community Advocacy Project; the Family Project; the School Health Project; the Youth Development Project; the International Program; and the Mary S. Calderone Library. Through these and other programs, SIECUS meets the need for sexuality information and education among young people, parents, educators, school boards, community leaders, policymakers, and health professionals. It advocates for federal and state policies that support comprehensive sexuality education and access to reproductive health care, and it partners with nongovernmental organizations overseas to help develop their sexuality education and reproductive health programs. SIECUS provides many publications, including the bimonthly *SIECUS Report*, a leading journal on sexuality issues; *Guidelines for Comprehensive Sexuality Education: Kindergarten–12th Grade*; the *Families Are Talking Quarterly* newsletter; *Innovative Approaches to Increase Parent-Child Communication about Sexuality*; the *State and Community Action Kit*; *Toward a Sexually Healthy America: Roadblocks Imposed by the Federal Government's Abstinence-Only-until-Marriage Education Program*; and *Making the Connection: Sexuality and Reproductive Health*.

South Carolina Advocates for Pregnant Women
164-D Market Street
Charleston, SC 29401-1984
(843) 579-0637
http://www.scapw.org

South Carolina Advocates for Pregnant Women (SCAPW) was established in 1999 to fight punitive policies and attitudes directed at pregnant and parenting drug-addicted women. Although many states criminalize drug use during pregnancy, South Carolina has the most punitive policy in the United States. SCAPW is a state-based nonprofit organization. Its mission is to decriminalize pregnancy, ensure access to abortion and other reproductive services, and ensure that substance abuse and other health problems that women face during pregnancy are treated through the health care system, not the criminal justice system. SCAPW uses public education, community organizing, advocacy, and litigation to bring about change in personal attitudes, thereby affecting health care policy. It believes that the road to treatment for drug addiction should be through health care, not the criminal justice system.

7

Print and Nonprint Resources

Books

Albury, Rebecca M. *The Politics of Reproduction.* Crows Nest, Australia: Allen and Unwin, 1999. 210 pages.

Albury provides an Australian feminist perspective on the politics of reproduction. The emphasis is on a woman's body as her own, sexual politics, choices about abortion and contraception, and issues of medicalized childbirth and technologies of gender. Albury draws on the experience of younger and older women and looks at the changing ways in which women negotiate fertility, contraception, abortion, assisted reproduction, adoption, and motherhood. She examines how the media, the medical profession, public policy, and the law constrain women's experiences.

Andrews, Lori B. *Future Perfect.* New York: Columbia University Press, 2001. 288 pages.

Andrews provides an analysis of the impact of human genetics on our lives and institutions. She presents several competing models for genetic policy (the medical model, the public health model, and the fundamental rights model) and shows how one's choice among these models will determines his or her decisions about genetic intervention. Andrews asks questions such as the following: Who should have access to these techniques? Should genetic interventions be used to enhance characteristics? and Should gene therapy be undertaken on embryos?

Baer, Judith A., ed. *Historical and Multicultural Encyclopedia of Women's Reproductive Rights in the United States.* Westport, CT: Greenwood Press, 2002. 238 pages.

Baer's book offers comprehensive coverage of issues, laws, court cases, technological advances, and prominent persons as they relate to reproductive rights, primarily in the United States. Entries representing racial and ethnic groups' experiences figure prominently, as do the effects of age, class, education, health, religion, and sexual preference on childbearing and child rearing. The pieces, which vary considerably in length and detail, are written by scholars from a wide range of disciplines.

Blank, Robert. *Regulating Reproduction.* New York: Columbia University Press, 1990. 269 pages.

In this comprehensive review of assisted reproductive techniques and the policy dilemmas that accompany them, Blank argues that rather than focus on a particular technique, we must look at their cumulative impact on social values and the way we view our fellow humans. The book attempts to provide a context within which to frame a reasonable public policy regarding reproductive technology and provides a useful review of policies in other countries. It is well written in language appropriate for both the clinical and nonclinical reader.

———. *Fertility Control: New Techniques, New Policy Issues.* Westport, CT: Greenwood Press, 1991. 164 pages.

Beginning with the eugenics movement of the early twentieth century, Blank provides an overview of contraception and sterilization policy in the United States. He examines in detail the legal context of voluntary and involuntary sterilization and contemporary issues in fertility control, including the debate over long-term subdermal implants such as Norplant and the abortion drug RU-486.

———. *Mother and Fetus: Changing Notions of Maternal Responsibility.* Westport, CT: Greenwood Press, 1992. 207 pages.

Blank focuses on the changing relationship between the pregnant woman and the fetus brought about by new technologies in assisted reproduction, prenatal screening and diagnosis, fetal surgery, and knowledge about the impact of maternal behavior on the health of the fetus. He examines the legal and public policy consequences of pregnancy in light of these changes, including torts for wrongful birth, fetal protection laws against workplace hazards, suits for prenatal injury, and criminal sanctions for maternal actions.

Blank, Robert, and Janna C. Merrick. *Human Reproduction, Emerging Technologies, and Conflicting Rights.* Washington, DC: Congressional Quarterly Press, 1995. 269 pages.

This book provides comprehensive coverage of policy issues related to human reproduction. The authors use a "rights" framework that focuses on both positive and negative rights. They include a right not to have children, a right to have children, and a right to make decisions concerning the quality and quantity of children. The text is highly readable, and the coverage is comprehensive.

Bonnicksen, Andrea L. *In Vitro Fertilization: Building Policy from Laboratories to Legislatures.* New York: Columbia University Press, 1999. 194 pages.

Bonnicksen provides a classic analysis of the early history of the practice and policies surrounding in vitro fertilization (IVF) in the United States. She suggests that public policy cannot be set until the practices of IVF in the clinical setting are better understood. This book is a good case study of the developing rights to reproduction assistance technology of infertile persons and other potential consumers of these services.

————. *Crafting a Cloning Policy: From Dolly to Stem Cells.* Washington, DC: Georgetown University Press, 2002. 232 pages.

Bonnicksen examines the political reaction to the science of cloning and the efforts to construct a cloning policy. She traces the various legislative and bureaucratic efforts at the federal and state levels to oversee this new area of research and demonstrates why it is so politically explosive. She also looks more briefly at the issues surrounding the related area of stem cell research.

Boston Women's Health Book Collective. *Our Bodies, Ourselves.* New York: Simon and Schuster, 1998.

Now in its third edition, *Our Bodies, Ourselves* is a comprehensive approach to women's health care, particularly women's reproductive health care. It includes such wide-ranging topics as substance use, emotional well-being, sexual orientation and identity, sexually transmitted diseases, childbearing, and menopause. It also provides information on symptoms of illness, conventional medical treatments, and alternative treatments.

Burfoot, Annette, ed. *Encyclopedia of Reproductive Technologies.* Boulder, CO: Westview, 1999. 404 pages.

The seventy chapters of this anthology provide a comprehensive review of a wide range of issues associated with reproduction and reproductive technology. Some chapters focus on philosophy, some on public policy, and some on clinical issues. Although the title references "technologies," some of the entries address nontechnological issues like breastfeeding, female circumcision, and so on.

Chadwick, Ruth, ed. *The Concise Encyclopedia of the Ethics of New Technologies.* San Diego, CA: Academic Press, 2001. 404 pages.

This edited book contains longer pieces written by experts across a range of areas, including contraceptive technology, cloning, embryology, fetal research, gene therapy, genetic screening, and reproductive technologies. It is designed for readers who want more details on the ethical arguments and dimensions of these issues.

Craig, Barbara Hinkson, and David M. O'Brien. *Abortion and American Politics.* Chatham, NJ: Chatham House Publishers, 1993. 382 pages.

Craig and O'Brien provide a comprehensive analysis of the history of abortion policymaking with special emphasis on the formation and activities of prochoice and prolife interest groups.

Daniels, Ken, and Erica Haimes, eds. *Donor Insemination: International Social Science Perspectives.* Cambridge: Cambridge University Press, 1998. 185 pages.

The editors provide a strong collection of chapters focusing on donor insemination and written by international scholars from a variety of fields. The volume considers a variety of perspectives, including those of the semen providers, the medical community, policymakers, and the children and families created through donor insemination. It also includes an overview of international regulatory context.

Gosden, Roger. *Designing Babies: The Brave New World of Reproductive Technology.* New York: W. H. Freeman, 1999. 260 pages.

Gosden provides a sophisticated and internationally based analysis of reproductive technology. With a scientific background as an eminent international reproductive research pioneer (having completed postdoctoral work with Robert Edwards, the English physiologist who developed in vitro fertilization techniques, and now serving as scientific director at the Jones Institute for Reproductive Medicine) and a strong grounding in classical literature, Gosden interweaves an analysis of the ethical, policy, and clinical challenges of major reproductive technologies, including in vitro fertilization, cloning, embryo diagnosis and selection, surrogacy, and so forth.

McFarlane, Deborah R., and Kenneth J. Meier. *The Politics of Fertility Control: Family Planning and Abortion Policies in the American States.* New York: Chatham House, 2001. 197 pages.

McFarlane and Meier examine fertility control policy in the United States by taking a policy approach to analyzing abortion and contraception.

McGee, Glenn. *The Perfect Baby: Parenthood in the New World of Cloning and Genetics.* Lanham, MD: Rowman and Littlefield, 2000. 153 pages.

The Perfect Baby focuses on cloning and genetic engineering and analyzes their impact on society, parenthood, and the family. McGee cautions that genetic alterations may not have the impact on these "altered persons" that one might think because social institutions like churches and schools have more immediate impact.

Peters, Ted. *For the Love of Children: Genetic Technology and the Future of the Family.* Louisville, KY: Westminster John Knox Press, 1996. 227 pages.

Peters's analysis of reproductive technology centers on Christian theology and focuses on the needs and well-being of children. He supports various forms of assisted reproduction with the understanding that all children—regardless of the circumstances of their conception or birth—should be treated with Christian love.

Purdy, Laura M. *Reproducing Persons: Issues in Feminist Bioethics.* Ithaca, NY: Cornell University Press, 1996. 255 pages.

In this tightly argued and provocative analysis, Purdy contends that feminist bioethics can help clarify controversies over abortion and reproductive technologies. Separate essays discuss such timely topics as rights and duties connected with conception and pregnancy, whether conceiving a child or taking a pregnancy to term can ever be wrong, and conflicting interests between men and women regarding abortion.

Rengel, Marian. *Encyclopedia of Birth Control.* Westport, CT: Oryx Press, 2000. 312 pages.

This encyclopedia comprehensively reviews contraceptive issues and includes more than 200 entries on a wide range of issues, including abortion, abstinence, population growth, religious views, menopause, and sexually transmitted diseases.

Robertson, John A. *Children of Choice: Freedom and the New Reproductive Technologies.* Princeton, NJ: Princeton University Press, 1994. 296 pages.

Robertson develops a sophisticated analysis of reproductive rights focusing on contraception and abortion, infertility, "quality control" of offspring, and use of reproductive capacity for nonreproductive ends, such as the use of fetal tissue for treating certain diseases. He views the issues surrounding reproductive policy from a rights-based perspective and concludes that it is best to let the individuals involved determine whether a given technology should be used.

Rothblatt, Martine. *Unzipped Genes.* Philadelphia: Temple University Press, 1997. 201 pages.

Rothblatt explores the tension between the possible benefits and hazards of emerging genetic technology, with special emphasis on the Human Genome Project. She advocates "personal eugenics," whereby individuals are allowed to choose sperm and eggs to create the child of their choice, and she believes that government policy should require insurers to cover such procedures. The most controversial aspect of the book is her advocacy of a policy in which all men would be sterilized after donating sperm for use at a later date. Doing so, she argues, would virtually eliminate the "disease" of unwanted pregnancies.

Rothman, Barbara Katz. *Recreating Motherhood: Ideology and Technology in a Patriarchal Society.* New York: W. W. Norton, 1989.

Rothman provides a classic feminist analysis of the changing roles of motherhood in a male-dominated society by focusing on the commodification of pregnancy and motherhood.

Journals

Educator's Update
http://www.plannedparenthood.org

Available from the Education Department at Planned Parenthood Federation of America, *Educator's Update*, published six times per year by the Planned Parenthood Federation of America, provides articles for the lay reader on various topics related to family planning. It also provides book reviews, descriptions of educational videos, dates for upcoming conferences, and addresses for other websites that deal with reproductive issues. It is available on-line at no charge or in printed form at an annual subscription fee of $30 ($38 for international orders).

Fertility and Sterility
http://www.asrm.org

Fertility and Sterility is an international journal for obstetricians, gynecologists, reproductive endocrinologists, urologists, scientists, and others who treat and investigate problems of infertility and human reproductive disorders. The journal publishes original scientific articles on clinical and laboratory research relevant to reproductive endocrinology, urology, andrology, physiology, immunology, genetics, contraception, and menopause. It encourages and supports meaningful basic and clinical research and facilitates and promotes excellence in professional education in the field of reproductive medicine.

The Guttmacher Report on Public Policy
http://www.agi-usa.org

The Guttmacher Report, published six times per year by the Alan Guttmacher Institute, focuses on public policy as it affects family planning in the United States. It is extremely valuable in keeping the reader up-to-date on the latest policy developments at both the federal and state levels. Recent editions are available on-line.

International Family Planning Perspectives
http://www.agi-usa.org

International Family Planning Perspectives, published by the Alan Guttmacher Institute four times per year, provides research articles on sexual and reproductive health and rights in Africa, Latin America, the Caribbean, and Asia with emphasis on contraception, fertility, adolescent pregnancy, abortion, family planning policies and programs, sexually transmitted diseases, including HIV/AIDS, and reproductive, maternal, and child health. All articles include summaries in Spanish and French. Recent editions are available on-line.

Journal of Assisted Reproductive Law
http://www.vgme.com/new.htm

The *Journal of Assisted Reproductive Law*, published by the law firm of Vorzimer, Masserman, and Ecoff in Beverly Hills, California, focuses on court decisions and litigation associated with reproductive issues.

Perspectives on Sexual and Reproductive Health
http://www.agi-usa.org

Published bimonthly by the Alan Guttmacher Institute, *Perspectives on Sexual and Reproductive Health* (formerly, *Family Planning Perspectives*) provides the latest research and analysis on sexual and reproductive health and rights in the United States and other industrialized countries.

Reproductive Freedom News
http://www.crlp.org

This journal is published monthly by the Center for Reproductive Law and Policy. It focuses primarily on statutes and court decisions affecting reproductive policies. It is available in printed form at no charge and online.

Videos

Abortion

Abortion for Survival
Type: VHS
Length: 33 minutes
Date: 1989
Cost: $19.95
Source: Feminist Majority Foundation
            http://www.feminist.org/store/ProductVideos.asp

This 1989 video reviews the need for safe, legal, and accessible abortion worldwide, highlighting the lack of access to affordable contraception and women's desires to limit their family size. The documentary opens with the performance of an abortion at six weeks that takes one minute and twenty-four seconds and reveals what was extracted from the uterus.

The Abortion Pill
Type: VHS
Length: 56 minutes
Date: 1997
Source: Abortion Access Project
            552 Massachusetts Avenue, Suite 215
            Cambridge, MA 02139
            (617) 661-1161; fax (617) 492-1915
            http://www.abortionaccess.org

This video examines the global politics of RU-486 and women's experiences with medical abortion.

Access Denied
Type: VHS
Length: 28 minutes
Date: 1991
Cost: rental, $50; purchase, $175
Source: Women Make Movies
http://www.wmm.com

This video addresses cutbacks in women's reproductive freedom and civil rights against the backdrop of Operation Rescue's religious antiabortion fervor. Produced by ReproVision, the media collective of Women's Health Action Mobilization, the video documents three years of direct actions by the antichoice movement. It covers the gag rule, parental consent laws, the U.S. Supreme Court decision in *Webster v. Reproductive Health Services* (1989), and menstrual extraction.

Counseling for Medical Abortion
Type: VHS
Length: 20 minutes
Date: 1996
Source: Abortion Access Project
552 Massachusetts Avenue, Suite 215
Cambridge, MA 02139
(617) 661-1161; fax (617) 492-1915
http://www.repro-activist.org/AAP/publica_
resources/videos.htm

Produced by Planned Parenthood of New York City, this video reviews professional counseling with a woman who is deciding whether to undergo a medical abortion.

Dear Doctor Spencer: Abortion in a Small Town
Type: VHS
Length: 26 minutes
Date: 1997
Source: Abortion Access Project
552 Massachusetts Avenue, Suite 215
Cambridge, MA 02139
(617) 661-1161; fax (617) 492-1915

http://www.repro-activist.org/AAP/publica_
resources/videos.htm
Also available from Concentric Media
http://www.concentric.org/projects/main.html

This video tells one provider's story of his practice in rural New York prior to the *Roe v. Wade* decision in 1973.

Fetal Indication Termination of Pregnancy Program
Type: VHS
Date: 1996
Source: Abortion Access Project
           552 Massachusetts Avenue, Suite 215
           Cambridge, MA 02139
           (617) 661-1161; fax (617) 492-1915
           http://www.repro-activist.org/AAP/publica_
           resources/videos.htm

Filmed in Wichita, Kansas, the video educates women and families about options in cases of severe fetal abnormality.

The Fragile Promise of Choice: Abortion in the U.S. Today
Type: VHS
Length: 57 minutes
Date: 1996
Cost: $39.95
Source: Concentric Media, http://www.concentric.org/
           projects/main.html
           Also available from Women Make Movies, http://
           www.wmm.com

Produced by KTEH for the Public Broadcasting System, the video addresses the crisis of abortion access and affordability, the atmosphere of harassment and violence toward providers, the impact of growing state and local legislative restrictions for women seeking care, and the complexity of religious issues.

From Danger to Dignity: The Fight for Safe Abortion
Type: VHS and 16 mm
Length: 57 minutes
Date: 1995
Cost: rental (VHS), $90; rental (film), $150; purchase
           (VHS), $175

Source: Women Make Movies
http://www.wmm.com
Also available from Abortion Access Project
552 Massachusetts Avenue, Suite 215
Cambridge, MA 02139
(617) 661-1161; fax (617) 492-1915
http://www.repro-activist.org/AAP/publica_
resources/videos.htm

This video weaves together two parallel stories: the evolution of underground networks, which helped women find safe abortions outside the law, and the intensive efforts by activists and legislators who dedicated themselves to legalizing abortion.

Help Wanted
Type: VHS
Date: 2001
Source: Abortion Access Project
552 Massachusetts Avenue, Suite 215
Cambridge, MA 02139
(617) 661-1161; fax (617) 492-1915
http://www.repro-activist.org/AAP/publica_
resources/videos.htm

For both activists and medical students, this video encourages health professional students to become abortion providers.

Jane: An Abortion Service
Type: VHS and 16 mm
Length: 58 minutes
Date: 1996
Cost: rental (VHS), $90; rental (film), $150; purchase
(VHS), $245
Source: Women Make Movies
http://www.wmm.com

This fascinating political look at a little-known chapter in women's history tells the story of "Jane," the Chicago-based women's health group that provided nearly 12,000 safe, illegal abortions from 1969 to 1973, using staff with no formal medical training. Archival footage and recreations mingle to depict how the repression of the early 1960s and social movements of the late

1960s influenced this unique group. The video was produced by the Independent Television Service (ITVS), with funds provided by the Corporation for Public Broadcasting.

Killing in the Name of Life: Terrorism against Abortion Clinics
Type: VHS
Cost: $19.95
Source: Feminist Majority Foundation
http://www.feminist.org/store/ProductVideos.asp

This short, educational video documents the domestic terrorism campaign carried out by the antiabortion movement against reproductive health clinics nationwide. The video includes actual footage of key players in the antiabortion movement participating in the harassment of doctors, clinic workers, clinic escorts, and patients.

Legal but Out of Reach: Six Women's Abortion Stories
Type: VHS
Length: 24 minutes
Cost: $25 for allied nonprofit organizations; $50 for institutions
Source: Civil Liberties and Public Policy Program
Hampshire College
Amherst, MA 01002-5001
(617) 559-5548

This video includes first-person testimonials from women who faced barriers to reproductive health care.

Legislating a Tragedy
Type: VHS
Length: 20 minutes
Date: 1996
Source: Abortion Access Project
552 Massachusetts Avenue, Suite 215
Cambridge, MA 02139
(617) 661-1161; fax (617) 492-1915
http://www.repro-activist.org/AAP/publica_
resources/videos.htm

This video covers the issues surrounding late abortion. It was made to counter the first act of Congress banning so-called partial-birth abortion. The bill was vetoed by President Bill Clinton.

Live Free or Die
Type: VHS
Length: 72 minutes
Date: 2000
Source: Abortion Access Project
552 Massachusetts Avenue, Suite 215
Cambridge, MA 02139
(617) 661-1161; fax (617) 492-1915
http://www.repro-activist.org/AAP/publica_
resources/videos.htm

This video documents a New Hampshire doctor's crusade to keep abortion accessible in his community and to keep sexual education in the local schools despite antichoice protesters and the merger of the community hospital with a Catholic medical center.

Never Go Back: The Threat to Legalized Abortion
Type: VHS
Length: 15 minutes
Cost: $19.95
Source: Feminist Majority Foundation
http://www.feminist.org/store/ProductVideos.asp

Produced by FMF board member Lorraine Sheinberg and narrated by Carrie Fisher, this video outlines the threat that upcoming Supreme Court retirements pose to accessible, legal abortion in the United States.

***Roe v. Wade* at Twenty-Five**
Type: VHS
Length: 60 minutes
Date: 1998
Cost: $12
Source: Center for Reproductive Law and Policy
120 Wall Street
New York, NY 10005
(212) 637-3600; fax (212) 637-3666
http://www.crlp.org

On January 22, 1998, the twenty-fifth anniversary of the U.S. Supreme Court decision *Roe v. Wade,* the Center for Reproductive Law and Policy hosted a national satellite teleconference to commemorate the occasion. In scenes from this landmark event, a panel of distinguished experts discussed the status of a woman's right to choose an abortion. Clips from the award-winning documentary, *From Danger to Dignity: The Fight for Safe Abortion,* add a human face to this timely production.

Silent No More
Type: VHS
Length: 45 minutes
Cost: $20
Source: Civil Liberties and Public Policy Program
          Hampshire College
          Amherst, MA 01002-5001
          (413) 559-5548
          http://hamp.hampshire.edu/~clpp

Women speak out on their experiences with abortion.

Silent Scream
Type: VHS
Length: 28 minutes
Cost: $19.95
Source: marianland.com
          3350-A Highway 6 South
          Sugarland, TX 77478
          http://marianland.com.

This video uses an ultrasound screen to show a first trimester abortion. It is narrated by Dr. Bernard Nathanson and is available in several languages and is appropriate for ages twelve years and up.

Speaking Out for Reproductive Freedom
Type: VHS
Length: 180 minutes
Date: 1996
Cost: $20
Source: Civil Liberties and Public Policy Program
          Hampshire College
          Amherst, MA 01002-5001

(413) 559-5548
http://hamp.hampshire.edu/~clpp

Twenty women address the issues of abortion and reproductive freedom.

Unholy Alliance
Type: VHS
Length: 22 minutes
Date: 1995
Source: Abortion Access Project
552 Massachusetts Avenue, Suite 215
Cambridge, MA 02139
(617) 661-1161; fax (617) 492-1915
http://www.repro-activist.org/AAP/publica_
resources/videos.htm

Produced by the Public Policy Institute of the Planned Parenthood Federation of America, this video focuses on the work and broad-reaching influence of Human Life International.

We Can Do It Better: Inside an Independent Abortion Clinic
Type: VHS
Length: 33 minutes
Date: 2002
Source: Abortion Access Project
552 Massachusetts Avenue, Suite 215
Cambridge, MA 02139
(617) 661-1161; fax (617) 492-1915
http://www.repro-activist.org/AAP/publica_
resources/videos.htm

A rare and intimate look at the daily work of an independent abortion clinic.

When Abortion Was Illegal: Untold Stories
Type: VHS
Length: 28 minutes
Date: 1992
Cost: $29.95
Source: Concentric Media
http://www.concentric.org/projects/main.html

A Public Broadcasting System video detailing personal accounts of the physical, legal, and emotional consequences of abortion during the era when it was a crime in the United States. The video includes profiles of doctors who risked imprisonment by providing illegal procedures, of women who experienced back-alley abortions, and of others who broke the law by helping women find safe care. These people speak frankly, some for the first time.

You're What? A Story of Teenage Pregnancy
Type: VHS
Length: 28 minutes
Date: 1986
Source: Abortion Access Project
552 Massachusetts Avenue, Suite 215
Cambridge, MA 02139
(617) 661-1161; fax (617) 492-1915
http://www.repro-activist.org/AAP/publica_
resources/videos.htm

This docudrama follows a teenager as she struggles to decide whether to continue an unintended pregnancy. It also discusses the repercussions of parental consent laws.

Assisted Reproduction

Creating Your Family—Hows and Whys of Surrogate Parenting
Type: VHS
Length: 40 minutes
Cost: $20
Source: Center for Surrogate Parenting
15821 Ventura Boulevard, Suite 675
Encino, CA 91436
(818) 788-8288
http://www.creatingfamilies.com

This video portrays the stories of seven surrogate mothers, as well as two couples whose children were born with the assistance of surrogate mothers. These individuals answer questions about surrogacy, and the viewer is guided through the surrogate parenting process.

Florence and Robin
Type: VHS
Length: 52 minutes
Date: 1994
Cost: $89.95
Source: Films for the Humanities and Sciences
PO Box 2053
Princeton, NJ 08543-2053

Produced by Andrew McLaughlin Associates, this frank program follows the extraordinary journey of a lesbian couple toward parenthood, from a sperm bank by lesbians for lesbians in San Francisco, to the traditionalism of Virginia, where a lesbian mother recently lost custody of her son. Florence and Robin give a unique insight into their struggle in a world that considers them abnormal. The program also features the children of lesbian and gay couples and talks to pupils at a nursery school where one in six has gay parents (Planned Parenthood of America of Southeastern Pennsylvania: http://www.ppsp.org/avcatalog/communication.htm).

Frontline: Making Babies
Type: VHS
Length: 60 minutes
Cost: $14.95
Source: Public Broadcasting System
http://www.shop.pbs.org/cust/cdeploy?ecaction=
ecwalkin&template=shoppbs/homepage/index.
en.html

This video analyzes the dramatic strides made in human reproduction by looking at genetic profiling, cloning, and other forms of reproductive technology. It evaluates the ethical and moral dilemmas that these new technologies raise.

On the Eighth Day
Type: VHS
Length: 51 minutes
Date: 1992
Cost: Rental, $90; purchase, $295
Source: Women Make Movies
http://www.wmm.com

On the Eighth Day, a two-part film series, poses disturbing questions about the new reproductive and genetic technologies and how they affect women and society in general. Part I, *Making Babies,* explores the origins and applications of in vitro fertilization. Part II, *Making Perfect Babies,* examines the application of genetic technology and the social and economic pressures that may influence the development of such technology.

Contraception

The Pill

Type: VHS
Length: 45 minutes
Date: 1999
Cost: Rental, $75; purchase, $245
Source: Women Make Movies
            http://www.wmm.com

This documentary chronicles little-known chapters in the history of oral contraceptives and examines the role of the pharmaceutical industry in the development and marketing of the pill. The video draws on archival and period footage, interviews with women from Puerto Rico who became unsuspecting test subjects for the early pill, insights from women's health activists who publicly questioned the high-dose version's safety, and testimony from scientists prominent in the drug's development. Also featured are Gloria Steinem and journalist Barbara Seaman, whose 1969 book, *The Doctors' Case against the Pill,* became a cause célèbre in the campaign for informed consent.

The Real Deal about Birth Control

Type: VHS
Length: 18 minutes
Cost: $45
Source: Planned Parenthood of the Mid-Hudson Valley
            26 West Street
            Newburgh, NY 12550
            (845) 562-3098
            http://www.plannedparenthood.org

Are the myths about hormonal contraception alive and well in your community? This video developed by teen peer educators from Planned Parenthood of the Mid-Hudson Valley helps female teens sort through the myths and rumors they have heard about hormonal methods and make their decisions based on "the real deal." This short video by and for teens lets viewers know that Planned Parenthood is a safe place to go for information, birth control, and nonjudgmental support.

The Roots of Roe
Type: VHS
Length: 57 minutes
Date: 1997
Cost: $19.95
Source: Abortion Access Project
            552 Massachusetts Avenue, Suite 215
            Cambridge, MA 02139
            (617) 661-1161; fax (617) 492-1915
            http://www.repro-activist.org/AAP/publica_
                resources/videos.htm

The Roots of Roe chronicles the history of birth control and abortion in the United States from the advent of the American Medical Association to the Comstock laws, including Margaret Sanger, and the landmark case of *Roe v. Wade*.

Skin Deep
Type: VHS
Length: 15 minutes
Date: 1997
Cost: rental, $50; purchase, $195
Source: Women Make Movies
            http://www.wmm.com

As diverse women share their experiences with Norplant, community leaders and public policy activists discuss the issues of informed consent, along with race and class discrimination regarding the use of this drug.

Speak EC: What Every Woman Needs to Know about Emergency Contraception
Type: VHS
Length: 11 minutes
Date: 2000
Cost: $10

Source: Center for Reproductive Law and Policy
            120 Wall Street
            New York, NY 10005
            (212) 637-3600; fax (212) 637-3666
            http://www.crlp.org

This video educates the viewer about emergency contraception. Widespread use of emergency contraception could reduce the annual need for abortion in the United States by 50 percent, yet studies show that only 11 percent of women know enough about emergency contraceptive pills to be able to use them.

Pregnancy and Childbirth

And Baby Makes Two
Type: VHS
Length: 60 minutes
Date: 1999
Cost: $29.95
Source: First Run Features
            153 Waverly Place
            New York, NY 10014
            (800) 229-8575
            http://www.firstrunfeatures.com

And Baby Makes Two follows a support group formed to share the trials and triumphs of becoming single mothers. From artificial insemination to adoption to the old-fashioned method of conception, this video looks at the successes and failures of various methods and the emotional consequences these women face in their attempts to become mothers. Single motherhood is no longer the exclusive province of poor, undereducated, and often minority teenagers. White, middle-class women in their thirties and forties are now joining its ranks—consciously and without shame—forcing society to look anew at the culture of the nuclear family.

The Birthing Experience and Life with Multiples
Type: VHS
Length: 75 minutes
Cost: $129
Source: Film Ideas
            308 North Wolf Road

Wheeling, IL 60090
(847) 419-0255; (800) 475-3456
http://www.filmideas.com/titlepages/pthrus/
sebastian.html;filmid@ais.net

This video provides information about labor, delivery, and life at home with multiple infants. It includes material on medical treatments, anesthesia, twin ultrasound, twin vaginal deliveries, triplet cesarean deliveries, and how to organize a home after a multiple birth.

C-Section Birth Day!
Type: VHS
Length: 17 minutes
Cost: $129
Source: Film Ideas
             308 North Wolf Road
             Wheeling, IL 60090
             (847) 419-0255; (800) 475-3456
             http://www.filmideas.com/titlepages/pthrus/
               sebastian.html; filmid@ais.net

This video provides information on cesarean deliveries, including the role of fetal monitoring, administration of anesthesia, the actual surgery, and recovery and postpartum care.

DES: The Timebomb Drug
Type: VHS and 16 mm
Length: 24 minutes
Date: 1983
Cost: rental (VHS), $60; rental (film), $60; purchase
               (VHS), $195
Source: Women Make Movies
             http://www.wmm.com

From 1940 to 1971, diethylstilbestrol (DES), a synthetic estrogen, was prescribed to millions of women as a "wonder drug" to prevent miscarriage. Today, some of the children of these mothers, particularly daughters, have cancer. This video is a case study of the questionable relationship between the medical profession and the pharmaceutical industry and their accountability for the effects of DES on women and their children.

A Healthy Baby Girl
Type: VHS and 16 mm
Length: 57 minutes
Date: 1996
Cost: rental (VHS), $90; rental (film), $150; purchase
            (VHS), $295
Source: Women Make Movies
            http://www.wmm.com

In 1963, the filmmaker's mother was prescribed the synthetic hormone DES, meant to prevent miscarriage and ensure a healthy baby. At age twenty-five, the filmmaker was diagnosed with DES-related cervical cancer. Shot over five years, this film tells a story of survival, mother-daughter love, family renewal, and community activism.

Her Own Law
Type: VHS
Length: 11 minutes
Date: 2000
Source: www.MediaRights.org or www.amazon.com

This video considers a woman's right to choose how and where to have her baby and the way in which those choices are threatened. It explores the practice and philosophy of homebirth and midwifery and considers ways in which doctors and midwives might work together to provide a continuum of care for all women.

**Preparing for Multiples with Nutrition and
Preventive Care**
Type: VHS
Length: 76 minutes
Cost: $129
Source: Film Ideas
            308 North Wolf Road
            Wheeling, IL 60090
            (847) 419-0255; (800) 475-3456
            http://www.filmideas.com/titlepages/pthrus/
                sebastian.html; filmid@ais.net

This video provides the viewer with information on proper nutrition and diet, the risks involved with multiple births, recognition of and treatments to prevent preterm labor, and warning signs that indicate further treatment.

Sex Education

Raising Healthy Kids: Families Talk about Sexual Health (Part 1)
Raising Healthy Kids: Families Talk about Sexual Health (Part 2)
Type: VHS
Length: 30 minutes each
Date: 2001
Cost: $99.95; if purchased with Part II, $149.95
Source: Family Health Productions
http://www.AboutHealth.com

Produced with the assistance of the Centers for Disease Control and Prevention, this video is designed to educate parents and help them feel comfortable talking with their children about sexual health. Videos include interviews with children, parents, and experts. Part I, *For Parents of Young Children,* addresses setting limits with children, telling children the truth, labeling body parts correctly, explaining how babies are made, and outlining the difference between appropriate and inappropriate touching. Part II, *For Parents of Preadolescents and Adolescents,* addresses values, what is meant by listening, condoms, how to avoid absolutes, whether we give children mixed messages, healthy relationships, and more. A facilitator's manual is included. (Planned Parenthood Federation of America: http://www.plannedparenthood.org.)

Substance Abuse

Different Directions: Understanding Fetal Alcohol Syndrome
Type: VHS
Length: 22 minutes
Date: 2000
Cost: $50
Source: Pat Spadetto
North for the Children
fax (705) 567-2466
Also available from the Assembly of First Nations
(AFN) Canada

http://www.afn.ca/Programs/Health%20Secretariat/
fas/fetal_alcohol_syndrome.htm

The Centre for Addiction and Mental Health in Toronto may lend
this video via interlibrary loan: (416) 535-8501, ext. 6987

Produced with the assistance of Health Canada, this video
looks at two children with fetal alcohol syndrome—one five-
year-old girl and one adult young man—and their remarkable
mothers, one a birth mother and one an adoptive mother.

Drug Babies
Type: VHS
Length: 30 minutes
Date: 1990
Cost: $99.95
Source: AIMS MultiMedia
            http://www.aimsmultimedia.com

Produced by Dolphin Productions, *Drug Babies* deals with the
physical and emotional problems of children exposed in utero to
drugs or alcohol or both. It addresses the problems of the mothers, social services, and foster care and also examines the treatments available for these children and the special demands they
will place on the educational system.

Fetal Alcohol Syndrome, a 3-part series
What Is FAS? Fetal Alcohol Syndrome (Part 1)
**Preventing FAS: A Pregnant Woman Never Drinks Alone
(Part 2)**
Living and Learning with FAS (Part 3)
Type: VHS
Date: 1991
Cost: $149 each
Source: Magic Lantern Communications
            (800) 263-1717; fax (416) 827-1154
            Also available from the Assembly of First Nations
              (AFN) Canada
            http://www.afn.ca/Programs/Health%20Secretariat/
            fas/fetal_alcohol_syndrome.htm

The Centre for Addiction and Mental Health in Toronto may lend
this video via interlibrary loan: (416) 535-8501, ext. 6987

This 3-part series provides an overview of fetal alcohol syndrome and encourages women not to drink during pregnancy. It has a message for everyone—professionals, family, and friends—who can help a woman make that choice. It also discusses meeting the special needs of children and adolescents with FAS.

Precious Gift
Type: VHS
Length: 16 minutes
Date: 1997
Cost: $15
Source: Saskatchewan Institute on Prevention of Handicaps
            1319 Colony Street
            Saskatoon, SK S7N 2Z1, Canada
            (306) 655-2512; fax (306) 655-2511
            Also available from The Assembly of First Nations
              (AFN) Canada
            http://www.afn.ca/Programs/Health%20Secretariat/
              fas/fetal_alcohol_syndrome.htm

The Centre for Addiction and Mental Health in Toronto may lend this video via interlibrary loan: (416) 535-8501, ext. 6987

This documentary, filmed on the Beardy's and Okemasis Reserve in Saskatchewan, deals with the issue of drinking during pregnancy. It documents the life of a young woman, Celeste, who believes she is pregnant and must decide whether she will drink during her pregnancy. Through the support of her partner, Kookum, her doctor, and her friends, Celeste decides that she will not drink while pregnant. Emphasis is placed on the roles played by all members of the community—including family, friends, and professionals—in producing a healthy baby.

Sebastian: An Extraordinary Life
Type: VHS
Length: 18 minutes
Date: 1995
Cost: $125
Source: Film Ideas
            308 North Wolf Road
            Wheeling, IL 60090
            (847) 419-0255; (800) 475-3456

http://www.filmideas.com/titlepages/pthrus/
sebastian.html;filmid@ais.net

Born to a fifteen-year-old mother, Sebastian suffers from fetal alcohol syndrome. Because this young boy has permanent brain damage, he requires almost constant medical care. Sebastian's sad condition could have been easily avoided. This is an excellent resource for expectant mothers who need to understand the potentially devastating consequences of alcohol intake during pregnancy.

Women of Substance
Type: VHS and 16 mm
Length: 55 minutes
Date: 1994
Cost: rental (VHS), $60; purchase (VHS), $195
Source: Women Make Movies
            http://www.wmm.com

A Video Action Fund documentary by Rory Kennedy and Robin Smith with narration by Joanne Woodward, *Women of Substance* examines the struggles and triumphs of women overcoming addiction during pregnancy and motherhood. More than 5 million women in the United States are affected by drug and alcohol addiction and 1,000 babies are born each day with drugs and alcohol in their systems. Although prenatal alcohol and drug exposure is believed to be the single most preventable cause of birth defects, nine out of ten pregnant addicts who want treatment never receive it. Following the stories of three diverse women, this film is a comprehensive portrait of the legal, moral, and health battles being waged to improve treatment opportunities for pregnant addicts and women with children. A thirty-minute version is also available.

Websites

Gallup Organization
http://www.gallup.com

Gallup Polls can be accessed at no charge through this site.

Legal Information Institute at Cornell University Law School
http://www.law.cornell.edu/lii.html

The Legal Information Institute site provides the texts of many court decisions and statutes.

National Institutes of Health
http://www.nih.gov/news/stemcell/primer.htm

The National Institutes of Health provide valuable resources in many fields, including especially good information on stem cell research. They also offer a variety of outstanding journals and reports.

National Women's Health Resource Center
http://www.healthywomen.org

The National Women's Health Resource Center has information on many women's health issues, including reproductive health issues. Its website has useful links to other websites that focus on women's reproductive issues.

University of Wisconsin at Madison
http://www.news.wisc.edu/packages/stemcells

The University of Wisconsin at Madison has been at the forefront of stem cell research. It provides a very informative website about stem cell research, with links to other websites.

Note: More websites with excellent research information can be found in Chapter 6.

Glossary

abortion Loss of a pregnancy, either accidentally or purposefully, before viability (twenty-four weeks).

adult stem cell An undifferentiated cell found in a differentiated tissue that can renew itself and (with certain limitations) differentiate to yield all the specialized cell types of the tissue from which it originated.

AIDS (acquired immunodeficiency syndrome) The late stage of the illness triggered by infection with human immunodeficiency virus (HIV). According to the official definition published by the Centers for Disease Control and Prevention, a person receives an AIDS diagnosis when he or she has a CD4 (helper T-cell) count of less than 200 and/or certain opportunistic infections common with advanced immune deficiency.

alpha feto-protein (AFP) A protein produced by a growing fetus that is present in amniotic fluid and, in smaller amounts, in the mother's blood. Larger than normal amounts are found in the maternal bloodstream if neural-tube defects are present in the fetus.

amniocentesis Removal of amniotic fluid by insertion of a needle into the amniotic sac; amniotic fluid is often used to assess fetal health or maturity.

amniotic fluid The liquid surrounding the fetus, composed of secretions from the placenta, fetal urine, and other minor constituents. It circulates constantly and is replaced every few hours.

anencephaly A type of neural-tube defect that occurs when the fetus's head and brain do not develop normally.

artificial insemination Insemination of women with semen samples from their husbands or from donors, using a syringe or other instrument.

assisted reproduction Any of a wide array of medical techniques designed to aid in the fertilization process and treat fertility problems.

blastocyst A preimplantation embryo of about 150 cells, reached at four to five days after fertilization. The blastocyst consists of a sphere made up of an outer layer of cells (the trophectoderm), a fluid-filled cavity (the blastocoel), and a cluster of cells on the interior (the inner cell mass).

cesarean delivery (C-section) Delivery of the fetus by means of an incision into the abdominal wall and the uterus; also called abdominal delivery.

chlamydia Fastest-spreading sexually transmitted disease in the United States. Up to 85 percent of infected women and 45 percent of men have no symptoms. If untreated, chlamydia can lead to serious consequences for women, including pelvic inflammatory disease, a leading cause of infertility among women.

chorionic villus sampling (CVS) A procedure in which a small sample of cells is taken from the placenta and tested.

chromosome Each cell has twenty-three pairs of chromosomes. They carry the genes, which carry all the inherited characteristics of a human being. A normal human has forty-six chromosomes.

clone A line of cells that is genetically identical (e.g., has the same DNA) to the originating cell.

conception The joining together of the sperm and egg. Fertilization.

contraception Any method used to stop the joining of the sperm and egg.

cryobank A storage facility for frozen sperm, eggs, or embryos.

cryopreservation Freezing tissues and storing them at -196 degrees C. They can later be thawed for assisted reproduction.

differentiation The process whereby an unspecialized early embryonic cell acquires the features of a specialized cell such as a heart, liver, or muscle cell.

DNA Deoxyribonucleic acid, a chemical found primarily in the nucleus of cells. DNA carries the instructions for making all the structures and materials the body needs to function.

Down's syndrome A genetic disorder caused by the presence of an extra chromosome and characterized by mental retardation, abnormal features of the face, and medical problems such as heart defects.

ectopic pregnancy A pregnancy in which the fertilized egg begins to grow in a place other than inside the uterus, usually in the fallopian tubes.

electronic fetal monitoring A method in which electronic instruments are used to record the heartbeat of the fetus and the contractions of the mother's uterus.

embryo In humans, the embryo is the developing organism from the time of fertilization until the end of the eighth week of gestation, when it becomes known as a fetus.

embryo reduction   Selective abortion or termination of fetuses in cases of multiple-fetus pregnancy in which continuation of the full pregnancy would cause serious health risk to the woman and the fetuses.

embryonic stem cells   Primitive (undifferentiated) cells from the embryo that have the potential to become a wide variety of specialized cell types.

estrogen   A female hormone produced in the ovaries that stimulates the growth of the lining of the uterus.

fallopian tubes   A pair of delicate tubes that lead from the cavity of the uterus to the area of the ovary and carry the mature eggs from the ovary to the uterus.

fertility   The ability to reproduce.

fertilization   Joining of the sperm and egg.

fetal alcohol syndrome (FAS)   A pattern of physical, mental, and behavioral problems in the baby that is thought to be due to alcohol abuse by the mother during pregnancy.

fetal anomaly   Fetal malformation or abnormal development.

fetal growth retardation   Inadequate growth of the fetus during the last stages of pregnancy.

fetal research   Any research carried out on a human fetus or an embryo.

fetal surgery   Surgery on a fetus, which can be done either in utero, using laparoscopy, or ex utero, in which the fetus is removed for surgery and then returned to the womb. This type of surgery has been used to insert shunts, remove urinary tract blockages, and do heart valve surgery.

fetus   A developing human, from usually two months after conception until birth.

gamete intrafallopian transfer (GIFT)   Eggs retrieved under laparoscopy are mixed with a prepared semen sample and introduced into the fallopian tubes.

gametes   Male and female reproductive cells; either the sperm or the egg.

gene   A functional unit of heredity that is a segment of DNA located in a specific site on a chromosome. A gene directs the formation of an enzyme or other protein.

genital herpes simplex   Herpes simplex infection involving the genital area. It can be significant during pregnancy because of the danger to a newborn fetus infected with herpes simplex.

genome All genetic material within the cells of an individual.

gestation Period of intrauterine development from conception through birth; that is, pregnancy.

human embryonic stem cell A type of pluripotent stem cell derived from the inner cell mass of the blastocyst.

hydrocephalus Excessive accumulation of fluid around the brain of the baby. Sometimes called "water on the brain."

implantation The embedding of a fertilized egg in the wall of the uterus approximately seven days after conception.

in utero Within the uterus.

in vitro Literally, "in glass"; in a laboratory dish or test tube; an artificial environment.

in vitro fertilization An assisted reproduction technique in which fertilization is accomplished outside the body.

infant A child under one year of age.

infertility Diminished ability to conceive. Inability to conceive after trying for one year. One in six couples are affected by infertility at some stage.

informed consent A legal concept that protects a person's rights to autonomy and self-determination by specifying that no action may be taken without that person's prior understanding and freely given consent.

intracytoplasmic sperm injection (ICSI) Injecting sperm directly into the egg to fertilize it. Considered a major advance in treating male infertility caused by low sperm count and low sperm activity.

intrauterine device (IUD) Long-term contraceptive device inserted in the uterus that interferes with implantation process.

karyotyping Technique for analysis of the chromosomes, in which they are visualized and arranged in order to see if and where anomalies exist.

labor Productive uterine contractions that produce dilation of the cervix, descent of the baby, and its expulsion into the world.

laparoscopy Surgical procedure performed using a slender fiber-optic scope for tubal ligation, diagnosis of pelvic pain, or diagnosis of ectopic pregnancy.

Medicaid Federal and state health funding program originally designed to fund care for the poor, especially women and children, but now largely going to the poor elderly.

microcephaly Abnormally small development of the head in the developing fetus.

neonatologist   A pediatric specialist who cares for premature or sick newborn babies.

neural-tube defects   Abnormalities in the development of the spinal cord and brain in the fetus. *See* anencephaly, hydrocephalus, and spina bifida.

oocyte   Female gamete or egg. In a natural cycle, only one or two eggs are produced.

oral contraceptives   Medical contraception techniques; the birth control pill.

ovulation   Cyclic production of an egg from the ovary. Superovulation is a technique used to override the natural ovulation limits of one to two eggs per cycle.

pelvic inflammatory disease (PID)   An infection involving the pelvic organs, that is, the ovaries and fallopian tubes. A common cause of infertility among women.

placenta   Organ inside the uterus that is attached to the baby by the umbilical cord; provides nourishment to and takes away waste from the fetus. It is also called the afterbirth.

placenta previa   Low attachment of the placenta, covering or coming very close to the cervix.

placental abruption   Premature separation of the placenta from the uterus.

pluripotent   The ability of a single stem cell to develop into many different cell types of the body.

preeclampsia   Combination of symptoms significant to pregnancy, including high blood pressure, edema, swelling, and changes in reflexes.

pregnancy   The condition of having a developing embryo or fetus in the body after fertilization of the female egg by the male sperm. Also, gestation.

premature delivery   Delivery before thirty-seven weeks gestation.

preterm   Born before thirty-seven weeks.

prostaglandins   A hormone that has profound effects on pregnancy as well as many other body systems. Prostaglandins break down the collagen in the cervix, softening it for dilation.

semen   Thick whitish fluid ejaculated by the male during orgasm and containing the spermatozoa and their nutrients.

sexually transmitted disease (STD)   Infection transmitted through sexual intercourse.

sickle cell anemia   Anemia caused by abnormal red blood cells shaped like a sickle or a cylinder. A genetic disorder with high incidence among individuals of African heritage.

somatic stem cells   Another name for adult stem cells.

sperm intrafallopian transfer (SIFT)   A procedure in which prepared semen is placed in the fallopian tubes.

spina bifida   A neural tube defect that results from improper closure of the fetal spine.

stem cells   Cells with the ability to divide for indefinite periods in culture and to give rise to specialized cells.

sterility   The inability to conceive or to produce offspring because of physical problems.

steroids   A group of medications of hormonal origin. Often used to treat various diseases and given to enhance fetal lung maturity. Includes estrogen, testosterone, progesterone, and prednisone.

stillbirth   Delivery of a baby that shows no signs of life.

surrogacy (biological or full)   A woman is artificially inseminated with the man's sperm of the commissioning couple and turns the baby over at birth to the genetic father. Unlike host surrogacy, in this type she is the biological and gestational mother.

surrogacy (gestational or host)   A woman carries to term an embryo produced by in vitro fertilization that is not hers and turns it over at birth to the genetic parents.

Tay-Sachs disease   An inherited disease characterized by mental and physical retardation, convulsions, enlargement of the head, and eventually death. This trait is usually carried by Ashkenazi Jews (the Jewish communities of Germany, France, Bohemia, Poland, and Russia).

teratogens   Agents that can cause birth defects when a woman is exposed to them during pregnancy.

totipotent   Cells that have unlimited capability and the capacity to form an entire organism, that is, the fertilized egg.

trimester   Any of the three three-month periods into which pregnancy is divided.

tubal sterilization (or ligation)   A method of female sterilization in which the fallopian tubes are closed by tying, banding, clipping, or sealing with electric current.

twinning   The process of splitting an embryo to create twins.

ultrasound   A test in which sound waves are used to examine internal structures. During pregnancy, it can be used to examine the fetus.

umbilical cord The cord that connects the placenta to the developing baby. It removes waste products and carbon dioxide from the baby and brings oxygenated blood and nutrients from the mother through the placenta to the baby.

uterus The organ in which the embryo/fetus grows. Also called a womb.

vasectomy A method of male sterilization in which a portion of the vas deferens is removed.

zygote Cell that results from the union of a sperm and egg at fertilization.

zygote intrafallopian transfer (ZIFT) Similar to GIFT, but the embryo, rather than the sperm and eggs, is transferred back into the fallopian tube.

Sources: Assisted Reproductive Medicine Glossary. www.infertility-info.org/gloslist.htm. Accessed December 14, 2002.

National Institutes of Health. "Stem Cell Primer—Glossary." http://www.nih.gov/news/stemcell/primer.htm#8. Accessed December 14, 2002.

WebMD Health. "Glossary of Pregnancy Terms." http://my.webmd.com/content/article/1680.51798. Accessed December 14, 2002.

Index

About the Authors

Janna C. Merrick earned her Ph.D. in political science at the University of Washington (1978) and is currently professor of government and international affairs at the University of South Florida. She teaches courses in public policy and conducts research in the areas of women's reproductive health policy and children's health policy. She has coauthored and coedited four books including *Compelled Compassion: Government Intervention in the Treatment of Critically Ill Newborns* (1992); *The Politics of Pregnancy: Issues in the Maternal-Fetal Relationship* (1993); *Human Reproduction, Emerging Technologies, and Conflicting Rights* (1995); and *The Encyclopedia of Biomedical Policy* (1996). She has served as guest editor for symposia published by the *Journal of Legal Medicine* and *Women and Politics* and currently serves on the editorial board of the journal *Politics and the Life Sciences*.

Robert H. Blank is professor of public policy at Brunel University in London. He earned a Ph.D. in political science from the University of Maryland (1971) and has specialized in biomedical policy. He has published numerous articles and books on reproductive policy including *The Political Implications of Human Genetic Technology* (1981); *Redefining Human Life: Reproductive Technologies and Social Policy* (1984); *Regulating Reproduction* (1990); *Fertility Control* (1991); *Mother and Fetus* (1992); *Fetal Protection in the Workplace* (1993), and *Biomedical Policy* (1995). He also coauthored, with Janna Merrick, *Human Reproduction, Emerging Technologies, and Conflicting Rights* (1995), *The Politics of Pregnancy* (1993), and *Compelled Compassion* (1992). Blank has been associate editor of *Politics and the Life Sciences*, a coeditor of numerous special issues in other professional journals, and coeditor of the Columbia University Press series Issues in Biomedical Policy. He was a member of the U.S. Office of Technology Assessment advisory panel on neuroscience research (1988–1991) and chaired its hearings on fetal tissue transplantation.

241